Causation and Persistence

Causation and Persistence
A Theory of Causation

DOUGLAS EHRING

New York   Oxford
OXFORD UNIVERSITY PRESS
1997

Oxford University Press

Oxford   New York
Athens   Auckland   Bangkok   Bogota   Bombay   Buenos Aires
Calcutta   Cape Town   Dar es Salaam   Delhi   Florence   Hong Kong
Istanbul   Karachi   Kuala Lumpur   Madras   Madrid   Melbourne
Mexico City   Nairobi   Paris   Singapore   Taipei   Tokyo   Toronto
and associated companies in
Berlin   Ibadan

Copyright © 1997 by Douglas Ehring

Published by Oxford University Press, Inc.
198 Madison Avenue, New York, New York 10016

Oxford is a registered trademark of Oxford University Press

All rights reserved. No part of this publication may be reproduced,
stored in a retrieval system, or transmitted, in any form or by any means,
electronic, mechanical, photocopying, recording, or otherwise,
without the prior permission of Oxford University Press.

Library of Congress Cataloging-in-Publication Data
Ehring, Douglas, 1952–
Causation and persistence : a theory of causation / Douglas Ehring
p.   cm.
Includes bibliographical references and index.
ISBN 0-19-510794-2
1. Causation   I. Title.
BD541.E37   1997
122—dc20   96-22282

1 3 5 7 9 8 6 4 2
Printed in the United States of America
on acid-free paper

*To the memory of James T. Moore, whose friendship
made philosophy possible for me*

For my parents, Connie and Eddie Ehring

Acknowledgments

Let's start with a worst-case scenario: I forget to thank someone who deserves to be thanked. And, in fact, since so many people have influenced this work for the better, chances are that will happen. I apologize in advance to those I forget to acknowledge.

Bernard Berofsky and Sidney Morgenbesser deserve both general and specific thanks, first for introducing me to the topic of causation, thereby shaping my career, and second for influencing my account of causal asymmetry, the topic of the last chapter of this book.

Some of this project was pursued while I was an academic visitor in the philosophy departments of Stanford University and the London School of Economics, and at the Centre for the Philosophy of the Natural and Social Sciences in London. I am grateful to these institutions, and I especially want to thank Nancy Cartwright for her invitations to visit at the LSE during the spring of 1993 and at the Centre in the summer of 1994. In London, I benefited from the lively Monday night discussions of the "Family," which included Tim Crane, Keith Hossack, Mike Martin, Lucy O'Brien, David Papineau, Sarah Patterson, Gabriel Segal, Barry C. Smith, Scott Sturgeon, and Bernhard Weis. I also discussed related topics with David-Hillel Ruben, who graciously helped me find a niche in London. And, while there, I was extremely fortunate to enjoy the encouragement of Hermione Gee, Tabitha Jackson, Neil Manson, Liz Mitchell, and Michelle Salis. Their friendship played a significant role in making this book possible. I am especially appreciative to Scott Sturgeon for his friendship and for introducing me to the philosophers of London as well as for many hours of very pleasurable philosophical conversation.

Much of this project was pursued in Dallas, at Southern Methodist University. At SMU, I benefited from the comments of my colleagues, including Eric Barnes, Alan Hausman, David Hausman, Mark Heller, Jean Kazez, Alastair Norcross, David Ring, and Steve Sverdlik. I am especially thankful to David Hausman, who provided constant support and encouragement throughout this project when he was chair of the philosophy department. I am grateful to Southern Methodist University for a number of sabbaticals and research grants.

I am also greatly appreciative to David Sanford, whose writings influenced my views on causal asymmetry, as did his comments on my work earlier in my career.

Three philosophers—Mark Heller, John Carroll, and David Papineau—read and commented on earlier drafts of this work. Their incisive commentary helped me avoid important mistakes and contributed much to the work's structure and content. I am profoundly obliged to them for their assistance.

The National Endowment for the Humanities provided a summer stipend to support my work on the topic of causation and identity, and the American Council of Learned Societies provided a fellowship to support my work on the topic of causal relata. I am also grateful to the members of the 1991 NEH summer seminar on causation and explanation and especially to Paul Humphreys, who ran this seminar.

In the final stages, I received very useful comments from three anonymous referees from Oxford University Press. Their amazingly detailed and extensive comments were responsible for the elimination of certain significant errors and for many (I hope) improvements. Lesley Lurie provided expert editorial assistance on the introduction.

Various sections of this book make use of material from some of my previously published articles. Parts of these articles are reproduced here with the permission of the publishers: "Causal Asymmetry," *The Journal of Philosophy*, 79, 1982; "Probabilistic Causality and Preemption," *British Journal for the Philosophy of Science*, 35, 1984; "Closed Causal Loops, Single Causes, and Asymmetry," *Analysis*, 46, 1986; "The Transference Theory of Causation," *Synthese*, 67, 1986; "Causal Relata," *Synthese*, 73, 1987; "Causal Asymmetry and Causal Relata," *Synthese*, 76, 1988; "Preemption and Probabilistic Counterfactual Theory," *Philosophical Studies*, 56, 1989; "The 'only t_1 through t_2' Principle," *Analysis*, 49, 1989; "Preemption, Direct Causation, and Identity," *Synthese*, 85, 1990; "Motion, Causation, and the Causal Theory of Identity," *The Australasian Journal of Philosophy*, 69, 1991; and "Preemption and Eells on Token Causation," *Philosophical Studies*, 74, 1994. Permission to use material from the *Synthese* and *Philosophical Studies* papers was granted by Kluwer Academic Publishers.

I am very much indebted to Christi Favor for her friendship and support during this project.

Contents

Introduction 3
  Background: Theories of Causation 3
  Background: Tropes 10
  Outline 15

1. *Preemption* 18
  Why Preemption, and What Is Preemption? 19
  Deterministic Theories 22
  Probabilistic Theories 32
  Singularist Accounts 43
  Objections 46

2. *The Significance of Preemption* 50
  Mechanism 50
  Against Arguments for Causal Realism 61
  Mechanism, Nonmechanism, and Methodology 68
  Persistence and Causal Relata 69

3. *Causal Relata* 71
  Davidson versus Kim 71
  Two Ways to Interpret Property Instances 84
  Summary 89

4. *Qualitative Persistence* 91
  For the Existence and Persistence of Tropes 91
  Against a Causal Account of Trope Persistence 104
  Summary 114

5. *The Alphabet of Causation* 116
  Mackie on Qualitative Persistence 116
  Partial Trope Persistence 117

      A Theory of Causation   120
      Summary   141

6.   *Causal Asymmetry*   *142*
      Two Preliminary Concepts   143
      A Definition of Causal Priority   147

Notes   *155*

Bibliography   *181*

Causation and Persistence

Introduction

Causal judgments are pervasive and apparently ineliminable in the sciences as well as in everyday life. We are almost never free of the task of making causal judgments in our practical lives, and in scientific settings, a high priority is assigned to determining the causal relations that structure our world. Nevertheless, there remains an air of philosophical mystery around this relation. What is the nature of this special tie that concerns us so greatly? What is the nature of the processes that connect causes with their effects? That is the main topic of my study—how causes bring about their effects. Traditionally, an approximate consensus held that causation consisted of a "generalist" component (for example, causal sequences falling under general laws) and a "singularist" component (intrinsic relations that do not depend upon what happens elsewhere or elsewhen). I am interested in the latter component of causation—the singularist tie, if any, that exists between particular causes and their particular effects. Received opinion reduces these singularist connections to certain unremarkable relations, like temporal proximity, and assumes that most of the interesting work is done by the generalist component. In this study, I question this assumption. I argue that cause and effect are locally tied together by more than spatio-temporal relations. Indeed, the central thesis of this work is that cause and effect are connected by way of a mechanism that is best characterized by reference to qualitative constancy and persistence or, more precisely, the persistence of individual properties or "tropes."

Background: Theories of Causation

The philosophy of causation includes a host of traditions, each motivated by a different feature of the causal relationship. A full treatment here of the extensive literature in each of these traditions is neither feasible nor necessary. However, an outline of the most important theories will give some sense of what goes into the construction of an account of causation, and a brief catalogue of the more important objections to and disagreements among these doctrines will highlight basic decision points in the philosophy of causation.[1] Key issues then can be brought into focus, allowing me to situate the theory of this study among these traditions. It is natural to begin with the historically most important tradition, that of Humeanism and neo-Humeanism.

The Humean Tradition

What Hume noticed about causation was that its most significant observable feature is that cause and effect are "constantly conjoined."[2] Regular sequences of events of one type all followed by events of the other include, for example, water freezing at very low temperatures, dry matches lighting when struck, and pin pricks followed by pain. The Humean then analyzes causation as derivative on such regular sequences. What is fundamental to causation are the general regularities. A particular sequence is causal by virtue of being an instance of a general pattern: c causes e on this occasion because on lots and lots of other occasions (in fact on *all*), when events like c occur, they are followed by events like e.[3] That's what makes *this* c-e sequence causal rather than noncausal. The same particular sequence, c-e, coupled with no general pattern, would not be causal. This is a top-down theory of causation, where the top represents the level of the general. It is this generalist component that is most central to the Humean tradition. The Humean adds some singularist features (causes must be temporally prior to their effects and spatially and temporally contiguous with their direct effects), but the core remains in the regularities. Most contemporary philosophers disagree with Hume about what the generalist component is but are still Humean in the broad sense of positing a generalist component to causation.

The traditional Humean stress on constant conjunction has been criticized at different levels. At the extreme end are objections meant to question the whole notion that constant conjunctions play a central role. The most radical of these criticisms give up on Humeanism altogether, rejecting the claim that there is any generalist component whatsoever to causation (from this comes singularist accounts). Less radical, but still fundamental, is the rejection of the need for perfectly uniform regularities (from this comes probabilistic accounts). Lesser objections lead into the neo-Humean program. The most obvious of these lesser complaints is that causal sequences are not always associated with Humean-style regularities. Even in the cases thought to fit the Humean picture best, there is slippage. Although I may cause this match to light by striking it on this occasion, match strikings are not invariably followed by match lightings, as all smokers know.[4] If causation really is closely associated with some generalist component, reading off the appropriate general truths is no simple matter. In the same reformist vein is the observation that general regularities are not always causal. Examples of merely coincidental correlations are a case in point—for example, sun spots coincidentally correlated with railroad workers' strikes. Accidental constant conjunctions do not ground any corresponding token causal sequence.[5] The Humean emphasis on a generalist component can be maintained only with significant refinement.[6]

Enter the neo-Humean. The neo-Humean tries to solve these problems by moving away from unqualified constant conjunction to laws of nature. With this shift, the less radical problems may have solutions. For example, on the one hand, there may indeed be a law of nature that is not immediately evident but is associated with our match striking-lighting sequence. On the other hand, there is not likely to be a genuine law linking sun spots and workers' strikes. Laws, rather than constant conjunctions, furnish causation's generalist component, and token causation is just a sequence that instances a causal law.[7] Causation is a matter of a cause event, in conjunction with the laws and background conditions, guaranteeing an effect event.[8] Causes are lawfully sufficient for their effects in the circumstances. With "laws" as the central analytic concept, the analysis of laws of nature becomes the principal issue for the philosophy of causation. Neo-Humean theories, then, get fleshed out either by way of a regularity theory of laws or an account of laws as relations among universals.

The neo-Humean account does mark an improvement in the Humean camp. Nevertheless, revised Humeanism still must face radical challenges to the claim that lawful sufficiency is the mark of causation. A challenge that perhaps stops short of a fundamental attack is the objection that lawful sufficiency does not always go with causation—that lawful sufficiency may not be sufficient for causation. Here we find the problem of joint effects and the problem of causal direction. Joint effects sometimes may be mutually lawfully sufficient (even though such effects are causally independent). In addition, an effect may be nomologically sufficient for its cause, if laws and circumstances guarantee that the effect could not have occurred otherwise than by being caused by this particular cause (even though effects do *not* cause their causes).[9] The question of preemption also falls into this problem set: preempted causes may sometimes be lawfully sufficient for their would-be effects.[10] However, the most radical challenge comes from the opposite direction. Lawful sufficiency may not be necessary for causation. Many philosophers doubt that causes must lawfully guarantee their effects. Causation in indeterministic settings seems possible, and probabilistic causes are not nomologically sufficient for their effects.[11]

Along with these criticisms of the Humean tradition have come a series of replacement philosophical programs. I briefly review the main ones here. The starting point for these alternatives is the rejection of nomological sufficiency as fundamental to causation. The two most important alternate accounts are counterfactual theory and probabilistic theory.

Counterfactual Theory

The Humean begins with the observation that causes are constantly conjoined with their effects, and the neo-Humean updates this observation with the principle that causes are nomologically sufficient for their effects. The counterfactual theorist begins with a different observation: causes generally make a difference. The world would have been different without the cause in the specific sense that its direct effect events would not have occurred. Causes are counterfactually necessary for their direct effects. If I strike a match and it lights, then it is true that had I not struck the match, it would not have lit. What makes this counterfactual true, assuming that the striking and the lighting do take place, is that in the most similar worlds without this striking, the lighting does not occur either. Such is the view of David Lewis, the best-known proponent of counterfactual theory.[12] Lewis also holds that interworld similarity is determined by both nomological and factual similarities across worlds. In the case of distant causally connected events, there will be a connecting chain of successively counterfactually dependent events.

These are the basics of counterfactual theory. As they stand, they immediately generate a series of challenges, some more pressing than others. On one side are difficulties that call for qualification and refinement. For instance, here we have Kim's various *noncausal* counterfactuals, such as, "If my sister had not given birth at *t*, I would not have become an uncle at *t*."[13] Under this same umbrella of noncausal counterfactuals lie the problem of joint effects and the problem of causal direction, both of which worried the neo-Humeans. With joint effects, it would seem, we sometimes find mutual counterfactual dependence—if you hadn't gotten a fever, you wouldn't now have a headache, although both are the result of an underlying virus and the two are not directly causally connected.[14] With the problem of causal direction, we sometimes seem to find causes that counterfactually depend on their effects: in some circumstances, had the match not lit, it would not earlier have been struck.[15] Perhaps even more worrisome, however, are cases of causation *without* counterfactual dependence. Individual overdeterminers are certainly *not* counterfactually necessary for their effects. Jones's overdetermined death by firing squad would have happened in the absence of any *one* of the shots fired. Preempting causes also seem to fail the counterfactual test. For example, if Fred kills Smith, but Failsafe Sally would have done the job in Fred's absence, then Smith's death does not counterfactually depend on its actual cause. I discuss the preemption problem extensively in chapter 1.

Probabilistic Accounts

The other major successor to the neo-Humean tradition is probabilistic theory. While neo-Humeanism requires that causes be nomologically sufficient for their effects, probabilistic theories are motivated by the growing recognition of causation in indeterministic settings. Quantum mechanics seems to support probabilistic theory in this respect. Nomological sufficiency fails in quantum mechanical settings without a failure in causation. If, for example, I activate a gun by way of a purely quantum mechanical process, with the result that your cat is shot, my actions cause the cat's death even if my actions do not nomologically guarantee the death. The same type of action repeated in indistinguishable circumstances might fail to issue in that same effect. Examples of this sort prompt probabilistic theories to abandon nomological sufficiency and to substitute the claim that causes increase the probability of their effects without necessarily determining them.[16] What the probabilistic theorist notices is that effects are more likely in the presence of their causes. This is what is basic to probabilistic accounts. This fundamental notion requires a great deal of elaboration and is developed differently by different theorists.[17]

As with neo-Humean and counterfactual accounts, probabilistic theories confront a number of problems of varying grades of severity, including some of the same problems encountered by these other theories. For example, they share the problem of joint effects and the problem of causal direction. With respect to the former problem, we find joint effects that are positively probabilistically mutually relevant in some circumstances (for instance, a fever and a headache caused by a virus), and with respect to the latter problem, we encounter the fact that effects raise the probability of their causes whenever causes do the same for their effects (for instance, the match's lighting makes it more likely that it was struck).[18] But greater difficulties must also be addressed. For almost any probabilistic theory, the really serious worry is that some causes *lower* the probability of their effects, as in this I. J. Good example: Moriarty is about to push a boulder from the top of a cliff in order to squash Holmes standing below, but Watson intervenes at the last moment to push the boulder in a safer direction. Unfortunately and improbably, Watson's push ends up causing the death of Holmes. Although what Watson does lowers the probability of Holmes's death, he still causes the death.[19] In chapter 1, I return to a related issue (that of causes that have no impact on the probability of their effects) in the context of preemptive causation.[20]

Singularist Accounts

The broadly Humean tradition takes causation to be largely a matter of general patterns: particular sequences gain their causal status by instancing regularities that unfold across world history. Whether c causes e depends on what happens elsewhere, including in the very distant future and the distant past. The singularist starts with a notably different intuition—with the observation that whether or not two particular events are causally connected cannot depend on what happens either in the future *after* those events have transpired or in the causally distant past. Whether you are enjoying that ice cream you are now eating (a causal relation) cannot depend on what happens next week. Whether you have just been hit by a ball (a causal relation) cannot depend on what happens in one hundred years, and whether the aspirin you took caused your headache to go away cannot depend on what might happen in ten thousand years. Causation is a purely local matter between particular events. By rejecting any generalist component to causation, singularism makes a complete break with Humeanism. A unique and unrepeated sequence can be causal, since the causal relation is independent of any generalist component, and specific causal sequences may fail to be subsumable under any laws, even a probabilistic law. Indeed, causal laws may be grounded on token causal sequences rather than the other way around.

Singularism is elaborated within either a reductionist framework or a nonreductionist framework. Singularist reductionists claim that singular causal statements of the form "c causes e" are reducible to and logically determined by noncausal facts about particulars alone, or, more precisely, by noncausal properties and relations of c and e and the local processes that connect these events. Nonreductionists deny that any such reduction is possible. For the nonreductionist singularist, causation cannot be explained in terms of anything but the singular causal relations between the relevant particular events. I will briefly review four versions of the singularist program.

Anscombe

Elizabeth Anscombe arguably can be considered a nonreductionist singularist. She certainly rejects traditional Humeanism, partly on the grounds of probabilistic causation.[21] She rejects the view "that any singular causal proposition implies a universal statement running 'Always when this, then that'."[22] Less clear is whether she believes that singular causal sequences must at least instance probabilistic laws. Some of her comments, however, seem to indicate that she intends singularism.[23] She argues that since causality is a matter of "deriving from or arising of," no corresponding universal generalization is implied by the fact that c causes e on a particular occasion.[24] If valid, this reasoning would also apply to probabilistic laws, because if "deriving from" does not entail what will happen generally, it should not entail what is even likely to happen on other occasions.[25] As Tooley suggests, the best way to make sense of

Anscombe's claim that *c*'s coming from *e* does not imply any universal generalization is that "Anscombe believes that causation is just a relation between concrete individuals . . . rather than, as Hume thought, something involving at least an implicit reference to corresponding *types* of individuals."[26] I would add that she appears to be a nonreductionist singularist, since "derives from" is very close to a synonym for "is caused by."

Tooley
Tooley is a much better example of a nonreductionist singularist, as he has a fully developed account of causation. For Tooley, causation is not reducible to the noncausal, but causation is analyzable. In support of his claim that causal relations are not reducible to noncausal facts, he presents a series of possible worlds that share all their noncausal facts but apparently differ causally. In order to justify his claim that causation, though not reducible, is analyzable, he argues that "causation" is a theoretical term and, like other theoretical terms in the sciences, such as "electron," can be analyzed through a technique developed by Ramsey and Lewis.[27] This formally elaborated account of causation as a theoretical relation is then situated within a singularist framework.[28] Causation is an irreducible theoretical relation that holds between particular states of affairs. Causation does not supervene on causal laws together with noncausal facts about particulars; it does not even presuppose causal laws: "events could still be causally related without falling under any relevant law."[29] In chapter 2, I will address some of Tooley's arguments for nonreductionism.

Ducasse
On the other side of the singularist camp is Ducasse, for whom causation is a *reducible* singularist relation. Like all singularists, Ducasse holds that causation is a relation between particular events with no generalist component. It is not, however, either a theoretical relation or irreducible. Causation is a directly perceivable and reducible relation. In particular, the reduction Ducasse proposes is roughly the following: the cause of a particular change *e* in a situation was the particular change *c*, which alone occurred in that situation immediately preceding *e*.[30] The striking of the match caused it to light by virtue of the fact that the striking was the only change in the circumstances that preceded the lighting.[31] His definition transmutes Mill's method of difference from an epistemological means for discovering causes to an ontological account of what causation is.[32]

Singularism, as much as nonsingularism, has its share of difficulties. Primary among them is the worry that causal relations may simply not be possible in a world without laws. Causation does seem to many philosophers to presuppose relevant covering laws, even if those laws are only probabilistic laws. A related difficulty with Ducasse's program, which applies to Anscombe's and Tooley's programs as well, is epistemological: we are prone to abandon individual causal judgments if later events unfold in unexpected ways, and this seems to support the claim for a generalist component. We would abandon the judgment that this *c* caused this *e* if in the future, under the same circumstances, *c* occurred but was not followed by *e* (assuming determinism).[33] Also related, and most germane to Ducasse's account, is a concern about relevancy. Ducasse's definition does not discriminate between causally relevant and irrelevant changes in the situation preceding *e*. If Jones ingests poison and some ice cream, then dies, an account of causation should reflect the fact that only the poison played a causal role in the death. For Ducasse, however, both the poison and the ice cream must be elements of the cause, since both are parts of the only preceding change.[34]

Transference Theory
As we have seen, the Humean begins with the observation that causes are constantly conjoined with their effects; the neo-Humean with the principle that causes are nomologically sufficient for their effects; the counterfactual theorist with the fact that causes generally make a difference; and the probabilist with the recognition that causes increase the probability of their effects. The transference theorist starts with an alternate observation: on close inspection of any physically possible causal process, one can find an actual transfer of something from cause to effect. The key to causation is physical transference. Transference theory shifts our attention to the underlying physical processes associated with causation in this and other physically possible worlds,[35] and the result is, arguably, a form of singularism. The actual transfers are local phenomena, which may or may not be law-governed. As such, transference theory does not supply a generalist principle at all (although versions of transference theory could, and typically do, have a separate generalist component).[36]

For Aronson, a contemporary proponent of transference theory, causation consists in the transfer of energy or momentum from one object to another at the point of contact between these objects.[37] The movement of one billiard ball (directly) causes the movement of a second if and only if the first hits the second and transfers to it some kinetic energy. The contact condition excludes action-at-a-distance, and the multiple objects requirement entails that changes internal to a single object are noncausal.

Transference theory, at least in this simple form, faces a number of serious difficulties: (1) there certainly are *caused* internal changes—for example, a chemical substance undergoing internal causal processes;[38] (2) there appear to be causal processes that don't seem to involve a transference of a physical quantity—for example, turning off a light switch causes the light to go out, but no electrical energy is transferred to the light;[39] (3) in cases of simultaneous causation—for example, two perfectly enmeshed rotating gears—causal direction is not easily established, since neither gear may have been moving prior to contact with the other gear; and (4) if backward causation is to be accommodated, then it must be distinguished from forward causation, but in transference theory there is no clear distinction, since in both cases, a quantity is possessed by one object at t_1 and by a different object at later time t_2.[40] Nevertheless, transference theory is still important, and it will play a significant role in my argument for a "mechanistic" account of causation's singularist component in chapters 1 and 2.

The Theory of This Study

The preceding brief compendium of theories makes possible the classification of this study's account.

My main concern in this study is with certain features of the causal relation that I call singularist. By a singularist relation between token events I mean a relation the realization of which does not depend on what happens in other regions or on how appropriate event types are related. These relations hold in virtue of purely local facts. I try to do two main things with respect to this topic. The first is to motivate the need for a theory of this singularist component according to which there is some local mechanism for the transmission of causal influence, and the second is to characterize this mechanism in terms of the persistence of individual properties. Where, then, does the theory of this study fit within the various traditional accounts?

In developing an account of causation's singularist component, I will assume that there is a generalist component to causation. In that respect, I am working within a broadly Humean tradition and not the singularist tradition. However, I make no attempt to explore the generalist component, but for the sake of definiteness assume it to be a matter of laws.[41] Although I assume there is a generalist component, I reject nomological sufficiency as a necessary condition for causation. I take probabilistic causation to be possible, and in fact, the most important examples I use are probabilistic. I also argue that nomological sufficiency is not sufficient for causation, even when combined with certain standard spatio-temporal restrictions. With respect to causation's singularist component, I reject traditional spatio-temporalist views. The singularist component of causation is not a matter of spatio-temporal contiguity or any spatio-temporal relations. My own positive account of causation's singularist component, however, does bear a family resemblance to transference theory, since I appeal to some persisting "entity" (persisting tropes), although no actual *transference* between objects is required.[42] Finally, I will help myself to counterfactuals, but only in my account of causal asymmetry in the last chapter. Counterfactuals play no role in accounting for the singularist component. In general, the overall theory of causation I propose is reductionist. I reject what Tooley calls "causal realism," understood as a form of nonreductionism: causation is *not* some further fact over and above the noncausal facts.

I now turn to the other main topic of this study: tropes. By way of introduction, I provide here a short overview of what has been said about tropes by their main supporters. I also discuss the different philosophical uses to which tropes are put in order to better locate my own project. This quick survey will make later discussions more accessible. I also outline my account of causation's singularist component in terms of trope persistence and indicate what problems it is meant to solve.

Background: Tropes

In traditional metaphysical discussions, concrete objects, such as tables and chairs, are listed as particulars, and properties, such as redness and wisdom, are classified (by realists) as universals. The trope theorist breaks with tradition and postulates a category of particulars that includes properties. Properties are real but are not universals (a different view from that of nominalists who deny properties altogether). At least some properties (trope nominalists say "all") are particulars, and as particulars, they cannot be shared.[43] A universal property can characterize more than one wholly distinct object at the same time, but tropes lack this capacity. The universal "greenness" may be instantiated by a piece of paper in Vermont and by a wall in London (that very same universal), but green tropes of spatially wholly distinct objects at the same time are necessarily nonidentical. The closest that tropes of wholly distinct objects that exist at the same time can ever get to identity is exact similarity. It is the absence of the possibility of multiple simultaneous instances that puts tropes on the side of particulars. This ball's roundness, conceived as a trope, is distinct from the roundness of any other ball, and the whiteness of this page is numerically distinct from the whiteness of the preceding page, no matter how similar it is. Balls and pages are particulars, but so too, it turns out, are roundnesses and whitenesses. Tropes are *particularized properties*.[44]

That tropes are properties but still particulars is their central feature. Nevertheless, three additional, less central aspects to the doctrine of tropes should also be mentioned. The first is the fact that tropes, at least of physical objects, are spatio-temporally located. Consider, again, the whiteness of this page. This individual property has a definite location and a definite duration, and the same is true of other tropes. For example, the specific shape trope of a specific tree is spread out across a certain spatial region and is realized during a certain time period. Tropes are like ordinary objects in having spatio-temporal locations.[45] The second, additional feature of this doctrine is that tropes are "abstract"—a feature of the view that may tend to mislead, since "abstract" is used differently in other philosophical contexts. Tropes are *not* abstract in the sense that numbers and sets are. The abstractness of tropes contrasts with the "concreteness" of ordinary objects.[46] Tropes can and usually do overlap with other tropes at the same spatio-temporal location, whereas concrete objects are not ordinarily thought to overlap with other concrete objects.[47] The color of a sphere, for example, occupies the same spatial location as the shape of the sphere, whereas the sphere itself "monopolizes," as Campbell says, its location, excluding other concrete particulars;[48] or, again, no other distinct object (as ordinarily conceived) co-occupies the location of the chair, but the chair's mass shares its location with the chair's density. The possibility of co-occupation makes tropes nonconcrete or abstract.

The third supplemental feature of trope theory is a little more esoteric: tropes are not "bare particulars." Some philosophers posit a kind of particular that in itself lacks all characteristics and is called a "bare particular." The philosophical function of bare particulars is to supply particularity to ordinary objects—to tie their universal properties to a definite "something." Hence, bare particulars lack a nature or a character in themselves. The same is not true of tropes. Tropes have a nature, since they are themselves properties. Put slightly differently, bare particulars, if they exist, would have the function of supplying an object with particularity but not a nature, whereas tropes could do both.

However, it is important *not* to picture a trope as including a separate component that determines its particularity, akin to a bare particular, and another that determines its nature, akin to a universal. The trope's nature is not separable from its particularity.[49] To think of tropes otherwise would collapse them into exemplifications of universals by bare particulars.

Indeed, tropes must be distinguished from exemplifications of universals by any object (whether a bare particular or not)—that is, from so-called states of affairs. The exemplification of a universal U by an object o at a time t is a particular of sorts and is also sometimes referred to, as are tropes, as a "property instance." Still, there are important reasons for distinguishing such exemplifications from tropes. First, consider that the constituents of an exemplification of a universal include the object, the property, and the exemplification relation (if it is a relation); and notice that the property-constituents are universals, not particulars. The state of affairs as a whole is a particular, but its property-constituents are not. In the case of a trope, the property itself is a particular. Second, and related to this point, the particularity of the exemplification of a universal derives not at all from its constituent property (a universal); it derives only from the object-constituent (and perhaps its time). The particularity of a trope, however, derives from the property itself, not from the object it characterizes.[50] Third, the nature of a state of affairs can be shared (by including the same universal-constituent), but not so the nature of a trope, since a trope's nature is inseparable from its particularity. Fourth, assuming that both tropes and exemplifications of universals are logically possible, there could exist tropes even if there are no exemplifications of universals (if, say, there are no universals), and, conversely, if there are no tropes, there may still be exemplifications of universals.[51]

Then what are tropes for, philosophically? Tropes play a role in three main philosophical programs: (1) to give a nominalist account of concrete objects, such as tables and chairs; (2) to explain the repeated instantiation of types without recourse to universals; and (3) to account for the nature of causal relata. The last is the one of greatest interest here, but a brief introduction to the other two will make clear what is *not* going on in this study.

Concrete Objects

Nominalist trope-theorists posit properties and relations, but only as particulars, and they claim that concrete objects can be built up either solely from tropes or from tropes and some other nonproperty particular. A trope-only ontology analyzes ordinary objects as bundles of tropes.[52] A chair is just the collection of its tropes—for example, its brownness, its hardness, and so on.[53] These sundry properties form a single concrete object in virtue of their mutual compresence in a certain location.[54] As Armstrong states the view, "Particulars *reduce* to bundles of compresent tropes."[55] A trope-bundle theory runs parallel to a universal-bundle theory of objects, with one definite advantage: with tropes as the elements of the bundles, it is possible for exactly similar, but numerically distinct objects to exist; otherwise it is not.[56] If the elements are universals, exactly resembling bundles must be identical.[57]

Types

The second metaphysical task for tropes is to account for the fact that distinct objects may fall under the same type. Consider two objects with the same color, say red. The realist postulates a shared "redness" universal to explain this fact, but the trope theorist who is a nominalist must resist this option. The trope theorist claims instead that these two objects are characterized by distinct red tropes but that these tropes (not the red objects) are members of a class of red tropes, and it is that common class membership of the red tropes that is the grounding for the common type labeled "red." This class of red tropes is then further characterized either in terms of unanalyzable "distributive unity" (Stout) or unanalyzable resemblance (Williams and Campbell).[58] For Stout, the members of the class of red tropes have an unanalyzable and primitive "distributive unity" that is not grounded in resemblance and cannot be further explained. For the Williams-Campbell camp, resemblance grounds the unity of the class of red tropes, but resemblance itself among tropes is primitive, not to be cashed out in terms of shared universals.[59]

Causal Relata

The third metaphysical task, which is central to this study, is to account for causal relata. What kinds of things does the causal relation relate? Some philosophers have suggested facts, others events, and some even sentences. Most trope proponents claim that causal relata consist in tropes. As Campbell observes, "If you are burnt by a hot wire it is, after all, not heat in general, or wires in general, or the other characteristics of this wire, but *the heat of this wire* which does the burning."[60] Or, more generally, "causes are always features (almost always a small selection from the host of features present) and every particular cause is a particular feature or constellation of features."[61] These features are identified with tropes: "the terms of the *causal* relation are always tropes."[62]

This third metaphysical use for tropes is independent from the other two. For example, a causal-relata-as-tropes view can be maintained without accepting a nominalist, one-category ontology. Of the three metaphysical tasks discussed above, I am interested only in the third: the project of accounting for causation in terms of tropes. What I am *not* doing is attempting (1) to analyze the nature of concrete objects as bundles of tropes[63] or (2) to defend trope nominalism, including a trope-based account of types. What I say here may be compatible with the existence of universals and is compatible with the rejection of universals. What is excluded is the possibility of accounting for causation without reference to tropes. In particular, we will not be able to get along with exemplifications of universals in place of tropes. Tropes have a nonredundant role in a theory of causation. In short, tropes are not reducible to exemplifications of universals, and the work done by tropes in a theory of causation cannot be done equally well by exemplifications of universals.

In addition to defending tropes as the sole causal relata, I use tropes to account for the singularist component of the causal relation. I exploit tropes' capacity for persistence to explain the singularist component. In one sense, this project is less ambitious than trope nominalism, because it includes only causation. In another sense, however, it is more far-ranging. Nominalists previously employed tropes only as causal relata, whereas here tropes take on a further, more central role in the theory of causation.

I will now bring these two topics, causation and tropes, together and outline the notion of trope persistence and my account of causation's singularist component.

Trope Persistence and Causation

The issue of trope persistence is not well articulated in the literature. There is a tendency, in fact, to treat tropes as momentary. In later chapters, I provide reasons for reversing that trend. A related issue is whether or not tropes' persistence is a matter of relations between trope-stages, an issue that is also addressed in subsequent chapters. At this point, however, it will be useful to introduce my views on trope persistence as a whole. This overall sketch will help the reader better understand the dialectical moves to come. Refinements and the necessary argumentation are added later.

Qualitative persistence is pervasive and unremarkable. A ball retains its shape. An electron retains its charge. And a chair retains its color. These are all cases of qualitative persistence, and of course there are countless others. Qualitative persistence is a widespread feature of the world. As philosophers we may well ask, in what does qualitative persistence consist? The answer, I believe, is that genuine cases of qualitative persistence are cases of trope persistence. The ball's persisting shape is a persisting shape trope. The electron's continuous charge characteristic is just the persistence of the same particularized property over time. The chair's color is a persisting color trope. That is the trope-theoretic account of qualitative persistence. Fundamental to this analysis of qualitative persistence is the claim that as with concrete particulars abstract particulars can and do persist. Tropes are not necessarily momentary, which is not to say that all tropes persist. For example, the blue of a movie-image sky is a series of nearly momentary tropes. Still, there are persisting tropes.

With any persisting entity, including tropes, different interpretations of what that persistence consists in are possible. On one view, a persisting trope has temporal parts, and the trope's persistence consists in the holding of certain relations, typically including causation, among these temporal stages. We are familiar with temporal-parts views from the literature on personal identity and physical object identity. The other interpretation is nonrelational. On this view, the persisting entity has no temporal stages. A trope's persistence will then consist in the trope's being present or realized wholly at each moment of its duration. I defend this three-dimensionalist perspective.

Trope persistence, although nonrelational, is not all-or-nothing. Tropes may exhibit partial persistence. Partial persistence is possible because there are compound tropes. Parts of a compound trope may survive while other parts fail to endure. In that event, tropes at different times will partially overlap. A compound trope may persist partially in the wake of the destruction of a part of that same trope. Partial trope persistence falls into certain basic patterns: fission and fusion. A fissioning compound trope breaks apart to form simpler tropes, which are partially identical to the original compound trope. For example, a fissioning charge property may be associated with a charged object that divides into two objects, each of which retains half of the original charge. Trope fusion is the reverse of trope fission: a compound trope is formed from simpler tropes. The fusing tropes are partially identical to the compound trope. Trope fusion and fission also may be combined, typically, in sequence.

The main goal of this study is to furnish an account of causation's singularist component. "Generalist" theories make causation between token events depend in part on certain type-type relations, but such relations cannot be all there is to token causation. Some "singularist" component is also necessary. I propose a "mechanist" account of that singularist component: causes and direct effects are locally connected by more than purely spatial and temporal relations. Indeed, I suggest that one common feature of causal processes—qualitative persistence—provides the key to causation's singularist component. Qualitative persistence, if conceptually recast as trope persistence in its various forms, supplies the backbone of such an account. The most elementary causal processes, for example, turn out to be individual properties persisting unchanged, and such unchanging properties form a causal chain linking the past with the future. From these simple cases, we can build up to complex causal processes. More complex causal processes, when scrutinized closely, can be seen to exhibit assorted patterns of partial trope persistence, including trope fission and fusion. Even interactions among intersecting causal processes demonstrate complex forms of trope persistence. Details of such processes are elaborated in chapter 5. In short, causes and effects are tropes, and the local tie between cause and effect is a matter of trope persistence.

The basic intuition underlying this view is that in causation there is something that is preserved, and this something turns out to be properties. Causal relata are tropes, and causation's singularist component is constituted by their persistence. Causal inquiry is a matter of providing first a breakdown or analysis of the constituents of the relevant trope at a time t, then a history that indicates how these components came to be realized in their incarnation at t through property persistence, fission, and fusion. A world with causation is not a world of purely momentary facts. Genuine causation requires persistence between episodes. Efficient causation is analogous to "material causation," in that a listing of the preexisting tropes that form the building blocks for the effect trope replaces material causation's listing of component objects that come to form a resulting object.

As indicated earlier, there are a number of stubborn problems that have continued to perplex theories of causation. I take the four most important to be those of indeterministic causation, joint effects, causal direction, and preemption. Preemption is the most significant of these persistent problems, and it gets the greatest attention in this study. Preemption is the undoing of the leading reductionist theories of causation, as demonstrated in chapter 1, and in its most acute form it raises the issue of causation's singularist component. Trope persistence resolves this issue in a very straightforward way: preempting causes show the requisite form of qualitative persistence with their effects, but preempted causes fail to exhibit any such persistence with respect to their would-be effects. The theory of this study does not directly address the problem of probabilistic causation, although what I say is compatible with indeterminism. The problems of joint effects and causal direction get resolved not by trope persistence but only by way of an account of causal asymmetry (of what makes it true that causes cause their effects, but effects do not cause their causes), as set forth in chapter 6.

Outline

In chapter 1, I present the first stage of an argument directed at demonstrating the need for a mechanist theory of the singularist component of causation. This argument consists of a comparative examination of various contemporary theories of causation in the context of preemptive causation. I conclude that only a certain kind of singularist theory has any hope of diagnosing the causal facts in such cases.

In chapter 2, I consider two different kinds of theories of this singularist component—spatio-temporalism and mechanism. Spatio-temporalism claims that the only token-level relations between cause and effect are temporal and spatial relations. Mechanism claims that the singularist component of causation consists of a mechanism for the transmission of direct causal influence, a mechanism that involves persistence over time. I argue that the results of chapter 1 support one component of the mechanistic view (over the spatio-temporalist view): that there is some means by which causes bring about their direct effects. I next consider various options for characterizing this mechanism. There are three possible ways of fleshing out this local mechanism. The first two cite either purely spatio-temporal relations (which would collapse mechanism into spatio-temporalism) or nomological relations. Neither of these approaches can resolve the problem of preemption. The third option makes use of the persistence or identity of some "entity" that carries causal influence. This third option is immune to the difficulties of preemption. Finally, I argue that the identity conditions for this causal-influence-carrying entity should not reintroduce spatio-temporalism. Identity, for this entity, is not a matter of spatio-temporal (or nomological) relations among its temporal stages. The remainder of the book contains the details of this mechanistic account of causation's singularist component.

In chapter 3, I take up the issue of the nature of causal relata. The two main accounts that have been discussed in the literature are those of Davidson and Kim. A Davidsonian takes causal relata to consist in concrete events that exemplify an indefinite number of properties, only some of which are relevant to any particular effect that the event brings about. A Kimian, on the other hand, takes causal relata to consist in exemplifications of properties by an object or objects at a time. Of these two views, I favor the Kimian on the grounds that only this view is compatible with the transitivity of the causal relation. In brief, I argue that if an event's causal relations can depend on any of its various exemplified properties, then we will be able to construct chains in which transitivity fails. Since, for the Kimian, events are not efficacious in virtue of any of their merely exemplified properties, these kinds of chains are ruled out, whereas for the Davidsonian they are not.

There are two ways to interpret a property instance view. The first, which Kim holds, is that causal relata are exemplifications of universals. The second is that causal relata are tropes at a time. I argue that we should favor the interpretation that is consistent with the best account of causation. By way of anticipating chapter 5, I claim that the best account of certain simple causal scenarios—in which an earlier property instance is causally responsible for a later incarnation of that same property—is in terms of the notion of a persisting property. Causation is analyzed in terms of persisting properties. The trope view is best suited to this account of causation.

The burden of chapter 4 is to fulfill an argumentative debt from chapter 3—to show that there really are tropes and that they can persist. I point to two metaphysical facts that, I claim, can be fully accounted for only if there are persisting tropes. The first is that properties of an object sometimes persist. The second is the fact that property persistence is distinguishable from "nonsalient qualitative change," a form of change illustrated in the following scenario: a destroyer machine destroys a property of an object at the same moment that a creator machine generates an indistinguishable property in that object. A theory of properties, or at least property instances, should give a noncircular account of property persistence and provide a basis for distinguishing cases of property persistence from cases of nonsalient qualitative change. Only a theory positing persisting tropes can accomplish both tasks.

In the second half of this chapter, I argue against relational accounts of trope persistence, especially causal accounts. Against causal accounts I present a Kripke-like argument with the following structure. An adequate theory of trope persistence provides a basis for determining whether a given trope is moving or stationary. On a relational theory of trope persistence, motion will consist in the relevant trope stages, which occupy different spatial locations, being appropriately related by whatever relations constitute the basis of gen-identity for tropes. The difficulty is that there are circumstances (those in Kripke-like cases involving homogeneous spheres) in which a causal account fails to properly diagnose the facts of trope persistence and motion. Any relational account of trope persistence will have this defect. This opens the way to providing an account of causation in terms of trope persistence without fear of circularity.

In chapter 5, I develop an account of the singularist component of causation. I suggest that different patterns of causal processes can be analyzed by reference to various forms of trope persistence. Under this conception I reconstruct some examples, the best of which are from chemistry. These cases show clearly the way complex tropes can be built up and broken down over time. I provide a definition of causation according to which tropes at different times are causally connected only if they are linked by processes of trope persistence, fission, or fusion.

In the final chapter, I give an account of causal asymmetry that does not presuppose that causes must precede their effects. Causal asymmetry is rather a matter of the mutual causal independence of the causal antecedents of an effect. A cause is a member of a set of events that possess, within that set, a certain causal independence, whereas the effect event is not causally independent of any of these events. In brief, causes do their work only in relevant conditioning circumstances, which also constitute causal antecedents. Causal asymmetry is generated out of the causal independence of causes from their conditioning circumstances, an independence that is not found between those circumstances and the effect.

1

Preemption

A theory of causation should tell us just what the nature of the causal relation is between particular events. Theories that are "generalist" require that causally connected particular events instantiate *types* of events that are suitably related (at the type level). But type-level relations cannot exhaust the nature of token causation, and even the generalist must acknowledge a "singularist" component. A "singularist" relation is a relation between events the realization of which does not depend on what happens elsewhere in the world. Spatial and temporal relations are possible candidates for this component, but there are other options. As indicated, the main purpose of this study is to provide an account of the singularist component of causation. Although I will make a working generalist assumption (to the effect that causally connected events instantiate lawfully connected types), only the nature of the singularist component will receive attention here.

The Humean view provides a straightforward illustration of the need for a singularist component in a generalist account. For David Hume, the type-level relation constitutive of causation is constant conjunction—c-type events must generally be found together with e-type events if a particular event c causes a particular event e. But constant conjunction of event types cannot determine by itself how to *pair up* particular events (call this a "pairing problem"). With which particular e-type event should we pair a particular c-type event, such as c, which occurs, say, here and now? This generalist component of constant conjunction is not sufficient for a causal connection between any c-type event and some particular e-type event. Some further token-level relation must be specified that will guarantee that most of the e-type events will be eliminated as direct effects of this token event c. Typically, certain spatial and temporal relations, such as spatial/temporal contiguity, are invoked to do this job. These singularist relations are intended to solve the residual problem of causally pairing particular events, a problem left over by the generalist core of the Humean account.

Given the working generalist assumption of this study, one way to think of an account of this singularist component, then, is as an answer to a pairing problem generated by this generalist component. However, it should (and will) be made clear that even a theory that is not explicitly generalist (such as counterfactual theory) may require supplementation with a suitable singularist component. Even theories that are not clearly generalist may face an unresolved pairing problem, and it is the pairing problem itself, rather than the source of that problem, that demands a singularist component.

My first task along the way to constructing an account of the singularist component is to demonstrate the need for a singularist component of a certain kind. The execution of this task will involve a two-step argument. This chapter presents the first stage of this argument. In this chapter I present a comparative survey of various leading reductionist theories of causation with the end of establishing which features of a theory make for failure and which features make for success with respect to a certain problematic causal phenomenon—that of preemption. Only one of the theories examined, transference theory, is any good in preemptive contexts. I will argue that this result is significant because it indicates the need for a certain kind of singularist component in any theory adequate to the phenomenon of preemption. In the next chapter I take up the second half of this two-step argument and generalize from the limited success of transference theory in order to provide a broad characterization of the kind of singularist component required by an adequate theory of causation. In the next chapter I also address the issue of nonreductionist theories of causation and what they might say about the problem of preemption.

Why Preemption, and What Is Preemption?

Much of what follows in this chapter and the next revolves around preemption. However, it is not obvious that preemption should play such a principal role in the construction of a theory of causation. After all, theories generally face an array of problem cases other than that of preemption (e.g., joint effects, backward causation, and spurious correlations), not all of which are equally important. Should not preemption be relegated to the less important end of the spectrum? This question is especially pressing given that in many traditional discussions preemption does not loom large. Some indication must be given as to why preemption should be promoted to center stage.

First, notice that in the last twenty-five years, preemption has enjoyed a higher standing in the causation literature than in traditional discussions. The perceived importance of preemption has been affected by the rise of counterfactual theories. Preemption is naturally the dominant problem for any theory that makes causation a matter of counterfactual dependence. Preemption serves as the main purported counterexample to this kind of theory, since the effect of a preempting cause *c* would have occurred, it would seem, even in the absence of *c*. The prominence of counterfactual theory raises the profile of preemption. However, there are deeper reasons for promoting preemption to a leading role, reasons not linked to the accidental features of the history of the subject. The issues raised by preemptive causation go to the heart of what a theory of causation should be like. Preemption presents more than a minor problem that can handled by some final noncentral revisions.

To see this, consider what the construction of a theory of causation involves. A central decision in any such construction concerns to what degree causation is or is not purely an intrinsic matter. As we have seen, theories can be assayed according to how much weight they place on generalist factors and how much on singularist factors. For a generalist, whether c causes e depends on factors that are extrinsic to the processes that connect c and e—certain regularities in the world at large, for instance. A singularist eschews such type-level factors and emphasizes intrinsic features of the connecting processes. The generalist-nongeneralist nexus is perhaps the key manifestation of the extrinsic-intrinsic distinction in this domain, but there are other aspects to the latter distinction. In addition to the global extrinsic factors extolled by the generalist, the causal theorist must decide how much weight should go to extrinsic factors that are much more local. Situational factors or extrinsic background factors may also be part of our account of causation (or they may not). Do we want the causal connection of c and e to depend on the presence of situational factors that are not a matter of intrinsic features of the processes that connect c and e? The enterprise of constructing an account of causation depends crucially on the issue of the appropriate mix of the extrinsic and the intrinsic, and this is where preemption comes in. These issues are tremendously sharpened through its lens, since preemption cases act as an acute test of the proper balance within this broad nexus.

The best way to demonstrate this point is to notice how theories run afoul of preemption: either by wrongly claiming efficacy of the preempted cause or by wrongly denying efficacy to the preempting cause. How is each of these errors generated? A theory that grants efficacy to preempted causes typically does so by overemphasizing generalist components. The preempted cause may fall under the same general truths or regularities, with respect to the effect, as does the preempting cause. A false appearance of efficacy is thereby induced. On the other hand, a theory that denies efficacy of preempting causes typically does so by way of an oversensitivity to situational, extrinsic factors. The mere presence of a preempted cause in the background shifts the theory's verdict on the preempting cause. In both of these cases, the theorist must consider giving more weight to the features of causal processes that are independent of the surrounding situation or broad global generalities. Preemption thus acts as a gauge of how far a theory has steered away from causation's intrinsic aspects—a necessary tonic against too much extrinsicness in our picture of causation—and thereby highlights a theory's deepest commitments.

What, then, is preemption? In cases of deterministic preemption, there are two causal lines, a main and an alternate line, both leading to the same effect. The main line, but not the alternate line, reaches completion and brings about this effect. However, had the main line failed to bring about the final effect, the alternate line would have brought it about. On the other hand, in cases of "probabilistic" preemption, it is *not* true that had the main line failed, the alternate line would definitely have run to completion. In cases of probabilistic preemption, had the main line not run to completion, the alternate line *might* have led to the final effect. Had the preempting cause failed, the alternate line would have raised the probability of the final effect to *the same degree* as the actual cause.

Preemptive causation also generally will include some blocking action: the main line blocks the efficacy of the alternate line. This interference can come in two forms. In the first, had the alternate line been free of this blocking action, it would have run to completion by way of some *additional* events—causal intermediaries between the last actual event in the alternate line and the final effect. I will call this "nonoccurrent preemption," since there are events (the intermediaries) that did *not* occur, but would have occurred had there been no blocking action. In the second form, the blocking action from the main line does not prevent the occurrence of any events in the alternate line. The blocking action prevents the last (actual) event in the alternate line from bringing about the final effect. The efficacy of this last event is blocked, but not by preventing the occurrence of any intermediary events between that event and the final effect. Unlike in nonoccurrent preemption, the final event in the alternate line would have *directly* caused the final effect (had it been efficacious at all). I will call this "occurrent preemption," since the main line does not block the occurrence of any *event* in the alternate line.

Certain kinds of causal phenomena, particularly preemption, are more likely than others to generate an unresolved pairing problem for a theory of causation. A theory of causation faces a pairing problem if there is more than one mutually exclusive candidate for the role of effect or cause, relative to a given event. As we have seen, preemptive settings include two events (the preempted and preempting cause) that are both candidates for pairing with the effect, and a theory may fail to solve this problem either by pairing *both* the preempting and preempted causes with the final effect or by pairing *neither* with that effect (or by reversing the correct pairing). As we shall see, only those theories that include a certain kind of singularist component are successful at this pairing task. The preemption pairing problem (as I will call it) arises not only for explicitly generalist accounts but also for other, quasi-generalist accounts (which say that the truth of singular causal statements is sensitive to certain type-type relations but not necessarily between types instantiated by the causal pair in question). Resolution of the preemption pairing problem will serve as the primary test of adequacy for an account of the singularist component. My eventual analysis of this component will be constructed largely in response to the preemption pairing problem faced by various contemporary reductionist theories of causation.

The theories of causation discussed in this first chapter can be divided into two kinds: those compatible only with determinism and those compatible with indeterminism. In the next section I consider accounts that assume the truth of determinism. Neo-Humeanism and traditional counterfactual theory fall into this group. In the section after that, I consider accounts that do not depend on determinism. There I review a sampling of probabilistic accounts, including probabilistic counterfactual theory. All of these theories are either generalist or quasi-generalist. In the third section of this chapter, I turn to what I interpret to be a singularist theory, transference theory. Almost all of these theories fail the test of preemption, with the exception of transference theory. The significance of this comparative success of transference theory to an account of the singularist component of causation is the topic of chapter 2.

Let us now consider how neo-Humean theory and counterfactual theory fare in preemptive settings. I warn the reader ahead of time that the discussions in this section and the next are fairly detailed. At the beginning of my examination of each theory, however, I will provide a general overview of that theory and its prospects for handling preemption. Following each such general overview will be a more detailed assessment. I return to a more general level of discussion in chapter 2, where the broader significance of these investigations will be made clear.

Deterministic Theories

Neo-Humean Theory

For the neo-Humean, causation is a matter of lawful connection. Token events are causally connected if and only if they are connected by law or subsumable under law. The striking of the match causes it to light just in case there are descriptions of each such that the occurrence of striking guarantees occurrence of the lighting, given the laws and accompanying circumstances. What I will try to show is that this line of analysis, which is accepted by many philosophers, runs into serious difficulty in contexts of preemptive causation. In brief, preempted (nongenuine) causes will sometimes be lawfully sufficient for the preemptively caused effect. What is significant about this breakdown of neo-Humeanism is the indication it gives of some further element to the causal relation, other than lawful connection. This further element is, unlike lawful connection, a singularist component of causation.

The neo-Humean view is the clearest example of a generalist account of causation. On this view, what makes singular causal statements true will include certain general facts. Singular causal statements such as "c causes e" are not only sensitive to events and relations realized at the time of c and e; they also have a nonlocal significance. This nonlocal sensitivity is a result of the fact that neo-Humean theories analyze causation in terms of laws of nature. The exact nature of this sensitivity will depend on how laws are analyzed. If laws are regularities, the truth value of singular causal statements will depend in part on how the world unfolds before and after the time of c-e—that is, on other particular facts not realized at the time of c-e. Even if laws are relations between universals (and even if these universal-universal relations are, in some sense, "singular facts"), singular causal statements still will implicate particular facts not realized at the time of c-e, because the laws under which they are subsumed will entail such regularities.[1] Suppose, for example, that it is a law that Fs are Gs, where F-ness and G-ness are universals. This relation of "necessitation" between these universals still "*entails* the corresponding Humean or cosmic uniformity: $(x)(Fx \supset Gx)$."[2] This entailment is compatible with the claim that laws do not supervene on facts about particulars.

What all neo-Humean accounts will agree on is that the truth of the singular causal statement "token event c causes token event e" depends in part on whether these events are subsumable under causal laws. The token events must exemplify types such that these types of events are lawfully connected. For example, the statement "c causes e" will be true only if there exist a law L, a statement of initial conditions I, and descriptions of these events, D_1 and D_2 respectively, such that a statement that D_1 occurs (in combination with L and I) entails a statement that D_2 occurs. In short, causally connected token events must exemplify types that are lawfully connected. What it is for types of events to be lawfully connected will be a matter of further analysis, but presumably such connections will not supervene on purely particular facts realized at the time of c-e.

Our question about this theory, which we will raise about several other contemporary accounts, is whether it can successfully handle preemptive causation. The answer to this question turns out to be negative, and that fact naturally generates a further question as to what features of this type of view give rise to this failure. I will make a diagnostic suggestion that will itself point us in the direction of a closer look at the singularist component of causation.

As I have already indicated, there are two main ways a theory may fail to solve the preemption pairing problem: by granting efficacy either to both or to neither of the preempting and preempted causes. If neo-Humeans are to avoid both of these extremes, they must guarantee generally that preempting causes are lawfully sufficient for their effects but that preempted causes are not lawfully sufficient for these same effects. The set of legal relations must exhibit just this asymmetry. The neo-Humean has no great difficulty satisfying the first conjunct—at least under determinism. Preempting causes presumably will be lawfully sufficient in the circumstances for their effects, if determinism holds. Or at least I will not question that presumption here. It is quite a different matter, however, when we turn to the legal relations of preempted causes. There is no way to guarantee that preempted causes are not also lawfully sufficient for preemptively caused effects, at least under certain circumstances.

This lack of legal asymmetry between preempting and preempted causes is illustrated in the following example:

> Oswald fires his rifle from the window of the book depository at such and such an angle and instantly kills the president. In the process LBJ is preempted from killing the president. Had Oswald not fired, LBJ's firing a second later would have killed the president anyway. The efficacy of Oswald's action is guaranteed for the neo-Humean by the fact that, assuming determinism, there will be circumstances and laws such that Oswald's firing guarantees the death. From appropriate descriptions of Oswald's firing, laws, and initial conditions, a statement of the occurrence of the death could be deduced, at least under a certain description. The difficulty is that the neo-Humean may have to say the same of LBJ's actions: we may also be able to deduce a statement of the death from a description of LBJ's actions, given the laws and circumstances. This deduction will hold whether or not Oswald's firing is included in a description of the circumstances. In the absence of Oswald's firing, LBJ's action is lawfully sufficient for the death, and if Oswald's firing is included, LBJ's actions in those circumstances will also be lawfully sufficient for the death.

The neo-Humean, then, seems compelled to grant efficacy to the preempted cause of death—LBJ's action.

Is this a fair criticism? There is a further characteristic of the neo-Humean account that may block this attribution of causal status to LBJ's actions. The neo-Humean also requires that the prospective cause be essential to the deduction—that if the statement of its occurrence is deleted from the argument, then the argument ceases to be valid. The statement describing LBJ's action, however, is not essential to the deduction, at least if Oswald's firing is included in the description of the initial conditions. The deduction remains valid if LBJ's firing is deleted from the premises. Since a statement of his actions is inessential, those actions do not cause the death.

But this way of disenfranchising LBJ's action may be too strong. The same reasoning applied to Oswald's firing is equally compelling: a statement of Oswald's firing is not essential to the deduction, if a description of LBJ's action is included in the circumstances. Given LBJ's action, the death is guaranteed even if Oswald does not fire. Oswald's action makes a difference only in how that death comes about, not whether it comes about.

There is a further possible move that the neo-Humean might make to produce the necessary legal asymmetry. He might suggest that we exclude LBJ's action from a description of the circumstances when evaluating the efficacy of Oswald's firing. This maneuver would restore the essentiality of the description of Oswald's firing. In the absence of this description, a statement of Oswald's firing is necessary for the validity of the deduction of the death. The efficacy of Oswald's action is thereby saved. The trouble with this move is that it is arbitrary to disallow a similar exclusion when evaluating the causal status of LBJ's actions. Unless causal assumptions are imported into the analysis, symmetry requires that we delete descriptions of Oswald's firing in any deduction invoked to demonstrate the efficacy of LBJ's action. If these prospective causes are to be evaluated on the same grounds, then descriptions of Oswald's firing must not appear in premises meant to demonstrate the efficacy of LBJ's action. But with the deletion of the description of Oswald's firing, LBJ's action will also qualify as a cause of the death (since it will appear essentially in a deduction of a statement of the death). In short, we are damned if we do and damned if we don't.

This dilemma facing the neo-Humean can be stated more abstractly. For the neo-Humean, the task of pairing the preempting, but not the preempted, cause to the effect is equivalent to the following task: demonstrate (1) that the preempting cause is lawfully sufficient for this effect but that the preempted cause is not lawfully sufficient, in the circumstances, and (2) that the preempted cause would have been lawfully sufficient in the absence of the preempting cause.

For the first part of (1), certifying that c_1 causes e, we need a causal law, L_1, to the effect that c_1-type events are followed by e-type events in circumstances H. This law, L_1, guarantees that in this situation, which is of type H, c_1 is a cause of e.

But it must also be shown that we cannot deduce e from a set of laws and c_2. If we are allowed to include c_1 in a description of the actual circumstances, then we will be able to deduce a statement that e occurs from a statement that c_2 occurs, a description of the actual circumstances, and L_1. However, if c_1 is included in a description of the actual circumstances, then c_2 is inessential to the deduction of e. So it might be suggested that this deduction does not show the efficacy of c_2.

The difficulty with this move, however, arises when we turn to (2). There must be a law that guarantees that c_2 would cause e in the absence of c_1. L_1 alone does not determine that c_2 would cause e in the absence of c_1. For this further implication, a causal law of the following form will do the job:

(L_2) c_2-type events in the absence of c_1-type events in circumstances H' are followed by e-type events.

The difficulty is this: if we include both L_1 and L_2 in our premises (and H and H' are compatible, as in some cases they will be), then we will be able to deduce a statement that e occurs from a statement that c_2 occurs, whether or not c_1 is included in a description of the actual circumstances. If c_1 is included in a description of the actual circumstances, then we can deduce e from c_2 and these two laws. And if we exclude c_1—on the same grounds of inessentiality we invoked to exclude c_2 from the deduction described—we will still be able to deduce e, since these two laws and c_2 guarantee e's occurrence whether or not c_1 occurs. On the other hand, if we reject this requirement against redundancy (and we allow c_1 into the premises), then we cannot demonstrate the efficacy of c_1 without also guaranteeing the efficacy of c_2, the preempted cause (since we cannot now exclude c_2 from a deduction of e that relies on L_1, c_1, and c_2).

One might object to this argument along the following lines. First, assume that the neo-Humean account must be formulated in terms of *states of affairs* and that only minimally sufficient states of affairs can be causes—where s is a minimally totally sufficient cause of e only if there is some L such that the occurrence of s, together with L, entails the occurrence of e, and no part of s has that property. Second, note that (where L includes L_1 and L_2) my underlying argument has this form:

(1) $(c_2 \& H' \& c_1 \& H \& L)$ entails e
(2) $(c_2 \& H' \& -c_1 \& H \& L)$ entails e
Therefore, $(c_2 \& H \& H' \& L)$ entails e.

Now one might object that though this entailment holds, it does not show that c_2 is a cause of e, since it does not show that c_2 belongs to any *state of affairs* of the required type. This is borne out, one might argue, by the fact that the only three possible relevant states of affairs are:

(1) $(c_2 \& H' \& H \& c_1)$
(2) $(c_2 \& H' \& H \& -c_1)$
(3) $((c_2 \& H' \& H \& c_1) \lor (c_2 \& H' \& H \& -c_1))$

But (1) is not minimally sufficient since c_2 is included, (2) is not actual since c_1 occurs, and (3) is disjunctive and there are no disjunctive states of affairs. Hence, the fact that the entailment goes through does not demonstrate that c_2 is part of a state of affairs with the requisite character.

This objection certainly carries weight in cases in which c_2 is not a preempted cause but an arbitrary event of no lawful relevance to e. In such cases, the fact that the disjunction in (3) makes it *seem* that c_2 is an essential part of a minimally sufficient condition for e could be dismissed on the grounds that there are no disjunctive states of affairs. Where c_2 is such an arbitrary event, there is no other possible state of affairs in which to include c_2 that might demonstrate its efficacy on this account. But in the case in which c_2 is an arbitrary event, it will not be true that $(c_2 \& H' \& -c_1 \& H \& L)$ entails e. That entailment, on the other hand, does hold when c_2 is a preempted cause. This additional entailment, combined with the fact that $(c_2 \& H' \& c_1 \& H \& L)$ entails e, allows us to specify another state of affairs, including c_2, that is both actual and minimal: $(c_2 \& H' \& H)$. I would need to appeal to the disjunctive state of affairs (3) to gain c_2 its false status only if the entailment—$(c_2 \& H' \& -c_1 \& H \& L)$ entails e—did not hold. That is what we would have to do if we attempted to generalize this argument to cover any arbitrary event—in order to show that the neo-Humean is forced to admit any arbitrary event as a cause of *e* if there are any causes of *e*. In that argument, the arbitrary event picks up its false status as cause only through its association with a genuine cause of *e* in a disjunction of this sort. But I am not attempting this more general argument. With preempted causes there is no need for disjunctive states of affairs, since c_2 with H' and H is a minimally sufficient condition for *e*, and c_2 & H' & H is an actual state of affairs.

We can conclude from this general discussion that the neo-Humean, at least in some cases, will be hard-pressed to pair just the preempting cause (rather than also the preempted cause) with the effect. Of greater significance, however, is the diagnostic question: what general feature of neo-Humean theory makes for this failure with respect to preemption? I would suggest that the source of this trouble is the fact that this theory is too willing to find causal efficacy wherever lawful sufficiency is found. As a consequence, this theory is too generous in its attributions of causal relevance. Preemption shows that being lawfully sufficient, even under causal laws, is not the same thing as being causally operative. Distinct events may stand in similar legal webs but play different causal roles; an event's legal role does not by itself determine that event's causal role.[3] Since neo-Humeanism will, in some cases, not be able to generate the necessary asymmetry between the legal relations of preempting and preempted causes, the latter will be wrongly tracked as efficacious. This diagnosis can be extended one step further. The failure to handle preemption is rooted in this theory's emphasis on the "general" component of causation: there is some feature of the causal relation that is not captured by this kind of law-based theory. What is missing is a certain kind of singularist relation that holds between preempting cause and effect, a relation that is absent between preempted cause and would-be effect. Or so I will suggest in subsequent discussion.

Counterfactual Theory

Although the neo-Humean account of causation is still very popular with philosophers, in the last twenty years much more attention has been paid to a different theory: counterfactual theory. The philosopher responsible for this shift in attention is David Lewis.[4] Lewis has succeeded in assuring counterfactual theory top billing by providing, with his counterfactual analysis of causation, a full-fledged possible world semantics for counterfactuals. The latter gives not only a basis for a substantial theory of counterfactuals but also the tools necessary for the resolution of many difficult and subtle causal questions, including the nature of causal asymmetry and the status of joint effects of a common cause. Our focus here is on how this theory handles preemption. As we shall see, Lewis's views on preemption have changed in important ways over time.

For the counterfactual theorist, causation is fundamentally a matter of counterfactual dependence. The striking of the match causes the lighting of the match in virtue of the fact that had the striking not occurred, the lighting would not have occurred. The counterfactual theorist, however, immediately acknowledges that counterfactual dependence cannot be made a necessary condition of causation because of preemptive causation. In a preemptive setting, had the actual preempting cause failed, the backup cause would have taken over its role. At best, only the ancestral of the counterfactual relation is necessary and sufficient for causation. Causally connected events must be linked by a chain of events such that each event is counterfactually dependent on its immediate predecessor. As David Lewis has pointed out, however, and as we shall see in further discussion, even the ancestral of the counterfactual relation will not guarantee success in all preemptive settings. There are settings in which even stepwise counterfactual dependence breaks down. As a consequence, David Lewis has weakened the requirements still further: events are causally connected if they are linked by a chain of events such that there is an intrinsically indistinguishable chain of events in some region or other (with different external circumstances) that does exhibit stepwise counterfactual dependence. However, as I will argue, this heavily revised form of counterfactual theory may save the efficacy of preempting causes, but it has the disastrous consequence that some preempted causes will also be judged efficacious. This much-weakened form of counterfactual theory, like neo-Humeanism, overlooks some element of the causal relation that ties preempting, but not preempted, causes to their effects. What is needed is an account of the singularist, purely local relations that connect genuine causes and effects.

For Lewis, occurrent event c causes occurrent event e if and only if there is a set of events, $(e_1, e_2, e_3, \ldots e_n)$, which may be empty, such that e counterfactually depends on $e_n \ldots$ and e_1 is counterfactually dependent on c ("stepwise counterfactual de-pendence"). e is counterfactually dependent on c just in case had c not occurred, e would not have occurred.[5] And this counterfactual is true just in case in the closest worlds in which c does not occur, e does not occur. The closeness of a world to our world is a function of how closely that world resembles ours factually and legally. Lewis presents a system of weights for judging overall world similarity according to which although it is important to "avoid even small, localized, simple violations of law," it is more important to "maximize the spatio-temporal region throughout which perfect match of particular fact prevails."[6] A greater degree of closeness is achieved by trading off small violations of law to guarantee this large region of perfect factual match than by trading off in the other direction.

Given this account of causation and this system of weights, causation is a matter of counterfactual dependence, and counterfactual dependence is a matter of similarity of worlds, which in part depends on laws. Singular causal statements are thus sensitive to certain type-type relations, the laws of nature (although not necessarily to type-type relations between the token events of the causal pair). An event pair may be causally connected in one world but not necessarily in another world with different laws. Different laws may make for different rankings of over-all comparative similarity and, hence, for differences in truth values for counterfactual statements (and thus causal statements). Lewis's theory is thus quasi-generalist.[7]

Lewis on Early and Late Preemption

Preemption poses a serious challenge to counterfactual theory. With (deterministic) preemptive causation, there is a backup or failsafe mechanism guaranteeing that the effect would have occurred had the actual cause failed to occur. Even if the cause had not occurred, the effect would have occurred anyway. In other words, it would seem that with preemptive causation, the appropriate counterfactual is simply false. And, indeed, various philosophers have cited preemption as a fatal counterexample to Lewis's account.

As one might expect, things are not so simple. Lewis has certain resources for mounting a defense against this charge. His defense can be divided into two different strategies corresponding to his distinction between *early* and *late* preemption. His defense varies from one form of preemption to the other. This distinction between early and late preemption has to do with the blocking action of the main line on the alternate line. In cases of early preemption, the alternate line is blocked before the final effect occurs, but with late preemption the alternate line is only blocked after the final effect has occurred. With early preemption, the blocking action from the main line is initiated at a time earlier than either that of the final effect or that of its direct cause (in the main line).

I will postpone my criticism of Lewis on early preemption until the section on probabilistic counterfactual theory. Here I will simply summarize his approach to early preemption and then move immediately into his account of late preemption. The reasons for postponing any criticism of his approach to early preemption are fourfold. First, as Lewis later acknowledged, his approach to early preemption does not work against late preemption, and as I will suggest, his approach to late preemption also works against early preemption (if it is adequate at all). Second, his approach to late preemption does not depend on his claim, not widely accepted, that "backtracking" counterfactuals (of a certain type) are false. Third, if his approach to late preemption is *not* effective (which I will argue), it matters little that he may have prevailed against early preemption. Fourth, it is easier to see the defects of Lewis's approach to early preemption in an indeterministic setting. More specifically, his no-backtracking principle, which is crucial to his approach to early preemption, may be somewhat credible under determinism but is demonstratively inadequate when transposed into an indeterministic setting.

Lewis's approach to early preemption is straightforward. He admits that there may be no counterfactual dependence of the final effect on the earlier preempting cause, as the charge makes out. Nevertheless, this effect will *stepwise* counterfactually depend on this cause. And, recalling the details of his account, he contends that stepwise dependence is sufficient for a causal connection.[8]

How does he attempt to demonstrate stepwise dependence? First, there will be at least one causal intermediary between the event that initiates the blocking action, against the alternate line, and the final effect. Second, by the time the intermediary event occurs (assume just one), the alternative process is already doomed. The occurrence of that earlier blocking-initiator event in the main line dooms the alternate line. Stepwise counterfactual dependence is thereby guaranteed. If the earlier blocking-initiator event had not occurred, the intermediary event would not have occurred. And if the intermediary event had not occurred, then *both* processes, main and alternate alike, would have failed to run to completion (and the effect would not have occurred).[9]

Lewis is aware that this defense against early preemption requires the falsity of the following "backtracking" counterfactual:

had the intermediary event not occurred, the earlier blocking-initiator event would not have occurred.

If this backtracking counterfactual is true, then the alternate line would have run to completion *even if* this intermediary event had not occurred. In that case, the final effect would have occurred (being brought about by the alternate line) even in the absence of the intermediary event. So if this backtracking counterfactual is true, the final effect is not counterfactually dependent on the intermediary event, and there is no stepwise dependence in the main line. Hence, as Lewis himself recognizes, his defense against early preemption requires that he show that this kind of backtracking counterfactual will always be false in cases of forward causation. Lewis's reasons for rejecting backtracking counterfactuals will be examined below in the section on indeterministic versions of counterfactual theory.

Late preemption is like early preemption except that there is no event in the main line, other than the final effect itself, that blocks completion of the alternate line. The alternative process is doomed only when the final effect occurs: "Shooting a man stalked by seven other gunmen would be a case of this kind, if it is a case of redundant causation at all, and if the other gunmen desist only when they see him dead."[10] If the main process had not run to completion, the alternate process would have taken up the slack. The effect would have occurred anyway, although perhaps somewhat later.

Why does Lewis's approach to early preemption fail for late? The reason is that there is no "intervening" event in the main process on which the final effect is counterfactually dependent. As a consequence, there is no stepwise dependence. There is no intervening event that occurs after the doomed fate of the alternate process is sealed. This is so because at no point before the completion of the main line is there a blocking-initiator event. The alternate line is blocked by the effect event itself, not by any earlier event. For every event in the main process, it is false that had that event not occurred, an earlier blocking event would still have occurred, cutting off the alternate line. Hence, for every event in the main process, it is false that had that event not occurred, the final effect would not have occurred. Without such an intermediary event on which the final effect depends, there is no room for transferring Lewis's approach to early preemption to late preemption: there is no room for the stepwise counterfactual dependence.[11]

His approach to late preemption (which he developed later), in fact, marks a significant departure from his original presentation of the counterfactual account. Here is Lewis's approach in his own words:

> Suppose we have processes—courses of events, which may or may not be causally connected—going on in two distinct spatiotemporal regions, regions of the same or of different possible worlds. Disregarding the surroundings of the two regions, and disregarding any irrelevant events that may be occurring in either region without being part of the process in question, what goes on in the two regions is exactly alike. Suppose further that the laws of nature that govern the two regions are exactly the same. Then can it be that we have a causal process in one of the regions but not the other? It seems not. Intuitively, whether the process going on in a region is causal depends only on the intrinsic character of the process itself, and on the relevant laws. The surroundings, and even other events

in the region, are irrelevant. Maybe the laws of nature are relevant without being intrinsic to the region (if some sort of regularity theory of lawhood is true) but nothing else is.[12]

Causal relations supervene on the intrinsic character of processes connecting events (with perhaps the exception of laws). Hence, it is enough for a causal connection between events that the intrinsic character of the processes connecting those events be the same as the character of processes that connect causally connected events in another region, which are not embedded in a late preemption matrix (given the same laws).[13] Even if the main-line process fails to exhibit stepwise dependence, that same process is causal if "its intrinsic character is just like processes" in other regions that exhibit stepwise counterfactual dependence (i.e., that are causally connected on the original counterfactual analysis).[14] In cases of late preemption, the final effect will satisfy this condition of stepwise "quasi-dependence" (but not genuine stepwise dependence) with the preempting cause.[15] On this "extended analysis" a causal chain is defined as a sequence of two or more events, with either dependence or quasi-dependence at each step. In cases of late preemption, the events in the main line form a causal chain in this extended sense.

The "extended" analysis also works for early preemption. With early preemption the main process will be intrinsically indistinguishable from processes in other surroundings (minus the alternative process) that display stepwise dependence.[16] And the extended analysis is satisfied in nonpreemptive cases, if it works at all. If e depends on c, then e quasi-depends on c, since there will be processes that are intrinsically indistinguishable from the c-e process and that exhibit dependence. The consequence is that we can treat Lewis as suggesting that the extended analysis is both necessary and sufficient for causation.

There is a major dividend accrued from using the extended analysis to analyze early preemption. The extended analysis does not depend on the no-backtracking principle. Hence, even if there are some true backtracking counterfactuals, the extended analysis remains immune to difficulties on that account with respect to preemption.[17] If true backtracking counterfactuals exclude stepwise dependence in some cases of early preemption, the main processes in those cases may still exhibit characters that are intrinsically indistinguishable from those of other causal processes that do display stepwise dependence. In short, even if Lewis's original approach to early preemption is defective, if the "extended" approach to late preemption is effective, Lewis can take care of early preemption. And if his strategy for late preemption fails, any success with early preemption on the earlier approach is of little interest. The central issue thus becomes: does Lewis's extended analysis work for preemption? The answer is negative.

Unextended counterfactual theory must reply to the charge that it treats preempting causes as nongenuine in cases of late preemption. The extended analysis fixes that problem. The final effect will quasi-depend on events earlier in the main process. And this will hold of both early and late preemption. Processes intrinsically indistinguishable from those of the main line will be found in different surroundings (minus the alternate line) in which there is counterfactual dependence of the final effect on these same main-line events.

The difficulty is that this reasoning applies equally well, in some cases, to events in the *alternate* line. In some cases, intrinsically indistinguishable processes, minus the *main* line, can be found in which there is counterfactual dependence of the final effect on those same alternate-line events. Events in the alternate line then satisfy the extended analysis. The result: some preempted causes are classified as genuine.

Is this objection sound? Perhaps not if nonoccurrent preemption is at stake. Recall that with nonoccurrent preemption, had the main line failed, the alternate line would have brought about the final effect by way of some new events. The alternate line would have run to completion by way of events that in fact did not occur. Hence, although there may be intrinsically *similar* processes connecting the final effect in stepwise dependence with the preempted cause, the match will not be perfect. These regions will include, in addition to the events of the alternate line, these new events.[18] Nevertheless, this objection is sound, at least for occurrent preemption. Recall that with occurrent preemption, the efficacy of the alternate line is blocked without blocking any events. There are no new events that would have occurred, in the alternate line, had the main line failed in some way. The main line blocks the last actual event in the alternate line from *directly* causing the final effect. Given the nature of occurrent preemption, we must expect that there are regions (with the same laws) in which there is realized a sequence intrinsically indistinguishable in character from that of the alternate line, but in which the final effect stepwise depends on events in that sequence. What spoils the dependence is something extraneous: the presence alongside the alternate process of the events of the main, efficacious process. Without them all would be well. Hold fixed the laws but change the surroundings, and we would have the dependence in the alternate line. In short, with occurrent preemption, the final effect will quasi-depend on events earlier in the alternate process. Some preempted causes are efficacious under the extended analysis.

In order to make this difficulty more vivid, consider the following example:

> Two qualitatively indistinguishable particles are on a collision course. Collisions of this type are governed by deterministic laws that dictate, in this case, that particle b will be completely annihilated and particle a will "jump" discontinuously to a point P at the next instant t. The laws also mandate that had either particle passed through the location of the collision in absence of the other, that particle would have jumped discontinuously to P. The effect of interest is the event of a particle of this type, which happens to be particle a, reaching P. The preemptive cause of that event is the pre-t movement of a. The pre-t movement of particle a preempts b's arrival at the point of the collision from causing it to be the case that a particle of that type reaches P at t: had a been absent, b would have reached P at t. And this is occurrent preemption. Given the laws, had the collision not taken place, particle b (in the absence of a) would have continued on to point P without traversing any intermediate points. There would have been no additional events in the alternate line (of b's history) between the actual final event in that line (b's arrival at the point of collision) and the final effect (the arrival of a particle of a certain type at P).

The main line, which consists of the movement of particle a, prevents the last actual event in the alternate line, the event of particle b arriving at the location of the collision, from *directly* causing the final effect, the arrival of a certain type of particle at P at t. The efficacy of the alternate line is blocked without blocking any events in that sequence. There will thus be regions, with the same laws, in which there is realized a sequence that is intrinsically indistinguishable from that of the alternate line and on which the final effect stepwise depends: there are regions in which a particle of the same type as b traverses space at the same velocity/momentum, arrives at the point of the would-be collision in the absence of a, and jumps to P. On the extended analysis, the final effect—the passing of a certain type of particle through P at t—quasi-depends on events in the alternate line in the actual case. Hence, the preempted cause, the pre-t movement of b, is a cause of the final effect.

The extended version of the counterfactual theory thus confronts an unresolved preemption pairing problem. What is the source of this pairing problem? In order to answer this question we need to look at what distinguishes the extended from the unextended analysis. The extended account exhibits a generalist strain absent in the original formulation. Under the extended view, causally connected events must exemplify types that are suitably related, such that tokens of these types are stepwise counterfactually dependent in intrinsically indistinguishable regions. With nonpreemptive causation, this generalism is trivial. In those cases, causal dependency does not depend on what happens in other regions. But in cases of preemption, (quasi-)causal dependency between token events *does* depend on what happens in other regions. It is just this move in the direction of a stricter generalism that opens Lewis up to the objection that some preempted causes, like preempting causes, qualify as genuine under his analysis. There will be other regions of the right sort in which the relevant types of events are stepwise counterfactually dependent. And like neo-Humeanism, this diagnosis raises the suspicion that some singularist relation has been overlooked that ties causes to their direct effects.

Probabilistic Theories

Alongside the great interest in counterfactual theory in the last twenty years, there has been a growing recognition that an adequate theory of causation must be consistent with the possibility that some causes bear at most a probabilistic relation to their effects. Many philosophers now believe that causation and indeterminism are not incompatible. As a consequence of this shift in perspectives, both neo-Humeanism and counterfactual theory (as initially formulated by Lewis) have been judged defective. In response to this relatively recently identified requirement, probabilistic theories of causation have been developed. These theories use the language of the probability calculus to explicate central causal notions.[19] The basic idea of all of these probabilistic theories is that causes raise (or change) the probability of their effects, or at least of their direct effects. This basic idea has been developed and refined in different directions by different philosophers. In this section I will explore three such variations. Our main concern, as before, will be with preemption or, more precisely, with the probabilistic analogue to preemption and with the capacity of a probabilistic account of causation to deal with this phenomenon. As with neo-Humeanism and counterfactual theory, probabilistic theories run into trouble in (probabilistic) preemptive settings. Under certain special circumstances, the preempted cause guarantees that the preempting cause does *not* raise the probability of the effect. In such cases the probabilistic theorist must wrongly render a verdict of inefficacy on the actual cause. Probabilistic relations are not sufficiently robust in preemptive settings. Whether or not there is a preempted cause waiting in the wings (without any change to the actual causal connecting process) can make the difference between a finding of efficacy or inefficacy. What this fact points to is the need to clarify the singularist relations that connect causes with their effects—relations that are robust in this sense.

Generalist Probability Theory

The first variation I consider will be called "generalist probabilistic theory." Under this variant, which may not correspond to any formulation in the literature, probabilistic theory is interpreted as descending from neo-Humean generalist theories by way of substantial modification. In place of the neo-Humean requirement that the relevant types exemplified by causally connected events be lawfully connected is the condition that those types be probabilistically related. Specifically, under this formulation the basic idea that causes raise the probability of their effects is given a generalist reading: a token event c causes a token event e only if there is a type exemplified by c that raises the probability of a type exemplified by e.[20]

However, this condition—exemplifying a type that raises the probability of a type exemplified by e—is not considered to be sufficient for c's causing e under this account. Some "spurious" causes will satisfy this condition. The classic example of a spurious cause is a barometer reading: the barometer reading increases the probability of a storm and may even precede a particular storm, but the reading itself does not cause the storm. "Spurious cause" is defined in various ways in the literature, but we need not consider the subtleties of these discussions. The following sufficient condition for a spurious cause will serve our purpose of exploring probabilistic preemption: there is an event f that occurs before c and e such that given this earlier F-type event, the probability of the later E-type event is independent of the occurrence of the earlier C-type event.[21] The earlier event f is said to "screen off" c from e. The probability of the storm given the barometer reading and earlier weather conditions is equal to the probability of the storm given those earlier weather conditions.[22] The barometer reading adds nothing to the probability of the storm once the weather conditions are given. The earlier weather conditions screen off the barometer reading from the storm. Probabilistic causes are nongenuine if screened off by earlier events.

How does a generalist probabilistic theory fare with respect to preemption? In order to address this question, we must recall the nature of probabilistic preemption. Unlike in deterministic preemption, here it is not true that had the main line failed, the alternate line would still have brought about the final effect. With probabilistic preemption what is true is that had the main line not been realized, the alternate line would have raised the probability of the final effect to the same degree as did the main line. The preempted cause is a *probabilistic* backup to the preempting cause, guaranteeing the same probability for the effect as does the preempting cause.

Probabilistic theory does not seem to be in danger of granting efficacy to preempted causes, the error made by neo-Humeanism. However, the second main way of mishandling preempting—by denying efficacy to preempting causes—is a different matter. Probabilistic theory will, in some cases, falsely mark the preempted cause as screening off the preempting cause from its effect. This will be so where the preempted cause occurs somewhat earlier than the preempting cause. The earlier occurrence of the preempted cause guarantees, in some cases, that the later occurrence of the real cause makes no difference to the probability of the effect. Given the earlier preempted cause, the probability of the effect is independent of its actual cause. Efficacy is thus denied to the preempting cause. The following example highlights this mistake:

> Both Fred and Cody attempt to electrocute Edgar by pulling electrical switches that are connected to Edgar's chair by wires that run through a mechanism. The probability of Edgar's death, given that Cody pulls his switch in time for his current to pass through the mechanism, is 1/2, and the same is true for Fred. Fred pulls his switch (f at t''), which is farther away, slightly earlier than does Cody (c at t'), and the current from Cody's switch passes through the connecting mechanism and breaks the circuit before Fred's current reaches the mechanism. Edgar dies of electrical shock (e at t) from Cody's current, which preempts the causal chain running from Fred's source. In this case the genuine cause, Cody's action, is screened off from the death by Fred's earlier action, the preempted cause, even though the probability of death given the type of action Cody performs (pulling an electrical switch) is greater than the probability of death simpliciter. This screening off is evident in the fact that the probability of death if both Cody and Fred pull their switches is equal to the probability of death if Fred pulls his switch. This equality can be seen as follows. If both pull their switches (or rather given events of such-and-such types), only Cody's current will get through, rendering the probability of death at 1/2. And the probability of death if Fred pulls his switch will be the same (1/2), since if Fred pulls his switch and Cody does not, then the probability of death is 1/2, and if Fred pulls his switch and Cody pulls his too, then the probability is still 1/2 (since only Cody's current will get through). Hence, the probability of Edgar's death given that both Cody and Fred pull their switches is equal to the probability of Edgar's death given that Fred pulls his switch. Or in symbols, $P(E|C,F) = P(E|F) = 1/2$. Cody's action is screened off from the death by Fred's earlier action, hence Cody's action is not a genuine cause of the death according to probabilistic theory. But in fact, Cody's action preempts Fred's action in causing the death.

What feature of generalist probabilistic theory generates this unfortunate result? The problem here arises because this theory makes causal relations overly sensitive to the surrounding web of probabilistic relations. On this theory the same causal pair, connected by the same kind of process, will be causally connected in some settings but not others. In some preemptive settings, the causal relevance of a cause may disappear even though the connecting processes are unchanged.[23] Type-level positive probabilistic relevance of the sort emphasized in this theory too easily vanishes in the wake of earlier preempted causes and *their* probabilistic relations. As a consequence, preempting causes can end up being screened off by earlier preempted causes. What is demonstrated by this breakdown of generalist probabilistic theory is that the causal relation involves some element or relation that cannot be so easily swamped by contextual probabilistic factors. The presence or absence of the relation of non-screened-off probability increase, interpreted along generalist lines, is too heavily dependent on what is happening elsewhere (i.e., in the alternate process). There is some feature of the causal relation that is missed by this kind of theory. What is wanting is a certain kind of singularist relation. But more on that later.

Nongeneralist Probability Theory

The failure of probability theory, interpreted along generalist lines, motivates an examination of nongeneralist formulations. The most interesting nongeneralist (but still quasi-generalist) variation is provided by Ellery Eells in *Probabilistic Causality*.[24]

The basic idea behind Eells's account of token causation is the same as that of generalist probability theory: token causes increase the probability of their effects. Eells, however, rejects the generalist claim that a token event x causes a token event y only if x exemplifies a type X and y exemplifies a type Y such that X increases the probability of Y. It is possible for a positive token cause to be of a type that is a type-level, probability-decreasing causal factor for a type exemplified by the token effect.[25] The basic idea of probability increase at the token level is rather a matter of how the probability of the later event "actually evolves around the time of the earlier event and between the times of the earlier and the later events."[26] If the token cause is x's exemplifying property or type X and the effect is y's exemplifying type Y, we should trace the changes in the probability of Y over a period of time from just before x until the time of y. Token causes increase the probability of their effects in the sense that this probability trajectory will rise over this time period. More precisely, but ignoring refinements that would turn this into a necessary condition, y's being Y is because of x's being X if (1) the probability of Y changes at the time of x, and (2) just after x the probability of Y is both high and higher than before x and that probability remains high until the time of y. The match's exemplifying the property of striking causes the match's exemplifying the property of lighting, since the probability of lighting changes at the moment of striking and the probability of lighting is high just after striking and is higher than just before striking, and that probability remains high until the time of the actual lighting. This is Eells's unqualified gloss on the basic idea of token causation. Some of the qualifications, which I will discuss shortly, bring into play quasi-generalist elements.[27]

Can this theory adequately handle preemption? Consider the following case, which involves a small variation on the last case. A patient who is very sick is hooked up intravenously to two sources of drugs. Each drug when released feeds into the patient through a common mechanism. This mechanism is designed so that there is a chance that if the drug from only one source passes through it, the other drug will be blocked from passing. The blocking drug preempts the blocked drug in causing the patient to survive in those cases in which the patient does survive and in which the second drug is (improbably) blocked. The patient has a high probability of death if his disease is untreated. Each drug source supplies a different kind of drug, each of which gives patients with this type of condition the same chance of survival—50%. Assume that the laws of biology make it physically impossible for patients in that condition to have a greater than 50% chance of survival. In addition, suppose that if both drugs enter the patient's system there is a 50% chance of recovery.

Here is what happens:

> The source of drug A is farther away from the mechanism than is the source of drug B. At t_3 a nurse (improbably) opens a valve and starts the flow of drug B, and at t_2, a short time later, drug A (improbably) is released. Drug A reaches the mechanism just before drug B. Drug A flows through the mechanism and reaches the patient. The flow of drug A through the mechanism (improbably) causes drug B to be blocked. The patient soon recovers from the disease. The cause of his recovery is the release of drug A: he survives because drug A was released from its source at t_2. The release of drug B, on the other hand, did not causally contribute to recovery.

What verdict must Eells's account render on the release of drug A at t_2? In order to answer that question, we must trace the trajectory of the probability of recovery across t_2. In particular, we must determine the probability of recovery just before t_2 and just after t_2.

What is the probability of recovery just before t_2, at a time between t_3 and t_2? The release of drug B guarantees a 50% chance of survival at that time. Why is that? If drug B reaches the patient, but drug A does not, he has a 50% chance of recovery. And let us also suppose that the setup gives a 100% chance that drug B will reach the patient unless drug A reaches the mechanism first (activating the blocking mechanism): if drug B were not to reach the patient, that would be because drug A had passed through the mechanism and entered the patient's system (and activated the blocking mechanism). We may also suppose that if drug A reaches the mechanism first, then drug A is guaranteed to reach the patient. And if drug A reaches the mechanism first but does not activate the mechanism, then both drugs reach the patient, giving him a 50% chance. Hence, at a time after t_3 but just before t_2, given the release of drug B, there is a 50% chance of recovery.

What is the probability of survival just after t_2, which is just after the release of drug A? Here again the answer is 50%. When drug A is released, it is guaranteed that either drug A or drug B will reach the patient. If either does, the chance of survival is 50%. And even if both drugs reach the patient, the probability of recovery is still 50%. Hence, the probability of recovery just before the release of drug A is the same as the probability of recovery just after the release of drug A. We may then conclude, at least tentatively, that Eells's theory entails that the release of drug A at t_2 is causally irrelevant to the patient's recovery, contrary to our assumption.[28]

But as I indicated, there are a number of qualifications to Eells's basic account of token causation. We must now determine whether the release of drug A comes out as efficacious when these qualifications are brought into play. It does not.

There are three qualifications. The first requires that we hold fixed all factors that are causally relevant at the type level to Y (survival) but are token uncaused by x (the release of drug A) when tracing the probability of Y.[29] The release of drug B is one such factor: this factor is type causally relevant to survival, and its exemplification is token uncaused by the release of drug A (since it is exemplified before the release of drug A). When the release of drug B is held fixed, the trajectory for the probability of survival does not vary from what we have already seen. The second qualification requires that we hold fixed any factor Z that interacts with X (release of drug A) with respect to Y (recovery) and is exemplified in the case at hand, but the exemplification of which is *not* token caused by x.[30] The most likely candidate for an interactive factor is the release of drug B.[31] But in fact the release of drug A does not interact with the release of drug B: (a) drug A's release does not lower the probability of survival given drug B's release, even though (b) drug A does raise the probability of survival in the absence of drug B, and (a') drug A does not raise the probability of survival in the presence of drug B, and (b') drug A does not lower the probability of survival in the absence of drug B. The third qualification requires that we hold fixed the relevant confounding factors to the degree to which those factors are token uncaused by x.[32] This third qualification does not apply to the release of drug B, since the release of drug B is not token caused *to any degree* by the release of drug A, since drug A is released after drug B.[33] It is hence unlikely that reference to these three qualifications will save the efficacy of the release of drug A.[34]

There are two features of this theory that give rise to this trouble with preemption. The first general feature is the fact that Eells's theory breaks down under *extreme* probabilities other than 1 or 0. Although Eells does admit that his theory applies only to cases in which the constellation of causes and interactive factors fail to confer extreme probabilities on their effects, he associates these extreme probabilities with 1 or 0 only.[35] He fails to note that a deterministic relation is only one way to confer an extreme probability on Y. If the physically maximum probability for Y is fixed by events earlier than x (the cause), then there will be no room for x's falling into place at t_x to affect the probability of Y. What is important about probability 1 in cases of determinism, in which his theory breaks down, is not that it is the logically highest possible probability but that it is the physically highest possible probability in those cases. What the example of indeterministic preemption considered here demonstrates is that Eells's theory does not work under certain forms of indeterminism for the same reasons that it doesn't work under determinism.[36]

The second feature, and the most important for our purposes here, is the fact that the probabilistic relations that this theory takes to be central to causation (the trajectory of the probability of the effect across the time of the cause) are too sensitive to factors that are extrinsic to the processes that connect cause and effect. Eells's nongeneralist form of probabilistic theory shares this feature with generalist variants. Eells's theory makes the causal relevance of the preempting cause overly sensitive to the presence or absence of the preempted cause. But the preempted cause is quite extrinsic to the processes that connect the preempting cause to its effect. The evolution of the probability of the effect factor over time is too easily influenced by such extrinsic factors, with the result that we wrongly judge the preempting cause to be inefficacious.

Probabilistic Counterfactual Theory

The third and final variation of probabilistic theory that I will discuss is a hybrid of probabilistic theory and counterfactual theory. Counterfactual theory, as originally presented by Lewis, is not compatible with all forms of indeterministic causation. This shortcoming stemmed from Lewis's assumption of determinism for purposes of initially developing the theory.[37] This defect was not long in standing. Probabilistic versions of counterfactual theory naturally followed, including one by Lewis. The central idea of probabilistic counterfactual theory is that if the cause had not occurred, the *probability* of its immediate effect would have been lower. This new counterfactual shares its antecedent with traditional counterfactual theory (the nonoccurrence of the cause-event), but the consequent clause is modeled on the probabilistic theory of causation. Richard Otte, for example, gives the following formulation (he relies on the notion of causes changing rather than raising the probability of their effects):

> c is a cause of e if c and e both occur and if t is the time at which c occurs, then $P(e|\text{all that is actual at } t) \neq P(e|\text{all that is actual at time } t \text{ minus all that would be not actual if } -c \text{ were to occur then}).$[38]

In determining the first probability we conditionalize on everything that is actual at the time of c's occurrence—the entire state of the world at t. The second probability is just the probability of e occurring if the world were changed just enough to permit $-c$ to occur.[39] If the second probability is higher than the first, then c is a positive cause of e.[40]

Our question about this variation on probabilistic theory is whether it does a better job with preemption than does traditional counterfactual theory. Initially, it would seem not, since this account inherits the limitations of traditional counterfactual theory under preemption: the relevant counterfactual is apparently false in preemptive settings. Consider that in cases of probabilistic preemption, the main line raises the probability of the final effect to a certain level, but had the main line failed, the alternate line would have raised the probability of the effect-event to that same level. The probability of the effect would have been the same without its actual cause, which amounts to causation without probabilistic counterfactual dependence.

But the matter does not stop here. As with traditional counterfactual theory, things are more complicated. Counterfactual theory may have certain resources for handling probabilistic preemption. I will focus on what this account may be able to say about early preemption. In particular, I will consider whether Lewis's approach to preemption in deterministic settings may be transposed to indeterministic cases and whether or not his strategy, once transposed, might be successful in this new setting.

First consider the indeterministic analogue to Lewis's approach to deterministic early preemption. Do we find stepwise probabilistic dependence in the main line in cases of early indeterministic preemption? If so, then probabilistic counterfactual theory is vindicated against this kind of early preemption. For stepwise dependence in the main line, three conditions must be met: (1) there must be a blocking-initiator event in the main line, (2) between this event and the final effect there must be at least one intermediary event (assume just one, i), and (3) it must be true that had the intermediary event *i* not occurred, the earlier blocking-initiator event would still have occurred and blocked the efficacy of the alternate line. (3) is required to guarantee that the probability of the final effect would have been different in the absence of the intermediary event, *i*. If we also assume that the intermediary event *i* probabilistically depends on the earlier blocking-initiator event, then there will be a causal chain from that earlier blocking event to the final effect.[41] That is how Lewis's approach to deterministic early preemption transposes onto the indeterministic analogue.

But there are reasons to think this strategy will not work in all indeterministic settings. The first reason has to do with certain significant differences between deterministic and indeterministic early preemption. The success of this strategy requires that the blocking action be *deterministic*. The earlier blocking-initiator event must guarantee interruption of the alternate line. This is so because if the effectiveness of the blocking-event (with respect to the alternate line) is merely probabilistic, then not all the closest worlds in which *i*, the intermediary event, fails to occur and the earlier blocking-initiator event occurs will be worlds in which the alternate line is blocked. In some of those closest non-*i* worlds the earlier (probabilistic) blocking-initiator event does not actually succeed in interrupting the alternate line. In *those* worlds, the probability of the final effect-event is the same (in the absence of *i*) as in the actual world, given the unblocked events of the alternate line. Hence, there is no stepwise probabilistic dependence of the final effect on events in the main line. But given that we are taking seriously the possibility of indeterministic causation, fulfillment of this deterministic requirement cannot be assumed. We cannot a priori rule out merely probabilistic blocking action from the main to the alternate lines.

There is a second reason for questioning the transposition of Lewis's approach onto early probabilistic preemption. There is strong reason to doubt that Lewis's no-backtracking principle holds under indeterminism. And recall that Lewis's strategy for early deterministic preemption requires that the following backtracking counterfactual be false:

(BC) had the intermediary event *i* not occurred, the earlier blocking-initiator event would not have occurred.

Only if this counterfactual is false will it be true that had *i* not occurred, the probability of the final effect would have been different. If this counterfactual is true, then in the absence of *i* the earlier blocking-initiator event would have been absent and the alternate line would not be blocked. But there are distinct problems with the extension of Lewis's reasons for rejecting backtracking counterfactuals to indeterminism.

Lewis reasons as follows in support of the rejection of (BC). Under determinism, to get rid of the intermediary event in the main line (call it "*i*") with the least overall departure from actuality, "it will normally be best not to diverge at all from the actual course of events until just before the time of" *i*. The greatest factual match with the actual world is thereby obtained. Diverging sooner rather than later will not help to avoid violations of laws, since "under determinism *any* divergence, soon or late, requires some violation of the actual laws."[42] If the laws were held sacred, there would be no way to get rid of *i* without changing all of the past. But surely, Lewis argues, such a world would not be as close to the actual world as a world in which the divergence takes place only just before i. Hence, it is false that had the intermediary event i failed to occur, the earlier blocking-initiator event would not have occurred.[43]

One might initially *suppose* that this system of priorities for comparing worlds provides a legitimate basis for finding stepwise counterfactual dependence in cases of probabilistic preemption. But consider a "mixed" world with both deterministic and indeterministic causation. Suppose that in the main line, the earlier blocking-initiator event, b, happens by chance but that this event deterministically causes the intermediary i, which then indeterministically causes the final effect. The relevant backtracking counterfactual is again:

> (BC) had the intermediary event, i, not occurred, the earlier blocking-initiator event would not have occurred.

This will be false only if there is a blocking-initiator-event, non-intermediary-event (b, non-i) world that is closer to the actual world than any non-blocking-initiator-event, non-intermediary-event (non-b, non-i) world. Now as we have seen, for Lewis it is more important to maximize the spatio-temporal region of perfect factual match than to avoid even small violations of law. Given these priorities, it might seem that a (b, non-i) world is closer to the actual world than any non-blocking-initiator-event, non-intermediary-event (non-b, non-i) world. The former worlds all contain law violations, since the blocking-initiator event deterministically causes the intermediary event. But in some of the latter (non-b, non-i) worlds, the blocking-initiator event fails to occur, as does i, without a law violation, since the blocking-initiator event occurs by chance. And a world in which the blocking-initiator event occurs but the intermediary fails displays a greater spatio-temporal region of perfect factual match than does a world in which both the blocking-initiator event and the intermediary fail to occur. Hence, one might *think* that given Lewis's priorities, since the closest (b, non-i) world contains a small miracle and the closest (non-b, non-i) world does not, but there is a greater match of particular fact in the (b, non-i) world, it follows that there is a (b, non-i) world that is closer to the actual world than any (non-b, non-i) world.

In fact, though, his system of weights does not have this implication. Consider again this "mixed world" case. The (b, non-i) world and the (non-b, non-i) world both display only a *slight difference* when compared to the actual world with respect to regions of perfect match of particular fact. The (b, non-i) world diverges from the actual world at the time of i, but the (non-b, non-i) world diverges only slightly earlier at the time of the blocking-initiator event; the difference along this dimension is negligible. On the other hand, the (b, non-i) world contains a law violation, and the (non-b, non-i) world does not. The blocking-initiator's nonoccurrence does not require a miracle, since its occurrence is spontaneous. And for the same reason, the nonoccurrence of the blocking-initiator event does not require or threaten any changes in the past. Hence, we do *not* find ourselves with two worlds such that in one there is a large region of perfect match of particular fact but a small miracle and in another there are no miracles but a *significantly smaller* region of perfect match. It is only in such cases that Lewis's weighting system requires that the world in which there is a law violation be ranked closer than the world in which there is no law violation. In the case at hand, Lewis's weighting system does *not* entail that there is more than sufficient compensation for the law violation in the form of a greater region of perfect match of particular fact, since the marginal increase in range of perfect factual match is so slight. These kinds of trade-offs are sanctioned only when the law violation guarantees a significantly larger region of perfect match. Hence, Lewis's system of weightings does not help to defend probabilistic counterfactual theory against early probabilistic preemption.

This failure of the weighting system to demonstrate the falsity of (BC) in our example, in fact, fits nicely with independent intuitions. We should not be so sure that there *is* a (b, non-i) world that is closer to the actual world than any (non-b, non-i) world. It is not possible to say confidently whether it is true or false that had the intermediary not occurred, the blocking-initiator would have occurred anyway. Given that the blocking-initiator event occurred spontaneously, there is as much reason, and perhaps even more, to think that the failure of i would be due to the failure of the earlier blocking-initiator event as there is to think that i's failure would be due to a law violation just before the time of i. Hence, we cannot say with confidence that there is stepwise counterfactual dependence in the main line in this case of probabilistic preemption.[44]

Extended Probabilistic Counterfactual Theory
There is, however, one more hope for dealing with early probabilistic preemption, which if successful will also work for late probabilistic preemption. We can construct a probabilistic analogue to Lewis's extended analysis of causation and try to apply it to early probabilistic preemption.

Earlier we concluded that Lewis's extended analysis will work, if at all, on both late and early deterministic preemption. Similarly, a probabilistic analogue of the extended analysis will presumably work for early probabilistic preemption. And it is easy enough to construct a probabilistic analogue to his "extended" analysis of causation:

> c causes e if and only if there is a set of events ($e_1, e_2, \ldots, e_n$) such that e probabilistically quasi-depends on $e_n, \ldots,$ and e_1 probabilistically quasi-depends on c.

And we can say that e probabilistically quasi-depends on c just in case c and e are linked by a process the intrinsic character of which is the same as that of processes in other regions, with the same laws but without any extraneous factors, which exhibit stepwise probabilistic counterfactual dependence (i.e., which are causally connected on the unextended version of the probabilistic counterfactual account). How will this extended analysis help with probabilistic preemption? Suppose that stepwise probabilistic counterfactual dependence fails in the main line, either because of the truth of a backtracking counterfactual or because of some form of *late* probabilistic preemption. Still, events in the main line will qualify as causes of the final effect on this extended probabilistic analysis. There will be events in other regions, with the same laws but without the alternate line, that are just like those in the main line and are connected by processes intrinsically indistinguishable from those of the main line but that display stepwise probabilistic counterfactual dependence. And it is worth emphasizing that even if the earlier blocking event in the main line counterfactually depends on the later intermediary event (a backtracking counterfactual), this extended analysis will still provide the verdict the probabilistic counterfactual theorist seeks. In other words, this analysis will work for late and early preemption even if the no-backtracking principle is rejected for indeterministic worlds.

This latest hope for handling early probabilistic preemption is short-lived, however. The same kind of objection raised earlier against Lewis's extended nonprobabilistic counterfactual theory applies here as well: some preempted causes come out as genuine under this analysis. The preemption pairing problem resurfaces in its other guise. Consider some event, *a*, in the alternate line, in a case of nonoccurrent preemption. Will *a* qualify as a cause of the final effect on the extended analysis? The answer is positive. There will be other regions, with the same laws but without the main line, in which an event just like *a* is connected by a process intrinsically indistinguishable from that which connects *a* to the final effect. And in those regions the final effect is stepwise counterfactually dependent on that event. The following example illustrates:

> There are two qualitatively indistinguishable particles with equal quantities of energy moving on a collision course. The laws mandate that if these two particles collide, one and only one particle will transfer its energy noncontinuously across a spatial gap to a third particle some distance away and that the energy of the other particle will simply be annihilated. However, each particle has some probability, less than 1, of transferring its energy or having its energy annihilated. Given the laws, whichever particle does the transferring, it is true that had that particle not transferred its energy to the third particle, the other particle would have. After the collision, both particles are devoid of these quantities of energy, and at some distance away the third particle has an increased quantity of energy, an increase equal to the amount of energy from only one of the particles. Also suppose that the laws dictate that had one particle alone passed the location of the collision, it would have transferred its energy noncontinuously to the third particle. Now as a matter of fact there is a collision, and one but not the other particle noncontinuously transferred its energy to this third particle and the other particle's energy was annihilated. The effect of interest is the possession of a certain amount of energy by the third particle, after the collision. Depending on which particle does the transferring, we have different causal stories. If the first particle does the transferring, then its possession of energy is the cause. And if the second makes the transfer, the second is the cause.

Suppose that the first particle does the transferring and that the second particle's energy is annihilated. The extended probabilistic counterfactual theory will correctly judge that the first particle's having a certain quantity of energy just before the transfer is a cause of the third particle's having a certain quantity of energy: there is a region R (with the same laws but without the second particle) in which the third particle's having a certain quantity of energy is probabilistically counterfactually dependent on an object much like the first's having a certain quantity of energy at an earlier moment. Region R is a region in which a particle of the same type as the first passes through a certain point alone and noncontinuously transfers its energy to a particle some distance away. Hence, the extended analysis will grant causal status to the first particle. The difficulty is that this theory entails the same thing about the second particle. There is also a region (with the same laws but without the first particle) in which the third particle's having a certain quantity of energy is probabilistically counterfactually dependent on a particle much like the second's having a certain quantity of energy at an earlier moment (in fact, it is the same region as region R). Since this is so, we are forced to say, contrary to our assumption, that the second particle is efficacious in the actual circumstances.

The extended version of probabilistic counterfactual theory thus does no better with preemption than does extended nonprobabilistic counterfactual theory. And the source of this pairing problem is the same: the extended account's generalist strain. Extended probabilistic counterfactual theory requires that causally connected events must exemplify types that are suitably related, such that tokens of these types are stepwise counterfactually dependent in intrinsically indistinguishable regions. The result is that in preemptive contexts, causal dependency ends up depending on what happens in other regions. This makes possible the mispairing of the preempted cause with the effect, since events in the alternate line will exemplify types that guarantee this stepwise quasi-counterfactual dependence.

Singularist Accounts

Enough has been said about generalist and quasi-generalist accounts to warrant a look at singularist theories. I begin with a brief mention of nonreductionist singularism and a brief discussion of Ducasse's reductionist singularist theory. The main focus, however, is on transference theory, a theory that may strike the reader as at least quasi-generalist. Although that assessment may be right, there are reasons, which I will indicate, for interpreting transference theory as singularist.

The nonreductionist singularist holds that there are irreducible causal facts about particulars that do not supervene on noncausal facts. On this view, occurrent preemption is handled by positing a brute causal difference between the preempting and preempted causes. The preempting cause stands in a nonreducible causal relation with the effect, but the preempted cause fails to stand in such a relation with that same event. I discuss nonreductionism in chapter 2, where I will argue that the best arguments for nonreductionism are unconvincing.

As indicated earlier, Ducasse claims that causation is a reducible and observable relation between particular events with no generalist component. He gives roughly the following analysis: the cause of a particular change e in a situation was the particular change c which alone occurred in that situation immediately preceding e.[45] The collision of the ball with the glass caused the glass to break in virtue of the fact that the collision was the only change in the circumstances that preceded the breaking. How does such an account fare with respect to preemption? Not well. Recall the objection from irrelevancies to Ducasse. If the only preceding change is complex, it may include some components that are clearly causally irrelevant to the effect-event. For example, the collision of the ball may have been accompanied by a change in color in the ball, which is in fact irrelevant to the breaking of the glass. This difficulty immediately translates into a problem for Ducasse's theory in preemptive settings. The problem is that in cases of preemption there will be two components to the "only preceding change," the actual cause-event and the preempted cause. Since Ducasse has no basis for excluding irrelevant preceding changes, he is not in a position to exclude the preempted cause from being at least a part of the cause of the effect-event.

Transference Theory

Transference theory is meant not as an analysis of the concept of causation but rather as a contingent claim about what causation is like in the actual world and in physically possible worlds. A naive form of transference theory requires that there be an actual transfer of energy or momentum between the cause-object and the effect-object. Preemption turns out not to be a problem for this theory. The causal facts can be read off from the facts about energy/momentum transfers in preemptive settings, even if they cannot be read off from the legal, counterfactual, or probabilistic relations. I don't take this result to be a general vindication of naive transference theory. Instead, I give transference theory a perhaps unorthodox reading as a singularist theory and argue that its greater success with preemption is further evidence that a theory of causation ought to include a significant singularist component. The point is to highlight the role and importance of a singularist component of a certain kind in a theory of causation. This point is explored in detail in chapter 2.

Transference theory stripped of all subtleties (naive transference theory) requires a transfer of energy or momentum from cause to effect. More precisely, c causes e if and only if some quantity of energy or momentum is transferred from the c-object to the e-object. The movement of billiard ball c causes the movement of billiard ball e in virtue of the fact that the first ball transfers a quantity of kinetic energy to the second ball at the point of contact. The effect-event itself (ball e's moving) is constituted by ball e's possessing a certain quantity of energy, which is acquired from the first ball. What is constitutive of the causal relation is the energy/momentum transference relation. More sophisticated forms of transference theory recognize more complex and less straightforward relations of transference. Our interest here, however, is in naive transference theory.

This theory certainly appears to be generalist, since energy/momentum transfers are law-governed processes. Why then suggest that naive transference theory is singularist? The reason is this: even though as a matter of fact such transfers are law-governed, that is not part of the theory. It is no part of this theory that there is a transfer of energy/momentum from billiard ball c to billiard ball e only if billiard balls of the same type undergoing the same type of collision in other regions involve the same type of energy transfer. Even if we find out that there is no type-type relation of this sort (no regularity), so long as there is a transfer of energy from c to e (even if it is not law-governed), this theory will declare that c and e are causally connected. This conclusion also extends to probabilistic type-type relations. Even if c-type events do not raise the probability of e-type events, and even if there is in fact no probabilistic relation whatsoever between types exemplified by these tokens, transference theory entails that these tokens are causally connected if there is in fact a transference. A token transfer of energy/momentum, even if not law-governed, is sufficient for a causal relation on naive transference theory. This feature of the theory also entails that naive transference theory is not even quasi-generalist. Such transfers of energy/momentum are sufficient for causation even if there are no laws whatsoever.

What about preemption? On this theory, effects consist in the manifestations of some quantity of energy/momentum. Causal ancestry is determined by the origins of the energy/momentum manifested in the effect. A preempting cause is distinguishable from a preempted cause in virtue of the fact that the energy/momentum of the effect-event is traceable back to the preempting cause-event, but not to the preempted cause-event. For example, if one billiard ball preempts another in causing a third to move, the energy acquired by the third ball will be traceable to the first ball but not to the second. This account of preemption will not vary between occurrent and nonoccurrent preemption. The preempting cause, in cases of occurrent preemption, is determined by whichever of the two events transferred energy/momentum to the final effect. The same is true of nonoccurrent preemption. If there is a transfer from both the main and the alternate lines, then there simply is no preemption, but only two lines of partial contributing causes. If there is no transfer from either line, then neither line is efficacious. Hence, preemptive causation does not present a serious problem for naive transference theory.

Consider an earlier example, which was problematic for probabilistic theories:

> Two qualitatively indistinguishable particles with equal quantities of energy are moving on a collision course. If there is a collision, one and only one particle will transfer its energy noncontinuously across a spatial gap to a third particle, and the energy of the other particle will simply be annihilated. Each particle has some probability, less than 1, of transferring its energy or having its energy annihilated. After the collision, both particles are devoid of these quantities of energy, and at some distance away the third particle has an increased quantity of energy, an increase equal to that amount of energy from only one of the particles. The laws dictate that had one particle alone passed the location of the collision, it would have transferred its energy noncontinuously to the "third" particle. There is a collision, and one but not the other particle noncontinuously transfers its energy to this third particle, and the other particle's energy is annihilated. The effect of interest is the possession of a certain amount of energy by the third particle, after the collision.

What is the cause of this later manifestation of energy? This energy traces back to one but not the other of the particles. That particle's possessing that energy at that earlier time is the cause of this later manifestation. If the first particle does the transferring, then its possession of energy is the cause. And if the second makes the transfer, the second is the cause. And this conclusion will not change even if we assume that the preemption here is occurrent—that is, even if we assume that the earlier manifestation of energy, by the annihilated particle, would have been a direct cause of the later manifestation.

Naive transference theory is thus more successful with the preemption pairing problem than are neo-Humean, counterfactual, and probabilistic theories. From this fact certain general lessons concerning the nature of a singularist component of causation will be extracted in the next chapter. The key difference among these theories, which we should note at this point, is that transference theory tells a certain kind of singularist story about the processes that connect causes with their direct effects. These other theories do not recognize this kind of singularist connecting process. We should also note that this limited victory for transference theory does not constitute a general vindication of transference theory. Indeed, the view I will defend is not transference theory.

Objections

Before these general lessons are considered, however, three objections to the argument of this chapter should be addressed. The first denies the possibility of preemption in general, and the second two deny the possibility of occurrent preemption. Since the argument of this chapter depends on preemption, it is vital that we reply.

Objection 1

Consider again our first example of preemption.

> LBJ fires in order to kill the president, but just a moment earlier Oswald fires and kills the president. Had Oswald not fired his gun, the president would still have been killed, but as a result of LBJ's firing. Oswald preempts LBJ. Oswald causes the death, and LBJ does not cause the death but would have caused that same death had Oswald not acted.

Or so it seems at first. But further specification of the facts may raise doubts about this appraisal. There are many ways in which the death would have differed had Oswald not fired. For example, if Oswald had not fired, the wound would have been deeper, given LBJ's gun. And if Oswald had not intervened, the death would have been later. The location of the death would have been closer to the grassy knoll, and so on. But if there are enough differences there is no preemption. Had Oswald not caused the death, it is not true that that *same* death would have come about by way of LBJ's action.[46] Finally, since in all cases of apparent preemption there will be many such differences, there are never any genuine cases of preemption.

We need not take this objection to heart for two reasons. First, this objection may rest on the dubious assumption that the same event could not have occurred otherwise than it did, or, at least, that all of an event's nonrelational properties are essential to it. Not all events are as fragile as this assumption purports. As David Lewis points out, the same death may, for example, have occurred somewhat earlier, or at the same time but more painfully, had the doctor not intervened.[47] Second, even if all of an event's nonrelational properties are essential, there is no reason to suppose that "perfect" preemption cases—cases in which the alternate cause would have produced a nonrelationally indistinguishable event—are not possible.

Support for this objection might come from a further principle, to the effect that an event's causal history is essential to it. No event could have occurred with alternate causes. Preemption is logically impossible under this principle. Preemption requires the possibility of alternative causal histories for the same event. This principle is even more dubious than the less extreme principle that all of an event's nonrelational properties are essential. On this extreme doctrine, even the slightest difference in the distant causal past of an event is incompatible with the occurrence of that event. But surely it is false that the Kennedy assassination would not have occurred had just one molecule moved differently in the distant causal past of Oswald's efforts, but his actions were otherwise the same.

Objection 2

Even if preemption in general is possible, *occurrent* preemption might be challenged. The possibility of occurrent preemption depends on the possibility of direct causation. In cases of occurrent preemption the blocking action acts on the alternate line by canceling the direct causal efficacy of the last actual event in that line. Occurrent preemption is possible only if it is true that had the main line not blocked the alternate line, the last event in the alternate line would have *directly* caused the final effect. Some philosophers deny that direct causation is possible.

This objection is not convincing. Direct causation is certainly possible. Causation will be universally indirect only if time is continuous, since only then will there be room for further relata between any two temporally distinct, causally connected events. However, if time is not continuous, if it is discrete, there will exist temporally nonoverlapping, causally connected events between which there are no intermediary events, assuming that there exist some temporally extended causal chains. Since it is at least logically possible that time is discrete, the possibility of direct causation must be admitted.

This defense of direct causation is not quite right. The discreteness of time does not in fact guarantee direct causation. Assume that e is the causally final member of an infinitely dense causal chain of simultaneous events at t_1. At t_2 we find another infinitely dense causal chain of simultaneous events, but without a first member. Suppose that the events at t_1 are causally responsible for the events at t_2. In particular, the causally final member of the chain at t_1 is a cause of the events that occur at t_2. Since there is no first member of the chain at t_2, the event that is the final member of the chain at t_1 is not a direct cause of any event at t_2. Hence, there exists a causal chain across time in which there is no direct causation. The supposition that time is discrete (that there are no temporal moments between t_1 and t_2) will not affect this conclusion.

This objection to my defense of direct causation, however, is itself weak for two reasons. First, we may concede that at the level of the subevents, both those that are simultaneous and those that are nonsimultaneous, there is no direct causation. There is, however, a direct causal connection between the total complex event at t_1, C, and the total complex event at t_2, E. C at t_1 causes the total complex event E at t_2. This causal relation is direct if time is discrete, assuming that t_1 and t_2 are neighboring moments. Second, even if such temporally distinct complexes of simultaneous events are not causally connected, there is a further reason for rejecting this objection to the claim that the possible discreteness of time entails the possibility of direct causation. This second reply concedes that discreteness alone may not be sufficient to generate direct causation, given temporally extended causal chains, but states that the addition of a further assumption will guarantee the entailment. This further assumption is that it is possible that there is no simultaneous causation. In a possible world in which time is discrete and in which there are temporally extended causal chains but no simultaneous causation, direct causation will be realized. Since a world of discrete time, devoid of simultaneous causation, is possible, direct causation is possible.

Finally, it is worth noting that the continuous nature of time, if it is continuous, does not by itself entail that direct causation is impossible. Causes and their effects may overlap temporally. Or between causes and their direct effects there may be temporal gaps that lack any causally intervening events.

Objection 3

There is a third objection that deserves some attention. One might object more directly to occurrent preemption. It might be claimed that genuine cases of preemption must always be such that the preempted cause, or some intermediary between the preempted cause and the final effect, does not occur. Hence, occurrent preemption is not logically possible. In order to defuse this objection, I will present a brief argument for the possibility of occurrent preemption.

The causal relation is generally acknowledged to have a "circumstantial" character, in the sense that specific causes and effects of an event will depend on the surrounding circumstances. Circumstances may play one of two causal roles in this respect, either by being necessary for an event's causing another specific event, or by being sufficient for preventing such a connection. For example, the striking of a match is causally connected to the lighting of the match only if oxygen is present. And if wet, the match will not light even if struck. Circumstances can enable or prevent a causal sequence.

Now suppose that f prevents c from causing e but that f does not actually prevent c from occurring. Also suppose that in the presence of f, g causes e. In other words, f relative to c acts to prevent e, but relative to g, f contributes to the production of e. If c and g both occur and f occurs, e will occur, being caused by g and f but not c. The causal relevance of c to e is blocked by f. This scenario is certainly possible. Suppose, for example, that c is the striking of a match, e is the lighting of the match, and f is the presence of some chemical on the striker that prevents the match from being caused to light through striking. g is the high temperature of the air, which causes the match to light when the efficacy of the striking is blocked. Whereas the presence of the liquid inhibits the striking's efficacy, it enables the high temperature to cause the match to light.

If this causal pattern is possible, we are a short distance from occurrent preemption. We need only now imagine that the separate roles assigned to f and g in this story are played by one event, say f. In that case, f both prevents c from causing e and itself directly causes e. Suppose, for example, that f, the presence of the liquid on the striker, prevents the striking from being efficacious but itself causes the match to light when it comes in contact with the match's surface. It is of course true that the striking is somewhat different in nature than it would have been without the liquid, but if the striking is a nonfragile event, it is the same event. In any case, it is at least logically possible that no event is missing in the chain but that f prevents the chain from being efficacious and that f itself independently causes e. The notion of occurrent preemption grows out of the circumstantial character of the causal relation—that is, out of the fact that the effects of a given cause depend on the circumstances in which that cause-event occurs.

In the next chapter, I will consider the significance of the conclusions of this chapter for a theory of the singularist component of causation. As we shall see, preemptive causation places certain definite demands on the general form which that component may take. In later chapters I will construct a theory that satisfies these requirements.

2

The Significance of Preemption

The general import of chapter 1 is that certain kinds of noncausal information about an array of events over time do not guarantee that we can trace the correct causal paths through this array. Some forms of guidance definitely are insufficient. Information about type-type relations in the form of laws of nature alone, for example, may produce fairly crazy pairings. Information restricted to probabilistic and counterfactual relations also is insufficient. In short, generalist and quasi-generalist theories have difficulties sorting out causal relations in preemptive settings. These shortcomings naturally give rise to an interest in the singularist component of causation. The superior performance of naive transference theory on this tracing task further highlights that interest.

Reductionist accounts of this singularist component can be divided into "spatio-temporalist" and "mechanist" accounts. "Spatio-temporalism" is the view that the local token-level relation between cause and direct effect can be fully characterized in spatial and temporal terms. The classical Humean provides the most familiar example: insofar as causation includes relations between token events, which do not supervene on relations between the types, all there is to causation is spatial/temporal contiguity and temporal priority. The mechanist denies that causes and direct effects are locally connected only by spatial and temporal relations. There is some other kind of local tie. There is a local mechanism for the transmission of direct causal influence which involves persistence over time and which cannot be fully characterized within the framework of spatio-temporalism. I will argue in this chapter that spatio-temporalism cannot be the proper account of the singularist component, since these relations are not sufficiently selective to solve the preemption pairing problem. The lesson of the first chapter's comparison of causal theories is that mechanism is to be preferred to spatio-temporalism. Resolution of the preemption problem requires a singularist component of this special kind. Preemption requires local relations between cause and direct effect which involve identity over time and which most definitely do not supervene on spatial and temporal relations or on type-level relations such as laws.

Mechanism

The mechanist thesis breaks down into four theses. The first specifies that there is a mechanism, and the other three specify in part the nature of that mechanism:

(1) *Mechanism Proper:* there is a mechanism for the transmission of an event's causal influence not only to its indirect effects but also to its direct effects.

(2) *The Identity-Based Character of Causal Mechanism:* the mechanism that carries causal influence from a cause to its direct effect must be characterized in terms of the notion of identity over time.

(3) *Non-Spatio-Temporal/Non-Nomological Theory of Identity:* the identity over time of the "entity" that carries direct causal influence cannot be analyzed in terms of spatio-temporal relations or laws.

(4) *Noncausal Theory of Identity:* the identity over time of the "entity" cannot be analyzed in causal terms.

Mechanism proper is trivially satisfied for indirect causation. There is always a further story to be told as to how a cause brings about its indirect effects—that is, by way of intermediary events. The intervening causal chain carries the causal influence. In the case of direct causation there are no causally intermediary events. Hence, there is no *causal* answer to the question of how a cause brings about its direct effects. The nonmechanist will say that without a causal answer, there simply is no answer whatsoever to the question of how (by what means) causes bring their direct effects. They just do. The only token-level relations are spatial/temporal, and these do not provide a "means," causal or otherwise, for carrying causal influence. For the mechanist, the lack of a causal answer does not entail that there is no mechanism whatsoever for propagating direct causal influence. Causes do simply bring about their direct effects in one sense (not *by* bringing about other events), but there is a *noncausal* means for propagating causal influence from causes to their direct effects. So says mechanism proper.

Mechanism proper affirms both that causation is mechanistic and that there are cases of direct causation that are mechanistic. It is possible to affirm the first half of this conjunction by denying that direct causation is possible. For those who reject direct causation, it will automatically be true that whenever one event causes another, there is some mechanism connecting these two events in the form of the causal intermediary events. The form of mechanism defended here includes the claim that direct causation is possible.

The second thesis of mechanism sets a constraint on the mechanism for transmitting direct causal influence. This mechanism must involve some "entity" that persists over time and carries causal influence. The nature of this "entity" is not specified at this level of abstraction. However, if this thesis is true, then a full analysis of causation must be predicated on an antecedently given concept of identity.

The third thesis states that the identity conditions for this entity, if any, cannot be specified solely in spatio-temporal terms or solely in terms of laws. The entity's persistence is not solely a matter of spatio-temporal or nomological relations among temporal stages. Persistence here cannot, for example, consist in spatio-temporal continuity of temporal parts.

This third thesis is of central importance to mechanism. If this third thesis is rejected, mechanism is not necessarily incompatible with spatio-temporalism. Even if direct causal influence were propagated by some persisting entity, if that entity's identity conditions were solely a matter of spatio-temporal relations, then the local token-level relation between cause and direct effect could be fully characterized in spatial and temporal terms. For our purposes here, this thesis also sets up an important task: to determine the nature of this persisting "entity" and to show how its persistence makes for causal influence.

The fourth thesis is necessary to avoid circularity. This thesis also has importance for the theory of identity. Not all "entities" that persist over time can be analyzed causally.

In Favor of Thesis 1: Mechanism Proper

There are two steps in my argument for mechanism proper. The first is to note that only the mechanistic theory, of the theories surveyed in chapter 1, is up to the demands of preemption. Preemption seems to require that direct causation be mechanistic in the "proper" sense. The second step further defends this claim that mechanism proper is necessary to take account of preemption. The second step addresses the question of whether there are any good arguments for the thesis that "causes" is an irreducible relation.[1] The "primitivist"—or, to use Tooley's expression, "causal realist"—provides an alternative resolution to the preemption pairing problem which is not mechanistic. The second step requires a critical examination of causal realism.

Step 1

If the arguments of the first chapter are sound, then counterfactual theory, probabilistic theory, and neo-Humean theory are not consistent with preemption. Naive transference theory, on the other hand, can handle preemptive causation.[2] What distinguishes naive transference theory from these other views and makes it particularly suitable for solving the preemption pairing problem? For the transference theorist, the preempted cause is distinguishable from the preempting cause in virtue of the absence of a transmission of energy/momentum from the preempted cause to the effect. There is no trail of energy/momentum from the preempted cause to the effect. What is so different about transference theory, then, is the following:

> naive transference theory tells a story about how causal influence is transmitted from cause to direct effect.

These other theories do not. Counterfactual theory, neo-Humeanism, and probabilistic theories do not tell us how causes bring about their direct effects. The transference relation is a noncausal physical mechanism for carrying direct causal influence. In short, naive transference theory is the only one of these theories that is mechanistic in the proper sense and does not confront an unresolved preemption pairing problem.

I do not suggest that transference theory is the only theory of this type. The requirement of mechanism proper is distinct from this specific form of mechanism, and the particular mechanistic story told by naive transference theory is probably incorrect. There are other ways to satisfy the mechanism proper thesis. This mechanism may not consist in energy/momentum transfers or in a spatio-temporally continuous process, or even in a deterministic process. At most we may conclude that there is some noncausal relation or mechanism that holds between a cause and its direct effect such that this relation resolves the preemption pairing problem. An accurate characterization of the nature of this mechanism needs further investigation. Whatever its nature, a mechanistic account will answer the question of how causes bring about their direct effects. This answer will make reference to some noncausal process that connects causes to their direct effects. We have still to establish that this mechanism must make use of the concept of persistence and is not analyzable in spatiotemporalist or type-level-only terms.

Step 2

As noted, primitivism (or causal realism) provides an answer to the preemption pairing problem that is not mechanistic. A causal realist maintains that causation is an irreducible and nonsupervening relation. She affirms the following thesis:

> *Realist Thesis:* The truth values of singular causal statements are not logically determinable without reference to any statement about causal facts about particulars.

There are irreducible causal facts about particulars that do not supervene on noncausal facts about particulars alone or on noncausal facts about particulars together with laws.[3] How does causal realism accommodate preemption, particularly occurrent preemption? There simply will be a brute causal difference between the actual situation and the counterfactual situation, with respect to the alternate line. In the actual situation, the last event in the alternate line does not bear a causal relation to the final effect, but in the counterfactual situation, that event does bear a causal relation to that effect-event, a relation that is not supervenient on further facts. In the actual situation, the final effect stands in a brute causal relation to an event in the main line, but not to any event in the alternate.

The causal realist thus distinguishes between preempting and preempted causes without mechanism proper. Even if the preempting and preempted causes do not differ with respect to any of the kinds of noncausal facts specified by the various theories of causation considered (including nomological, counterfactual, and probabilistic truths), and do not differ with respect to any fact concerning a mechanism for transmitting causal influence from cause to direct effect, there is still a basis for distinguishing preempting from preempted causes. There are irreducible causal facts about particulars, and one such fact may be that the preempting event, but not the preempted event, is causally relevant to the final effect. Two cases may share all their noncausal facts but differ in that one involves preemption but the other does not. Causal realism is thus compatible with forms of preemption that go beyond anything we have considered. In the cases discussed, preempting and preempted causes have at least differed with respect to noncausal facts about energy transfer and the like.

Is there any good reason for adopting causal realism? Various philosophers such as Tooley, Woodward, and Carroll have proposed arguments for this view, the best of which I consider toward the end of this chapter. My conclusion will be that these arguments are inadequate, and hence I conclude here in favor of mechanism proper, in anticipation of that discussion. Mechanism proper can be summarized as follows:

there exists a mechanism or relation S that causes bear to their direct effects with the following characteristics: (1) S is the means by which causal influence is transmitted to direct effects, (2) S does not consist in a causal chain, since that would collapse direct causation into indirect causation, and (3) given our anticipated rejection of causal realism, S is not the causal relation itself.

The Second Thesis: The Identity-Based Character of the Causal Mechanism

The second thesis of mechanism partially specifies the nature of the mechanism. This mechanism must be characterized in terms of the notion of identity over time. I argue for this claim by considering what I take to be the three possible options for characterizing this mechanism. Only one of them, the one that supports this second thesis, is correct. The three possible characterizations of S are the following: S is some spatio-temporal relation, S is some nomological relation, or S is some relation of identity.

Option 1

The first interpretation of S is that it is some spatio-temporal relation. Causes must stand in just that specific spatio-temporal relation to their immediate effects. This interpretation of S would turn mechanism into a variant of spatio-temporalism. Mechanism so interpreted is a species of the view that the only singularist relations between cause and direct effect are spatial and temporal relations. Different specific forms of S (different spatio-temporal relations) will generate different forms of spatio-temporalism. For example, if S consists in spatial/temporal contiguity and temporal priority, then with respect to the singularist component of causation, mechanism is equivalent to the classical Humean view.

This classical Humean view, however, has not been immune to criticism. Each component of this account has been thoroughly scrutinized. The requirement that causes precede their effects, for example, is rejected by some philosophers through appeals to actual cases of simultaneous causation (such as moving a pencil with one's hand) and the possibility of backward causation (such as time travel into the past).[4] The requirement of spatial contiguity also is thought to be too strong. The possibility of action at a spatial distance militates against any a priori adoption of this condition. And temporal contiguity may fail to be universal if phenomena such as hysteresis (direct causal action at a temporal distance) are at least possible and perhaps actual.

But these kinds of criticisms are peculiar to a certain brand of spatio-temporalism—Humeanism, here seen under the guise of our first interpretation of mechanism. In fact, there are more general reasons for doubting any spatio-temporalist interpretation of S. Consider, first, that if spatial relations are made mandatory, then causally connected nonspatial events are excluded a priori. However, if *Cartesian dualism* and *idealism* are at least coherent, causation outside the spatial realm is possible. For example, for Cartesians, mental-mental causation is nonspatial. And for the idealist, the world lacks any spatial properties but not causal relations. A theory of causation should try not to legislate in these matters.

Second, consider that there may be only a contingent correspondence between direct causation and spatial/temporal relations. There may be possible worlds in which this correspondence is different than in the actual world or in which the correspondence is not stable. In some possible worlds, for example, at one point in time gravitational forces may operate at a distance, but at another time they may operate through spatially continuous causal chains. And in some worlds there may be no consistent correlation between spatial relations and causation even at a time. Spatial contiguity may reign at one place but not at another. A moon's gravitational effects on a planet may be direct, but a sun's gravitational effects are propagated through a spatially continuous chain. These possibilities cannot be excluded a priori.

Finally, but most important, spatio-temporalism cannot resolve the preemption pairing problem. The easiest way to make this point is by reference to probabilistic preemption. Suppose that two events, c_1 and c_2, independently raise the probability of an effect-event to its maximum P, which is less than one, and that the probability of this effect-event is P given one or both of these events. For detail, apply this assumption to our earlier case of two qualitatively indistinguishable particles with equal quantities of energy that collide, with the consequence that one and only one particle transfers its energy noncontinuously across a spatial gap to a third particle and the energy of the other particle is simply annihilated. As far as these probabilistic relations go, as we have seen, it is left open whether c_1 or c_2 (respectively, the collision of each particle) is the preempting cause, assuming preemption. This underdetermination of the causal facts is borne out by the following: c_1 (or c_2) by itself, in otherwise identical circumstances, will sometimes be efficacious and sometimes not be efficacious. The addition of c_2 does not change that fact. The addition of c_2, in particular, does not guarantee efficacy for c_1. We cannot simply assume that c_1 is efficacious when c_2 also occurs. Given the probabilistic relations (and assuming that there is some causal fact and that this is a case of preemption), there is no basis for determining which of these events is efficacious. Nevertheless, there is a causal matter of fact. The addition of spatio-temporal information of a certain kind does not provide a basis for sorting out the causal facts. In particular, if both events, c_1 and c_2, bear the favored spatio-temporal relation to the effect-event, the causal facts are still underdetermined. It remains possible that c_1 but not c_2 is the cause or that c_2 but not c_1 is the cause.[5] On two different occasions the same setup, including the same spatial and temporal relations, may correspond to very different causal facts. Hence, interpreting S spatially or temporally cannot resolve the preemption pairing problem.[6]

Option 2

The second possible interpretation of S is that it is some nomological relation L. Causes bear L to their direct effects. The "mechanism" for propagating direct causal influence is simply lawful connection. And the preemption pairing problem will be resolved as follows: preempting causes stand in L to their direct effects, but preempted causes do not stand in L to their would-be effects.

This nomological interpretation moves us back to type-type relations and away from a singularist relation, unless there is a way to understand lawful connection as a purely local matter. This proposal is very close to the neo-Humean theory of causation and, indeed, shares the same defect. Nomological relations are ill-suited to solving the preemption pairing problem. Preempted causes may stand in just the same nomological relations to their would-be effects that preempting causes bear to their direct effects. For example, there may be a probabilistic law, indeed the same probabilistic law, that links both the real cause and the preempted cause to the effect.

Option 3

The third possible interpretation of *S* is that it is some relation of persistence. There is some "entity" that persists over time and somehow connects a cause with its direct effect. Naive transference theory is one example. Here, the persisting "entity" is energy/momentum, which is transferred from cause-object to effect-object. Cause and effect consist in manifestations of this same energy/momentum.

This third option, however, may be developed in other ways. *S* may be differently specified. The persisting "entity" may not be energy/momentum. And the relation between the cause/effect and that entity may not fit the model of transference theory. In order to clarify the general pattern, it will be useful to consider briefly two other theories under this third option.

Castañeda's Account

Hector-Neri Castañeda's theory of causation is very close to naive transference theory.[7] Central to his view is the claim that "in causation there is a transfer (or metaphysical replication) of something in the setup containing the cause to the setup containing the effect."[8] The transferee is "causity." Causity is, as a matter of fact, energy, but "this equation manifests a contingent identity" and is a subject for scientific investigation.[9] There are, however, certain general truths about causity that are accessible to the philosopher. For example, causity is a measurable, divisible quantity. We can also ascertain from philosophical investigation that the transference of causity from cause-object to effect-object is a necessary condition of causation. Again, we see a parallel with naive transference theory. From this condition it follows that an object's continued possession of causity over time does not constitute causation. The relation between causity and causes/effects, however, is less clear than in transference theory. On the latter account, causes and effects are "manifestations" of the transferee, energy/momentum. Castañeda does not seem to take this view. At most, he says that the causity of an object is dependent on its properties but that causity is not identical with any of an object's properties.[10]

Salmon's Account

Wesley Salmon's account bears a more distant resemblance to transference theory. Nonetheless, his account falls into the class of "persistence" theories. Here are the essentials of Salmon's view.

Two events ("interactions") are causally connected if there is a causal process that connects them. A causal process transmits its own structure and is capable of transmitting a mark. A pseudo-process lacks the capacity to transmit a mark. A moving car is a causal process (we can produce a persisting dent with one blow), but a shadow is a pseudo-process (a distortion produced at one point will not persist without further interactions).[11] A characteristic is transmitted by a process only if that characteristic is manifested by all stages of the process. Finally, causal processes are the means by which a causal influence is propagated from one space-time point to another.

Causal interactions, which play the role of causes/effects, consist in the intersections of processes. Interactions give rise to mutual, correlated modifications in each process. More precisely, two intersecting processes, P_1 and P_2, causally interact just in case there are characteristics of each process (Q of P_1 and R of P_2) such that those processes would have continued to exhibit these characteristics had they not intersected, but these characteristics are modified (Q to Q' and R to R') at the point of intersection, and these modified characteristics go on to characterize each process. Causal processes are the means by which causal influence is propagated, and causal interactions are the means by which processes are modified in structure.

The concept of a causal process puts this theory in the mechanist camp: there is a story to be told about how direct causal influence is propagated, and that story involves the concept of persistence. Indeed, Salmon contrasts his view nicely with a nonmechanist account: "[t]he propagation of causal influence by means of causal processes *constitutes*, I believe, the mysterious connection between cause and effect which Hume sought."[12]

What then is the general pattern of "persistence" theories? The following is a common feature. Events are causally connected only if there is some process that connects these events and only if this process is constituted by the persistence of some "entity." For transference theory, the persisting entity that constitutes the connecting process is energy/momentum. For Castañeda that entity is causity, and for Salmon, it is a structure or a characteristic. These theories, however, are not united by requiring transference of this "entity" from one object to another. Transference theory and Castañeda require cross-object transmission, but Salmon does not. At most, Salmon requires transference from one space-time point to another. Given this lack of agreement, I do not include cross-object transference, but only persistence, as an element in the general type. There must be some persisting entity that connects cause and effect.

Less clear is how the relevant persisting "entity" figures into the constitution of the causal relata. For naive transference theory, the cause-effect events are *manifestations* of the persisting entity, the energy/momentum. For Salmon, the cause-effect events seem to be instantiations of the relevant "entity"—persisting structures or characteristics, before and after modification, that are transmitted in a causal process. For Castañeda, the relation between causity and the cause-effect events is not obvious. In any case, a persistence theory ought to tell us how the persisting entity enters into the constitution of causal relata.

Is the connecting process constituted by a persisting "entity" posited by each of these theories singularist? Is the connecting process sensitive to what happens elsewhere or to type-type relations, such as laws of nature? I have argued that naive transference theory can be interpreted along singularist lines. The energy/momentum transference relation is only as a matter of fact law-governed. The same considerations support a singularist reading of Castañeda and Salmon, whatever they themselves might say. If it is logically possible for causity or characteristics to be transferred or persist in a lawless world, then these processes should be thought of as singularist, even if as a matter of fact they are law-governed. I will not, however, venture to evaluate

Castañeda's and Salmon's own views on this issue. What is important is the question of whether the persisting processes posited by this type of theory should be singularist in nature. I argue below that these processes must be local if the preemption pairing problem is to be solved. This is not to say that there is no generalist element in an adequate theory of causation. Nevertheless, there must be a singularist component.

What brings these theories together is the claim that the persistence of something is the substance of causation. Beyond that the details diverge. This third option, interpreting S in terms of persistence, is supported by a process of elimination. The spatiotemporalist and nomological interpretations of S are inadequate. That leaves the persistence interpretation. S is not some nomological relation or spatio-temporal relation but, rather, a relation of cross-temporal persistence. Combining theses 1 and 2, we have the following:

> there exists a mechanism or relation S that causes bear to their direct effects with the following characteristics: (1) S is the means by which causal influence is transmitted to direct effects, and (2) S consists in the persistence of something.

What that something might be and how its persistence is related to causes and effects are questions for further discussion in later chapters.

The Third Thesis: Non-Spatio-Temporal, Non-Nomological Theory of Identity

The third thesis constrains the theory of persistence for this "entity." The third thesis of mechanism mandates that persistence cannot be a matter of spatio-temporal or nomological relations among temporal parts of that entity (if it even has temporal parts). Hence, a persistence theory of causation excludes certain accounts of persistence.

There are two parts to this third thesis. The first part bars purely spatio-temporal accounts. This restriction can be defended by reference to the preemption pairing problem. In brief, a purely spatio-temporal account will not enable a mechanist to handle preemptive causation. For example, if the "entity's" persistence is simply a matter of a series of spatio-temporally continuous stages, then preemption remains problematic.

Transference theory provides a simple example that demonstrates this limitation of spatio-temporal accounts. Let us suppose that quantities of energy are constituted by temporal stages and that gen-identity is determined by some spatio-temporal relation among these stages. Recall the example involving the collision of two particles in which the energy from one of the colliding particles is transferred discontinuously to some third particle. The other particle's energy is annihilated. The effect of interest is the appearance of a certain quantity of energy at that distant location. Only one of the particles is causally responsible for this effect, and that is the particle the energy of which persists and is transferred. However, if our criterion of persistence for quantities of energy is spatio-temporal, each quantity of energy will have an equal claim to persistence and transfer. There is no difference of degree of spatio-temporal continuity or significant difference or asymmetry in spatial or temporal relations. Each quantity-of-energy stage at the moment of collision bears spatial and temporal relations to the later quantity-of-energy stage, and there is no basis for a significant asymmetry in these relations. A naive transference theory, backed by a spatio-temporal account of energy persistence, generates the result that the energy of each particle is a cause of the later energy state (or that neither is), contrary to our assumption. A persistence theory that rests on spatio-temporal continuity is not able to solve the preemption pairing problem.

The second part of the third thesis bars a nomological account of persistence, for the relevant entity. This constraint can also be defended by reference to the preemption pairing problem. A nomological account will not enable a mechanist to handle preemptive causation. The entity's persistence must not be simply a matter of a series of nomologically connected stages.

Again, naive transference theory demonstrates this liability. Suppose that the genidentity for quantities of energy is constituted by the nomological relations between successive stages of these quantities. Now reconsider the colliding particle case. There are probabilistic laws that govern the collision. Each particle stands in the same probabilistic relations to the later quantity-of-energy stage. There is no difference in the probabilistic relations dictated by these probabilistic laws. Nevertheless, only the energy of one of the particles persists and is transferred. The laws provide no basis for preferring one particle to the other. As far as the probabilistic laws go, then, both particles are causally efficacious (or neither is), contrary to our assumption. Transference theory breaks this tie only if there is some non-nomological basis for the persistence of quantities of energy/momentum.

These conclusions can be generalized beyond transference theory to any mechanistic account. A mechanist believes that there exists a mechanism or relation S that causes bear to their direct effects such that (1) S is the means by which causal influence is transmitted to direct effects, (2) S consists in the persistence of something, and (3) the persistence of that "entity" is not solely a matter of spatio-temporal or nomological relations. An adequate theory of causation must include a story as to how causes bring about their direct effects in terms of some persisting entity, and the persistence of this entity must not be solely a matter of spatio-temporal relations of temporal stages or nomological relations among such stages. Otherwise a persistence theory of causation will not be adequate to preemption. S supplies a singularist component to a theory of causation. Each of these three conditions is dictated largely by the requirement that a satisfactory theory not generate a preemption pairing problem. This sketch of the singularist component of causation must be filled in during subsequent chapters.

The Fourth Thesis: Noncausal Theory of Identity

An analysis of causation must not make use of concepts that themselves are analyzed causally. In particular, a persistence theory of causation must not make use of causally analyzed concepts. In other words, the persistence of the relevant "entity" should not be analyzed causally. The entity's persistence must not be a matter of a series of causally connected temporal stages. This condition is required to avoid circularity. It is circular to suggest that c directly causes e only if some entity is transferred from c to *e* if we then go on to claim that stages of this entity form a persisting entity only if these stages are causally connected. Cashing in the notion of a mechanism for carrying causal influence by reference to a persisting "entity" is acceptable only if the persistence of this entity is not analyzed causally.

These four theses form the core of any mechanistic account. There are, however, two further restrictions that any mechanistic theory should satisfy.

The argument in support of the third thesis does not show that nomological relations are not necessary for identity over time (of the relevant entity). What has been shown is that such relations are not sufficient for identity. However, there are additional reasons for thinking that nomological relations are not even necessary for persistence (of the relevant entity). These considerations, however, do not entail that nomological relations are not necessary for causation. What they show is that nomological connections are not necessary for S, the singularist component of causation. This leaves open that these relations are necessary for causation.

There are two arguments against the claim that laws are necessary for persistence. The first argument appeals to what I take to be a persuasive principle, the "only t_1 through t_2" principle:

> whether *a* at t_1 and *b* at t_2 are identical depends solely on facts about *a* and *b* and on properties that are realized between t_1 and t_2.

This principle implies that what happens before t_1 or after t_2 can make no difference to whether *a* and *b* are identical. Two worlds that agree on all their particular facts from t_1 to t_2 but differ otherwise will agree on whether *a* at t_1 and *b* at t_2 are identical. Temporally, persistence is a purely local matter. Persistence questions cannot depend on matters that are *temporally extraneous*.

This principle can be supported by the fact that its denial generates absurdities. Consider, for example, two worlds, w_1 and w_2, that differ only after t_2. Assume that *a* at t_1 is identical to *b* at t_2 in w_1. What rejection of this principle allows is that there could be some event that occurs after t_2 in w_2 which has no causal influence on any events that occur in the t_1 through t_2 period but makes a difference to what exists during that period. Suppose that there is some such event in w_2 such that w_2's counterpart to *b*, b^*, is not identical to *a* in w_2. In that case, given the transitivity and necessity of identity, since *a* is identical to *b* in w_1, we must say that *b* is not identical to b^*. Hence, *b* does not exist in w_2 even though *b* and b^* are indistinguishable. With the denial of this principle, the existence of *b* can be made to depend on temporally extraneous events that exert no causal influence over *b*.[13] As Harold Noonan puts a similar point, what is absurd is the implication that a situation differing "in a mere Cambridge way with respect to what happens in the location of *c* . . . may be a situation from which *c* is absent."[14]

Whereas persistence questions are temporally bounded in this way, questions of law are not. There is no analogous principle that applies to laws. The question of what laws are true of a certain process during a definite time period depends also on what happens in other temporal regions. The laws connecting *a* and *b* can vary depending on what happens before t_1 and after t_2 (since what laws are true in a world at all can so vary). This is certainly true for a regularity theory of laws. And it is perhaps also true for the view that laws are relations between universals, since on this view, a relation of necessitation between universals (appropriate to laws) entails the corresponding regularity.[15] Given this difference between the truth conditions for identity statements and law statements, it follows that nomological connections are not necessary for persistence. In other words, since laws either supervene on or at least entail temporally global facts, but identity is solely a matter of temporally local facts, nomological relations are not a necessary condition of identity over time. Even if the laws varied by virtue of different possible pasts (pre-t_1) or futures (post-t_2), but the t_1-t_2 local facts were kept constant, the facts that make for identity would not. Indeed, even if the past and future were such that there were no laws true of the processes connecting a and b, that would not exclude the possibility that a and b are identical. Given the "only t_1 through t_2" principle for identity, nomological relations are not necessary for persistence. It follows that nomological relations are not necessary for the persistence of the entity posited by a mechanistic theory of causation. This is the fifth condition satisfied by mechanistic accounts.

There is a second argument against nomological relations as necessary for persistence that also supports this fifth condition. This argument has to do with the logical possibility of certain kinds of worlds. There are certainly worlds devoid of laws. Some of these lawless worlds have persisting objects and states. Consider, for example, a lawless world with a single persisting particle. The state of this particle at any given time is not lawfully related by deterministic or indeterministic laws to any other state of the particle at other times. Although lawless, this same particle may persist for a period of time and remain stable. Its stability is not a matter of law but merely accidental. In short, accidental persistence is possible. Nomological relations are not necessary for persistence.

This fifth condition, it is worth noting, also rules out certain kinds of *causal* theories of persistence (for the relevant entity). In particular, a causal theory of persistence for this "entity," which is backed up by a neo-Humean theory of causation, is excluded. A neo-Humean causal theory of persistence would say (1) that stages of this entity are gen-identical only if they are causally connected and (2) that they are causally connected only if lawfully connected. What is ruled out is this second component of the neo-Humean theory (as part of an account of the singularist component of causation, but not necessarily of causation).

A further condition of adequacy for a persistence theory of S is dictated by the fact that events generally have multiple causes and multiple effects. The mechanism for carrying direct causal influence must be compatible with such many-one and one-many causal patterns. The entity that persists must be capable of partial identity over time, in the form of fission and fusion. Naive transference theory again provides an example. For this theory to have a chance of success, at least some quantities of energy/momentum must be fissionable and fusible. Multiple causes are made possible by the fusion of energy packets, and multiple effects are made possible by the fissioning of quantities of energy.

Against Arguments for Causal Realism

I now return to step 2 of my defense of mechanism proper. There are two reasons to consider causal realism in the context of my argument for mechanism. The first is that causal realism provides an alternate understanding of the preemption pairing problem that differs from that of mechanism. The second reason is that causal realism entails that mechanism is false. This latter entailment depends on the fact that mechanism, as understood here, is a reductionist doctrine, while causal realism is nonreductionist. Causal realism entails nonreductionism because it entails the nonsupervenience of the causal on the noncausal. My main focus here will be on arguments that are meant to support the nonsupervenience thesis of causal realism and, by implication, nonreductionism.

One positive reason to reject, or at least not to quickly embrace, nonsupervenience is its relative lack of informativeness. Reductionist programs, if successful, are more philosophically enlightening. With reductionist accounts, we gain philosophical insight into the nature of causation and its link with other important aspects of the world. Nonsupervenience cannot offer this. Hence, unless there are fairly strong arguments for nonsupervenience, we ought to pursue a reductionist program. I will argue that there are no such strong arguments.

Causal realists reject causal reductionism because reductionism entails that the causal supervenes on the noncausal and causal realists reject supervenience. Causal realists claim that there are examples in which different possible causal facts are associated with noncausally indistinguishable worlds. If convincing, such cases refute supervenience and thereby any reductionist program for causation. A number of philosophers, including Tooley, Woodward, and Carroll, present similar arguments for nonsupervenience.[16] Mechanism, a thesis about causation's singularist component, when combined with a generalist component (which is not nonreducibly causal), will be part of a reductionist program and thus possibly vulnerable to these examples.

The best of these cases for nonsupervenience involves probabilistic causation. These probabilistic cases plumb the same intuition: an event e has more than one possible causal history given all the noncausal facts, but supervenience requires just one. In these cases, it is claimed that the laws and noncausal facts do not fix the causal history of an event on a particular occasion, thus causation is not fully determined by the noncausal facts. In short, this line of argument rests on the possibility of a *type* of situation in which an event e can have different possible causal histories. Different *token* situations of this type are supposed to instantiate different causal histories for e but are not noncausally distinguishable. Supervenience would thereby be refuted.

Let's look at what I take to be the two best cases.

> *Case 1.* There are probabilistic laws linking C_1 with E and C_2 with E. On a particular occasion, tokens of C_1 and C_2 and E all occur, and the probability of e is higher than it would be in an otherwise similar situation in which c_1 is absent or in which c_2 is absent.[17]

The realist contends that for any particular situation of this type, different causal histories are possible, apparently including (1) c_1 alone causing e and (2) c_2 alone causing e. In some but not other case-1 worlds, c_1 causes e, even though these worlds, we may suppose, share all their noncausal facts.[18] Hence, all the noncausal facts fail to fix the causal facts, and supervenience fails. The second example is similar to the first.

> *Case 2.* There is a probabilistic law that there is a 75% chance of C_1 causing E. E can also occur spontaneously. On a particular occasion, c_1 occurs and is followed by e.[19]

The realist again maintains that for any particular situation of this type, there are two possible causal stories, including (1) c_1 alone causing e or (2) e occurring spontaneously. In some but not other case-2 worlds, e is caused, even though these worlds share their noncausal facts. The causal facts fail to supervene on the noncausal facts.

These are the strongest cases for nonsupervenience, but they are inconclusive. Their inadequacy can be demonstrated by reference to certain responses which are open to the supervenience theorist and for which the nonsupervenience theorist has no adequate reply. These responses entail that the causal facts do indeed supervene on the noncausal facts in these cases, contrary to any initial, naively realist intuitions. Let's focus on case 1. There are two prosupervenience responses I want to consider. Both claim that there is only one causal possibility in each of these cases, but they differ as to what that possibility is. The first response says that both c_1 and c_2 cause e in case 1; call this the "both-are-causes" response. The second claims that the causal facts are indeterminate; call this the "indeterminacy" response. If the proponent of these cases cannot successfully exclude both of these responses, then the best arguments for nonsupervenience are inadequate.[20]

First, note that both of these responses have some support. For example, that both c_1 and c_2 cause e in case 1 is supported by the fact that each of these events raises the probability of the effect.[21] The indeterminacy response also has some intuitive plausibility in case 1. The separate causal contributions of c_1 and c_2 may plausibly be seen as indeterminate, even if together they cause e. In this vein, the supervenience theorist could claim that the disjunctive event (c_1 or c_2) determinately causes e, although there is no determinate causal truth for each disjunct. For those philosophers who reject disjunctive events, including Tooley, we can substitute a "mereological" alternative, according to which the cause of e is the mereological sum of c_1 and c_2.[22] Only the causal roles of the part-events are indeterminate. Indeed, there is some positive support for this mereological response: if this mereological event had been wholly absent, e would not have occurred, but e does not counterfactually depend on the part-events separately (at least if we don't assume realism).[23] On the indeterminacy response, there is no causal fact of the matter about c_1 (or c_2) with respect to e. Once we know all the laws and noncausal facts, there is nothing else factual left to know, and it is, at best, a matter of decision whether a causal role is assigned to these separate events. Supervenience is preserved, since all case-1 worlds are similarly indeterminate.

The important question, then, is whether the nonsupervenience theorist can block the both-are-causes response and the indeterminacy response to case 1. If not, nonsupervenience is not established. There are two ways he might try to check these responses, but neither works.[24]

The Counterfactual Reply

The first way that a nonsupervenience theorist might try to block these responses is by reference to counterfactuals. Perhaps one can demonstrate that there is some counterfactual difference across case-1 worlds and use that fact to support the claim that there is a causal difference across these worlds. If, for example, in one case-1 world but not in another, it is true that had c_1 not happened then e would not have happened, that might show a difference in the efficacy of c_1 with respect to e.

This counterfactual response, however, is problematic. First, it will not be acceptable to the nonsupervenience theorist who places counterfactual conditionals in the noncausal base. For those nonsupervenience theorists there had better not be counterfactual differences in the case-1 worlds to match the causal differences. Otherwise, the case-1 worlds do not constitute a counterexample to supervenience. But even if counterfactuals are not part of the base, we must be given some reason to believe that case-1 worlds differ counterfactually in this way. We must be given some reason for thinking that what counts as the closest non-c_1 world differs among case-1 worlds. In this context, there are two conflicting candidate criteria for determining closeness. One discounts causal information and the other doesn't. On the first, any fact of the matter about whether c_1 or c_2 causes e is ignored in comparing worlds. With this discounting clause, we find that relative to any case-1 world, some of the closest non-c_1 worlds will be worlds in which e is caused probabilistically by c_2 and that in others, e does not occur because it is not caused by c_2. The case-1 worlds will then agree on the counterfactual status of c_1 with respect to e, since no counterfactual difference across these worlds has been found.

The second criterion abandons the discounting clause. e's causal history in w_1 is a factor that makes for similarity. If, in w_1, c_1 causes e and c_2 does not, that is relevant to what counts as the closest non-c_1 world.[25] With this criterion, if we assume causal differences among case-1 worlds, counterfactual differences can be found. The difficulty is that this second strategy is blatantly question-begging. The counterfactual "had c_1 not occurred, e would not have occurred" comes out true on this second approach only if we already have a determination that c_1 really does cause e and c_2 does not cause e in the relevant world. That begs the question at issue and against the supervenience view. The "counterfactual" approach cannot be used to block the both-are-causes response to case 1 (nor to block the indeterminacy response).

The Invariance Reply

The other way to resist the both-are-causes and indeterminacy responses is to appeal to what Woodward calls "invariance."[26] Causal invariance consists in the supposed fact that whatever tendency a cause has to cause a particular type of effect is an approximately *invariant* tendency across various contexts; such tendencies will exhibit some degree of context-independence.[27] Invariance seems at least to require that if a given cause in some contexts—for example, in isolation—*only sometimes* brings about its effect (an imperfect tendency), then c_1's tendency to cause E is imperfect, at best, in all contexts in which it produces E.[28]

How might invariance exclude the both-are-causes response to case 1? Here's how:

> Suppose that whenever c_1, c_2, and e occur together, c_1 is always efficacious with respect to e. That implies that c_1 has a *perfect* tendency to cause e in such contexts. But this would run contrary to c_1's imperfect tendency to cause e in other contexts—for example, in the absence of c_2. The claim that both c_1 and c_2 are efficacious in all case-1 worlds must be rejected.[29]

This initially appealing argument contains a fallacy. c_1's context-independent imperfect tendency requires that even in the c_2-context, c_1 only sometimes causes e. In fact, this remains true even on the both-are-causes response. What this argument fails to note is that c_2 does not guarantee that c_1 will cause e. When c_1 and c_2 occur together, sometimes e occurs, but sometimes e does *not* occur. So c_2 does not guarantee that c_1 will cause e, since c_2 and c_1 together do not guarantee that e will occur at all. c_1's imperfect tendency to cause e remains invariant across the c_2 context, even if whenever c_1, c_2, and e occur together, c_1 causes e.[30]

Another version of the invariance argument may not be similarly fallacious. Consider a more precise tendency, rather than the nonspecific imperfect tendency, to cause e: a particular probability of causing e. Invariance might require, roughly, that if c_1 has a probability P of causing e in one context, it has that probability of causing e in all (extrinsic?) contexts.[31] When we apply this argument to the both-are-causes response, we get the following argument:

> If whenever c_1 and c_2 occur together and one of them causes e, then so does the other, the probability of c_1's causing e will be higher than P when conjoined with c_2.[32] "It follows that we must suppose that in the presence of c_2, the characteristic tendency of c_1 to produce e is somehow transformed and enhanced from what that tendency is in the absence of c_2."[33]

Although not fallacious in the same way, this argument is equally deficient. We can bring out its deficiency by considering a specific version of the supervenience thesis.

To see the deficiency in this argument, assume that causation supervenes primarily on facts about probabilities. Invariance might then consist in the invariance of C_1's causal contribution to a type of effect, E, in different contexts, where this means that C_1's probabilistic contribution to E remains constant.[34] Does the both-are-causes response conflict with this kind of invariance? In fact, it does not. c_1's probabilistic contribution to e is the same whether or not it occurs with c_2 even if whenever c_1, c_2, and e occur together, both c_1 and c_2 cause e. And since "probabilistic contribution" is what causation is for the probability supervenience theorist, c_1's causal contribution remains constant.[35] Hence, the invariance argument can get a grip up on the both-are-causes response only by begging the question.

Perhaps, however, an invariance argument will work against the indeterminacy response. Here's such an argument:

> If an event sometimes causes e in one context, there is no context in which whether it causes e is always indeterminate. Since c_1 causes e sometimes in the absence of c_2, then c_1 must cause e sometimes in the presence of c_2. So it cannot be indeterminate whether c_1 causes e in *every* case-1 world.

In the end, however, this argument too is not compelling. First, we are not given any reason to think that invariance even applies when causation goes indeterminate. When there is no fact of the matter about c_1's causal relation to e, invariance may simply not apply. Second, even if it can apply, there is a sense in which the indeterminacy response in case 1 *does* preserve invariance. Consider that in a non-c_2 context, sometimes c_1 does not cause e and sometimes it is not true that c_1 does not cause e (because c_1 does cause e). This imperfect tendency *as described* remains invariant in c_2 contexts, given the indeterminacy response. In a c_2 context, sometimes c_1 does not cause e (since sometimes c_1 and c_2 together are not followed by e at all), and sometimes it is not true that c_1 does not cause e (because it is indeterminate whether or not c_1 does cause e). We need to be told why this isn't sufficient.[36] I conclude that the best arguments for causal realism, understood as nonsupervenience, are not convincing.[37]

Causal Realism as Antisupervenience

My discussion thus far has focused on causal realism's commitment to nonsupervenience, but there is some reason to think that some causal realists go beyond mere nonsupervenience.[38] Some causal realists seem to hold that the truth values of singular causal statements are not logically determined by or supervenient on *any* noncausal states of affairs—that causation is some further fact, independent of whatever the noncausal facts are.[39] For example, this thesis appears to be attributed by Tooley to himself qua causal realist.[40] Singular causal relations are *never* determined by noncausal facts. Call this thesis "antisupervenience," the nonepistemological side of what we can call "strong causal realism."[41] This thesis is much more demanding than mere nonsupervenience and, I would suggest, is implausible in its own right. I begin with two preliminary worries about what is required to defend antisupervenience.

First, consider that arguments for causal realism typically center around examples (like cases 1 and 2) designed to support the nonsupervenience thesis. Insofar as these cases form the only argument for causal realism, there is obviously an argumentative gap. Nonsupervenience does not entail antisupervenience. Even if there are pairs of worlds that agree noncausally but not causally, it does not immediately follow that no set of noncausal facts determines any set of causal facts.

Second, cases are easily constructed in which *causal* laws plus the noncausal facts entail certain singular causal statements.[42] If causal laws reduce to or supervene on noncausal states of affairs, then such cases would confound the antisupervenience thesis, since in those cases the truth of a singular causal statement would ultimately be determined by the noncausal states of affairs that make the causal law true and by the remaining noncausal facts. Causal realism about singular causal statements thus can be established only if it can be demonstrated that causal laws do not supervene on the noncausal. This is a significant argumentative obligation. But the argumentative liability is worse than that. Antisupervenience for causal laws also must be demonstrated. Without a general assurance that causal laws are *never* determined by noncausal facts, there is no guarantee that the noncausal facts in some of these kinds of cases do not determine the causal laws of their worlds.[43]

In addition to these concerns, there are cases that directly clash with antisupervenience. For example, counterexamples can be generated from noncausal functional laws or from causal laws by reinterpreting these laws as merely stating functional relationships. As reinterpreted, the laws provide for prediction without stating any kind of causal connection. Consider the causal law that C_1 and C_2 separately are causally sufficient for E, and Es occur only if caused by either C_1 or C_2. Reinterpret it as saying that Es occur only if preceded by either C_1 or C_2 and that each is lawfully sufficient for E. Our example then goes as follows:

Case 3. Suppose that this is the only law in the world and that c_1 occurs and is followed by e. In addition, assume that there are no other events in this world.

More concretely, make e the movement of a particle and C_1 and C_2 applications of different kinds of forces. What must the causal realist say about this case? If causal facts are really "further facts" over and above the noncausal facts, it would seem that the realist should posit at least two causally different worlds: in one, c_1, the only application of force, is causally connected to the movement of the particle, and in the other, the application of that same force and the movement are wholly causally independent. I find this claim to be highly counterintuitive. Worlds that are indistinguishable with respect to these very simple noncausal facts and "neutered" causal laws will agree on the causal status of c_1 with respect to e, whatever that might be. This intuition is independent of what those causal facts may be.[44]

The realist might reply that he need not claim, for example, that there are any such worlds in which these events are causally unconnected, as long as these noncausal facts do not determine which is the cause and which is the effect (that is, as long as it is left open whether c_1 causes e or e causes c_1). Then the causal realist can say that no specific singular causal statement is fixed even if the truth of the disjunction is fixed. I find this response unmotivated. If causation really is always some "further fact," why should the causal disjunction be fixed by noncausal facts (even though the disjuncts are not fixed)?

Cases can also be generated from merely functional noncausal laws.

Case 4. Suppose that it is a law that property C_1 varies directly with property E and there are no other laws. Assume that the world contains just this one particle, x, the only properties of which are C_1 and E, which vary together. There are no other events.

Causal realists must say that in some case-4 worlds c_1 is causally connected to e, but in others c_1 and e are causally independent. This assessment is counterintuitive. The covariations in C_1 and E are either causally connected in all such worlds or causally unconnected in all such worlds.[45]

Even more obviously, causal facts are sometimes fixed by facts about identity and energy/momentum transference. Suppose that it is a law that a particle will continue to have property P if there are no forces at work or other particles. Imagine that this is the only law and that there is just one particle, x, which has P at both t and t'—neighboring times. The causal realist, it would seem, must deny the intuitively obvious fact that the particle's having property P at these two times must be causally connected (in one direction or the other or as mutually causally dependent such that the same disjunct is satisfied in all of these worlds). If causation is some further fact, it would seem that noncausal facts, even about property persistence, should never fix the causal facts in this way. Energy transference cases also clash with causal realism. Suppose there is a law that if one billiard ball is in motion and comes into contact with a second billiard ball, energy from the first will be transferred to the second. Assume also that billiard ball A comes into contact with billiard ball B and transfers kinetic energy to the latter and that there are no other events. The causal facts in this case seem clear: in all such worlds, billiard ball A's movement causes billiard ball B's movement, or the other way around. There is no room for the possibility of no causal connection once the noncausal facts are fixed in this way.[46]

Mechanism, Nonmechanism, and Methodology

Our conclusion thus far is that an adequate theory of causation's singularist component should be mechanistic. We have also gone some way toward giving the general characteristics of such a theory. Our characterization is, however, still quite abstract (prior to specifying the details). Nevertheless, enough has been said to bring out some of the significance of this move in the direction of mechanism, at least at the methodological level.

A theory of causation will have methodological implications. An account of causation will determine that certain kinds of causal questions are legitimate or important and that others are not. For example, the neo-Humean view mandates that causal inquiry should in part be taken up with determining the causal laws under which event pairs are subsumable. On the other hand, a probabilistic theory will dictate certain kinds of statistical investigations. One way to get a sense of the differences between theories of causation is to consider differences in methodological significance.

How does a mechanistic account differ methodologically from a nonmechanistic account? The ontological differences between these kinds of theories will determine the scope of certain methodological principles. Consider, for example, the following possible methodological principle:

> do not accept a causal claim without an acceptable account of how the purported cause brings about its effect.

This principle requires details about the process by which the purported cause brings about its effect, in addition to any other evidence one might have for this claim, especially statistical evidence. Mechanists and nonmechanists who accept this principle will disagree about its scope. For the nonmechanist, this principle applies only to indirect causation: "further details" will consist in further intermediary links in the chain. The evidence for direct causal claims cannot be of this type. For the mechanist, however, there is room for applying this principle even to direct causation, since there is a story to be told about the processes that connect causes to their direct effects. For a mechanist who accepts this methodological principle, all causal hypotheses fall within its scope.

What this methodological difference highlights is a deeper difference between mechanist and nonmechanist, a difference on which we have already remarked. A mechanistic theory does not (but a nonmechanist does) reject questions of the form "how does c cause e?" in the case in which c directly causes e. A nonmechanist can make sense out of such questions only when asked about indirect causation. A mechanist claims that there is a singularist, noncausal process that connects a cause to its direct effect such that that process explains how causes bring about their direct effects. The nonmechanist rejects questions of this form. There are no such processes linking causes and direct effects. Questions of how one event causes another have answers only if there are causally intermediary events between them. At some point (that of direct causation), says the nonmechanist, such questions become inappropriate.

Persistence and Causal Relata

Given our general endorsement of a mechanist theory, we must now turn to the details of such an account. There are certain questions that must now be answered. The first concerns the nature of causal relata. What sorts of things stand in causal relations? The second concerns the nature of that which persists in causation. What exactly persists in causal sequences?

These are not unrelated questions. A mechanist account must specify the connection between causal relata and that which persists. For example, in naive transference theory, that relation is fairly clear. Causal relata are *manifestations* of energy/momentum, and energy/momentum is that which persists in causation. At the very least, our account of causal relata must be compatible with our account of that which persists. An account of causal relata constrains an account of the persisting entity, and vice versa. In the next chapter I examine the nature of causal relata. There I divide theories of causal relata into two kinds. One class posits explanatorily relevant properties, and the other class does not. On the "explanatory" model, there will be properties exemplified by causes and their effects such that those events are causally related in virtue of those properties. On the nonexplanatory model it is not the case that if c causes e, this is so because these events exemplify certain properties. I argue for the nonexplanatory approach, and within the nonexplanatory camp I push for the view that tropes (particularized properties) are the sole causal relata. This emphasis on tropes provides a clue for identifying the "entity" that carries causal influence—persisting tropes themselves. I pursue that approach to the causal-influence-carrying "entity" in chapters 4 and 5.

Preliminary to a detailed discussion of causal relata, it is important to clarify what we are and are not committed to at this point on the question of relata. What we have accepted thus far is mechanism. Does mechanism commit us to any particular account of causal relata? In particular, are we committed to an explanatory account?

Mechanists are not committed to explanatory accounts of relata. A mechanist theory deems legitimate the following question: how does c cause e, when c causes e directly? This question of how causes bring about their direct effects, however, should not be confused with the following why question: why does c cause e, where c directly causes e? These are independent questions. Even if a theory of causation answers the how question, it may not answer the why question, and an answer to the why question does not guarantee an answer to the how question. The why question about direct causation has an answer only if there is generally an explanation for why an event c causes another event e. Whether there will be such an answer depends on whether causal relata exemplify explanatorily relevant properties—on whether, in general, if c causes e there will be properties exemplified by c and e such that those events are causally related in virtue of those properties. Mechanism does not address the issue of whether there is generally this kind of explanation for why c causes e. Even if there is a singularist, persisting process that connects cause with direct effect, as mechanism asserts, causes may or may not exemplify any explanatory properties. It may or may not be the case that there are properties exemplified by c and e in virtue of which c causes e. And even if the cause exemplifies such explanatory properties, there may or may not be such a connecting process. I have committed myself to mechanism but have left open the question of whether such a theory should be explanatory.

In these first two chapters I have argued that a theory ought to provide an answer to the how question in the case of direct causation and an answer of a certain kind (involving persistence, etc.). What I will propose in the next chapter is that a theory of causal relata should *not* provide a basis for answering why questions in the case of direct causation. I will deny that where c directly causes e there are properties exemplified by c and e in virtue of which c causes e. The theory of causation being developed, hence, cuts against the grain of most contemporary views in two respects. It is mechanistic but nonexplanatory, rather than nonmechanistic and explanatory.

...ews. ("Feature" views will also be considered.) Davidson's view is that causal relata ...e events and that events are concrete occurrences that possess an indefinite number ...features over and above the ones we hit upon for describing them. For Kim, causal ...ata (which are "events") are the exemplifications of universals (including n-adic ...ations) by a concrete object (or n-tuple of objects) at a time.[1] (The feature theorist ...o takes causal relata to be exemplifications of properties by objects can be read as ...roponent of "Kimian events.")

For Davidson, causal relata are individual, concrete occurrences and, as such, are ...atio-temporal particulars that exemplify multiple properties.[2] Causes are efficacious ...virtue of their properties, but not in virtue of all their properties.[3] Some of c's prop-...ies, but not others, are explanatorily relevant to c's causing e. This is spelled out on ...vidson's neo-Humean view as follows. Two events are causally connected if and ...ly if these events are lawfully connected. Two events are lawfully connected if and ...ly if they exemplify properties in virtue of which they can be subsumed under a ...sal law. But not all of the properties exemplified by the events in a causal pair will ...relevant to their lawful connection. A cause will be characterized by many irrel-...nt properties with respect to a given effect. The striking of a match on a particular ...asion possesses many features that are irrelevant to the effect of its lighting, such ...he fact that it is the striking of a *blue* match. The color of the match does not help ...lain why the striking caused the lighting. So causes will exemplify both explanato-...relevant and explanatorily irrelevant features.

Any theory of causal relata, such as this one, which implies the following thesis, ...hat I have called "explanatory":

> the "in-virtue-of" assumption: a direct cause is efficacious in virtue of the features that it and its effect exemplify.

...w might this assumption be expressed under different theories of causation? A neo-...nean who accepts this assumption will assert that there is some property exem-...ed by c and some property exemplified by e in virtue of which the event pair is ...sumable under a law. For a probability theorist who accepts this assumption, there ...me property exemplified by c and some property exemplified by e in virtue of ...ch c raises the probability of e. And for a counterfactual theorist, the assumption ...unts to the claim that there is some property exemplified by c and some property ...nplified by e in virtue of which had c not occurred, e would not have occurred.

This thesis requires that whenever some token "event" c directly causes some other ...n "event" e, there will be some explanatorily relevant properties exemplified by ...e events: there is some property F and some property H such that c's exemplify-...$^{.}$ (and e's exemplifying H) explains c's causing e. This thesis is not equivalent to ...laim that every causal sequence instances some causal law. Indeed, the notion of ...anatorily relevant properties at stake here should be cashed out in terms of ...terfactuals—roughly, exemplified properties such that had those events lacked ..., the causal relation would not have been realized (see the later discussion). The ...rtue-of thesis excludes causal relata without explanatorily relevant features—that ... causing e without there being properties exemplified by c and e that explain c's ...ng e.[4]

3

Causal Relata

In chapters 1 and 2, I argued for a mechanistic theory, but I did no[t] for a nonexplanatory theory of causation. In this chapter I argue th[at cau]sation should *not* be explanatory—direct causes should not be th[e exem]plifying properties in virtue of which they bring about their effect[s....] the question of the nature of causal relata. On some accounts of ca[usation] others, causation is explanatory. The first part of this chapter con[tains my] argument against explanatory theories. My argument for this concl[usion turns] on a certain logical feature of the causal relation: its transitivity. F[or this] discussion I contrast a Davidsonian view of causal relata, which is [not, with a] Kimian view, which is not. I reject the Davidsonian view, and o[n the way] will also reject certain versions of a "feature" view of relata, accord[ing to which] relata are not events but features of events or objects. "Feature" [views share] the assumption that causes are efficacious in virtue of their (hig[h-level features)] are also inconsistent with transitivity. Indeed, any account of cau[sation that makes] this assumption will run afoul of transitivity. The conclusion of [the argument is that] Kimian events (as well as feature views that reject this assumptio[n) are ruled out] by causal transitivity. The second part of this chapter is taken u[p with deciding be]tween two different forms of what might be called the "property[view" of relata. On] the first (presumably that of Kim), causal relata are exemplificat[ions of properties by] objects. On the second, causal relata are tropes at a time. I defenc[the view that causal] relata are restricted to tropes at a time. This conclusion is closel[y related to the] question of just what it is that persists in a causal process, the topi[c of chapter 4.]

Davidson versus Kim

At the broadest level, theories of causal relata can be divided bet[ween those for which] causal relata are dated particulars, usually events (but also feat[ures of objects or] events), and those for which causal relata are facts, where facts a[re conceived of as] propositions. Some accounts recognize both fact and event caus[ation; others are con]cerned solely with causal relata understood as dated particular[s....] Within the "event" camp we can further distinguish between Da[vidsonian and]

3

Causal Relata

In chapters 1 and 2, I argued for a mechanistic theory, but I did not give an argument for a nonexplanatory theory of causation. In this chapter I argue that a theory of causation should *not* be explanatory—direct causes should not be thought of as exemplifying properties in virtue of which they bring about their effects. This brings us to the question of the nature of causal relata. On some accounts of causal relata, but not others, causation is explanatory. The first part of this chapter concerns itself with an argument against explanatory theories. My argument for this conclusion is predicated on a certain logical feature of the causal relation: its transitivity. For purposes of this discussion I contrast a Davidsonian view of causal relata, which is explanatory, with a Kimian view, which is not. I reject the Davidsonian view, and on this same basis, I will also reject certain versions of a "feature" view of relata, according to which causal relata are not events but features of events or objects. "Feature" accounts that share the assumption that causes are efficacious in virtue of their (higher-order) features are also inconsistent with transitivity. Indeed, any account of causal relata that shares this assumption will run afoul of transitivity. The conclusion of the first part is that Kimian events (as well as feature views that reject this assumption) are not excluded by causal transitivity. The second part of this chapter is taken up with deciding between two different forms of what might be called the "property instance" view. On the first (presumably that of Kim), causal relata are exemplifications of universals by objects. On the second, causal relata are tropes at a time. I defend the view that causal relata are restricted to tropes at a time. This conclusion is closely connected with the question of just what it is that persists in a causal process, the topic of chapters 4 and 5.

Davidson versus Kim

At the broadest level, theories of causal relata can be divided between those for which causal relata are dated particulars, usually events (but also features of objects and of events), and those for which causal relata are facts, where facts are something like true propositions. Some accounts recognize both fact and event causation. Here I am concerned solely with causal relata understood as dated particulars ("event" causation). Within the "event" camp we can further distinguish between Davidsonian and Kimian views. ("Feature" views will also be considered.) Davidson's view is that causal relata are events and that events are concrete occurrences that possess an indefinite number of features over and above the ones we hit upon for describing them. For Kim, causal relata (which are "events") are the exemplifications of universals (including n-adic relations) by a concrete object (or n-tuple of objects) at a time.[1] (The feature theorist who takes causal relata to be exemplifications of properties by objects can be read as a proponent of "Kimian events.")

For Davidson, causal relata are individual, concrete occurrences and, as such, are spatio-temporal particulars that exemplify multiple properties.[2] Causes are efficacious in virtue of their properties, but not in virtue of all their properties.[3] Some of c's properties, but not others, are explanatorily relevant to c's causing e. This is spelled out on Davidson's neo-Humean view as follows. Two events are causally connected if and only if these events are lawfully connected. Two events are lawfully connected if and only if they exemplify properties in virtue of which they can be subsumed under a causal law. But not all of the properties exemplified by the events in a causal pair will be relevant to their lawful connection. A cause will be characterized by many irrelevant properties with respect to a given effect. The striking of a match on a particular occasion possesses many features that are irrelevant to the effect of its lighting, such as the fact that it is the striking of a *blue* match. The color of the match does not help explain why the striking caused the lighting. So causes will exemplify both explanatorily relevant and explanatorily irrelevant features.

Any theory of causal relata, such as this one, which implies the following thesis, is what I have called "explanatory":

> the "in-virtue-of" assumption: a direct cause is efficacious in virtue of the features that it and its effect exemplify.

How might this assumption be expressed under different theories of causation? A neo-Humean who accepts this assumption will assert that there is some property exemplified by c and some property exemplified by e in virtue of which the event pair is subsumable under a law. For a probability theorist who accepts this assumption, there is some property exemplified by c and some property exemplified by e in virtue of which c raises the probability of e. And for a counterfactual theorist, the assumption amounts to the claim that there is some property exemplified by c and some property exemplified by e in virtue of which had c not occurred, e would not have occurred.

This thesis requires that whenever some token "event" c directly causes some other token "event" e, there will be some explanatorily relevant properties exemplified by those events: there is some property F and some property H such that c's exemplifying F (and e's exemplifying H) explains c's causing e. This thesis is not equivalent to the claim that every causal sequence instances some causal law. Indeed, the notion of explanatorily relevant properties at stake here should be cashed out in terms of counterfactuals—roughly, exemplified properties such that had those events lacked them, the causal relation would not have been realized (see the later discussion). The in-virtue-of thesis excludes causal relata without explanatorily relevant features—that is, c's causing e without there being properties exemplified by c and e that explain c's causing e.[4]

For Kim, causal relata (which are "events") are the exemplifications of universals (including *n*-adic relations) by a concrete object (or *n*-tuple of objects) at a time. Kim contrasts his view of properties and events with that of Davidson. Kim distinguishes between the property the exemplification of which by objects is the event from properties merely exemplified by the event. The former he calls the event's constitutive attribute. Every event has a unique constitutive attribute.[5] For Kim, the event of Socrates' dying at *t* has as its constitutive property "dying," but in addition that event exemplifies other properties, such as occurring in a prison, which are not constitutive of it. Davidson, Kim says, does not make such a distinction. As Kim puts the point, the inner structure of events is not analyzed, and consequently, Davidson does not associate with each event a unique constitutive property. For Davidson, no distinction is made between properties constitutive of events and properties exemplified by them, and an event's causal relations may be determined by any number of an event's properties. In sharp contrast, for Kim, an event's causal relations to other events are determined by its unique constitutive property and not by its merely exemplified properties.[6] In Kim's Humean view, the primary condition for two events' being causally connected is that their unique constitutive attributes fulfill the requirement of lawlike constant conjunction.

Do Kimian events satisfy the in-virtue-of assumption? Kim makes heavy use of this distinction between those properties an entity *exemplifies* and those properties of which it is an *exemplification*. Consider that a Kimian event consisting of the exemplification of the property of running by a person, for example, does not itself exemplify the property of running. Its "constitutive" object, not the event itself, does the exemplifying. Properties that an event exemplifies are not properties of which the event is an exemplification. And as we have seen, Kimian events are not efficacious in virtue of their merely exemplified properties. Events are efficacious in virtue of the unique property by which they are constituted. For Kim, although causal relations presuppose laws, causally connected events are not subsumable under laws in virtue of their merely exemplified properties. None of an event's exemplified properties are relevant to its causal relations, but all of its constitution is causally relevant. This thesis is significantly different than the in-virtue-of assumption, according to which direct causes bring about their effects in virtue of properties these events *exemplify*. So Kimian events do not satisfy the assumption, since none of the merely exemplified properties of a Kimian event go into an accounting of its causal relations. There is no property merely exemplified by a Kimian event such that had that event not exemplified that property, its causal relations would have been different.

The in-virtue-of thesis (endorsed by Davidson but not Kim) that there is no causation without explanatorily relevant properties has great appeal and is perhaps widely assumed. But there are reasons for doubting its truth. Such doubts, as we shall see, are linked to a pervasive feature of the causal relation: its transitivity. Causal transitivity cannot be guaranteed if causal relata exemplify explanatorily relevant features. The best place to start this argument is with Davidsonian concrete events. Other theories that share this assumption will also be rejected.

Our question is this: are Davidsonian events compatible with the transitivity of causal chains? In order to address this question we must first clarify the structure of a causal chain, at least for proponents of multifaceted concrete events. For the concrete-event theorist, a causal chain consists in a sequence of events such that each event causes its successor in virtue of properties exemplified by that event (and of its effect). What is not required is that the properties of an event in a causal chain which are explanatorily relevant to its immediate *effect* are the same properties which are explanatorily relevant to its immediate *cause*. Consider a causal chain of three concrete events. The first two events in this series will have multiple properties, and they will be causally connected in virtue of some of these properties but not others. The same will be true of the causal connection of the second event to the third. However, there is no requirement that the property of the second event, in virtue of which that second event is causally tied to the first, be the same property in virtue of which that event causes the third. c may cause e in virtue of c's being F and e's being H, but e may cause f, the third event, in virtue of the fact that e exemplifies R, a different property than H.

The question that I have posed, then, amounts to this: do causal chains, so conceived, guarantee causal transitivity? The answer is no. At least some chains satisfying this schema fail to exemplify transitivity. How might transitivity fail? The quickest way to show a transitivity failure is to begin with *complex* Davidsonian events composed of multiple events. We can then move on to more subtle cases of noncomplex Davidsonian events.

Complex Events

The key to generating a breakdown of transitivity for complex events is to set up a three-event chain in which the second event is caused in virtue of one of its component event's being caused by the first event but in which the second event brings about the third event by virtue of a *different* component event of itself:

> d causes complex event c in virtue of some part-event of d causing some part-event, c_1, of c, and c causes e in virtue of some different part-event of c, c_2, causing some part-event of e.

Transitivity can fail in such cases. Consider the following way of filling out this schema:

> (1) d is a chess championship consisting of three games (the subevents), including the event of Fred's playing in one such game (d_3).
> (2) c is the event of a party consisting of the subevents of toasting Fred's performance (c_1), Mark's dancing (c_2), and various other unrelated events.
> (3) e is a complex event of a medical emergency that includes Mark's having a heart attack (e_1).

d is a cause of c in virtue of the fact that Fred's playing (d_3) is a cause of the toasting of Fred (c_1), where d_3 causes c_1 in virtue of some feature of itself (which we can suppose happens also to be a feature of the complex event d, of which d_3 is a component). The remaining subevents of the chess championship are causally unconnected to the party-events. The medical emergency (e) is caused by the party (c) in virtue of the fact that Mark's heart attack (e_1) is caused by Mark's dancing (c_2), where c_2 is so efficacious in virtue of some but not all of its properties. No other party subevent is causally connected to the medical emergency.

Given transitivity, it should follow that the chess championship (d) is a cause of the medical emergency (e). But in fact, that is not so. The chess championship contributes not at all to the emergency. The chess championship is not causally linked to any subevent of the emergency. The only possible candidate is Mark's heart attack. But when we trace back from the heart attack, we find Mark's dancing as the direct cause, and when we trace back from his dancing, this does not lead to any subevent or aspect of the chess championship. Mark did not attend the championship, and he did not come to the party or dance at the party because of the championship. Even if the chess championship had not occurred, the party would have occurred anyway (we can suppose). It may be true that had there been no chess championship there would have been no toast to Fred, but Mark would still have danced, and as a result, the heart attack and medical emergency would have occurred. There is simply no causal link between the medical emergency and the championship. Hence, although the schema for causal chains of concrete events commits us to saying that the championship is a cause of the party and the party is a cause of the medical emergency, we cannot conclude as required by transitivity that the championship is a cause of the medical emergency. The point is that without certain restrictions, the concrete-event theorist's account of causal chains is incompatible with transitivity.

The proponent of concrete events might suggest further restrictions on causal chains with complex events (to restore transitivity). The most likely restrictions, however, move us in the direction of rejecting the assumption that events exemplify explanatorily relevant properties. For example, the following dubious principle presupposed in this case might be rejected:

> if a proper subpart of a complex event c causes a proper subpart of a complex event e, c is a cause of e.

This principle might be replaced with a different principle:

> complex event c causes an event e only if every component of c is a cause of e.

If this restriction is adopted, our example will not go through. The chess championship will not qualify as a cause of the party, and the party will not qualify as a cause of the medical emergency. Not every component of the championship is a cause of the party, and not every component of the party is a cause of the emergency. The issue of transitivity, then, does not even get started.

There may be other restrictions along these lines. This response, however, does not really undermine the point of this example. The point of this case is not to burden the concrete-event theorist with an implausible view—that is, that complex event c causes e so long as some part-event of c causes some part-event of e. The example makes clear that some restrictions on this principle are necessary if the schema for causal chains is to apply to complex concrete events. But just the kinds of restrictions proposed concede the main thrust of the criticism under discussion—that is, that causal relata may not contain both "relevant and irrelevant" component events if transitivity is to be guaranteed. The suggested restriction tries to solve the problem by requiring that the complex event include no irrelevant part-events. This condition will temporarily save the concrete-event view, but only at the price of focusing greater attention on the kinds of restrictions concrete events must satisfy if they are to be substituted into the schema we have described. The present restriction by itself does not undermine the concrete-event view. But what we will find is that when we move to noncomplex concrete events, similar considerations will force us to abandon the concrete-event view altogether—that is, analogous restrictions meant to save noncomplex events from violations of transitivity will not work, and the only workable restriction will amount to the abandonment of the in-virtue-of assumption itself and, hence, the view that concrete events are causal relata.

Noncomplex Events

Let us move on to noncomplex concrete events. A three-event causal chain will, on the concrete-event view, consist in a sequence of events (d, c, and e) such that each event causes its successor in virtue of properties exemplified by those events: d causes c in virtue of properties exemplified by d and c, and c causes e in virtue of properties exemplified by c and e. Will such chains always be consistent with transitivity? The answer again is no. The key to generating a breakdown of transitivity is to describe a three-event chain in which the second event is caused in virtue of one of its exemplified properties but in which the second event brings about the third event by virtue of a *different* exemplified property of itself:

> d causes event c in virtue of property H of c, and c causes e in virtue of some different property of c, F.

Consider the following way of filling out this pattern:

(1) d is the event of Davidson putting potassium salts in a fireplace.[7]
(2) c is the event of a purple fire in the fireplace a little later.
(3) e is Elvis's death, which results still later from the fire.

In addition to these three events, just at the moment that Davidson puts potassium salts into the fireplace, Jenny puts a lighted match into the fireplace.

What about the causal relations among d, c, and e? First, assume that the fire causes the death of Elvis (c causes e). What about Davidson's action and the purple fire (d and c)? Are these events causally connected? Davidson's adding potassium salts certainly has *some* direct effect. That effect must be some concrete event with an indefinite number of properties, on the concrete-event view. The reasonable candidates for this effect are the purple fire immediately after the action and the death of Elvis some time later. But the death, given that it occurs later, cannot be a *direct* effect of Davidson's action. We are left with the purple fire as the direct effect of Davidson's action. And, in fact, a proponent of concrete events should give this answer. Davidson's action possesses a feature (its involving potassium salts) that is causally relevant to a feature of the fire (its being purple). We can conclude that since Davidson's action has some direct effect, and the purple fire is the only event that could be reasonably taken as a direct effect of that action, his action causes the purple fire. Although the feature theorist will disagree, treating the purple feature of the fire rather than the concrete event of the fire as the effect, such a description is not open to the concrete-event proponent. Thus let us conditionally accept this characterization of the case: Davidson's action causes the fire, and the fire causes the death.

By transitivity it should follow that Davidson's action causes the death. But this is surely false. We can test this causal claim by asking what would have happened had he not acted. The answer is that the death would have occurred anyway. Even if potassium salts had not been added to the fireplace, Elvis would still have died from the fire. And given that this is a short causal chain involving no preemption, this counterfactual test is a reliable guide to the causal facts. We can conclude that even granting the perhaps counterintuitive claim that Davidson's action is a cause of the purple fire, Davidson's action is not in any sense a cause of Elvis's death. Indeed, there is an alternative to Davidson's action for the role of indirect cause of the death: Jenny's act of putting a lighted match into the fireplace. Jenny started the fire that caused Elvis's death. Davidson's action is completely irrelevant to Elvis's fate.

It is worth noting that the Kimian and the feature theorist will not be forced to the conclusion that Davidson's action causes the death. The fire's exemplification of the property "being purple," which is caused by the exemplification of a property of Davidson or of Davidson's action (its involving potassium salts), does not cause that feature (being a dying) of the final event or of Elvis. But the concrete-event theorist does not have this luxury.

This example shows that if causes are concrete events with multiple features, only some of which are explanatorily relevant, violations of causal transitivity are possible. The question that naturally arises is whether there is any way for the concrete-event theorist to avoid this conclusion. Here are some possible moves.

Possible Responses

Transitivity with concrete events can be preserved if one denies that for any given effect, not all of a cause's aspects are relevant to that effect: *all* of a cause's properties are relevant to any given immediate effect. Our Elvis example works only if not every aspect of the fire is relevant to Elvis's death. This way of saving transitivity simply denies that such cases are possible. But this strategy for preserving transitivity with concrete events is wildly implausible. If we take the concrete-event view seriously, then each event has an indefinite number of properties, and it is highly reasonable to expect that for any specific effect e of a concrete event c, some of c's properties are explanatorily irrelevant to e.

A second possible strategy is to reject the assumption that more than one of an event's properties are relevant to its different causal relations. This second response denies that each event c typically has multiple causal relations to other events and that those relations are grounded in various properties exemplified by c. Only one of an event's many exemplified properties has explanatory relevance. On this new assumption, our Elvis example carries no weight. The Elvis case works only if the fire (the intermediary event) is assumed to exemplify various properties, some of which are relevant to the fire's being caused by Davidson's action and others of which are relevant to the fire's causing the death. On this new assumption, the property of the fire that is relevant to its being caused by Davidson's action must be the same property relevant to the fire's causing the death of Elvis. Hence, our example embodies an impossible configuration of causal factors. This second response to the problem of transitivity, however, is less plausible than the first. Concrete events exemplify an indefinite number of properties, and these events stand in multiple causal relations. It would be miraculous if only one of these properties was explanatorily relevant to *all* those causal relations. Once we grant relevancy to merely exemplified properties (the in-virtue-of assumption), it is arbitrary to decree that only one of an event's multiple, exemplified properties will have causal relevance. This strategy, like the first, does not fit very well with the concrete-event view.

This second strategy can be made more plausible if combined with a further maneuver. This auxiliary tactic consists in bringing into play Kim's distinction between the properties an event exemplifies and the property in which it is an exemplification. Each event will consist in the exemplification of a single property. Additional properties of the event will be those that are merely exemplified by the event. The death of Socrates is constituted by a single property's exemplification (dying) but will be characterized by multiple properties exemplified by it (such as happening in prison). This distinction between the property of which the event is the exemplification and the multiple properties exemplified by the event can be combined with the second strategy, which rejects the assumption that more than one of an event's properties are relevant to its causal relations: each event will consist in the exemplification of one property, and each event will stand in causal relations in virtue of that one property alone. But as the reader is aware, this double maneuver moves us from the Davidsonian view of events to the Kimian view. Although this approach may help with transitivity, the resulting view is not a species of the concrete-event approach. This attempt to save the Davidsonian view is tantamount to the rejection of just that account of causal relata. In addition, this strategy amounts to the abandonment of the in-virtue-of assumption. Given these two amendments to the concrete-event view, events are efficacious not in virtue of properties which they exemplify but in virtue of properties of which they are exemplifications. The resulting view is worthy of consideration, but not as a form of the concrete-event approach.

The last defense of the concrete-event view is to reject the in-virtue-of assumption without also moving in the direction of Kim. No distinction is made between the properties an event exemplifies and the property in which it is an exemplification, and events are not efficacious in virtue of the latter class of properties alone. Events are not efficacious in virtue of any of their properties. We simply abandon the in-virtue-of assumption but hold onto Davidsonian events as causal relata. Without this assumption, Davidsonian events are efficacious *independently* of their properties. Our Elvis example must then be rejected. The fire does not have properties relevant to its being caused by Davidson's action, nor does it have properties relevant to its causing the death. The fire has no explanatorily relevant properties. This proposal, however, is the least plausible of those considered. If events stand in causal relations independently of their properties, then events stand in causal relations independently of any properties whatsoever. But that cannot be right. Causation is *feature-driven* in some sense. Properties must play some role. This proposal strips properties of their explanatory role but substitutes no other role. If merely exemplified properties have no explanatory relevance, then constitutive properties must have some kind of relevance—either they must have explanatory relevance or they must constitute the causal relata themselves. What is ruled out, given the feature-driven character of causation, is no role for properties of any kind.

The *feature-driven* thesis is not equivalent to the thesis that causal relata *have* features. If causal relata possess features but these features play no role in the causal story, such as explaining the causal efficacy of the relata, causation might fail to be feature-driven. However, the *feature-driven* nature of causation is *compatible with but not equivalent to* the view that causal relata *have* no features in virtue of which these relata are efficacious, but that these relata *are themselves* features or individual properties. Even if causal relata are individual properties and also have properties, but their efficacy depends not on the properties they *have* but on the individual properties in which they *consist*, causation will be feature-driven. The in-virtue-of assumption is sufficient but not necessary for the feature-driven character of causation. However, the feature-driven character of causation does not by itself entail that causal relata are themselves features. If, for example, causal relata are events but not features, and the in-virtue-of assumption is true, then causation will be feature-driven.

Concrete Features: Features with Explanatory Features

Let us set aside concrete events. I will return to Kimian events shortly. Before doing so, however, we should consider another possible view that bears an important resemblance to the concrete-event view. I will call this the "concrete-feature" account.

Not all philosophers who accept that causation is a relation between dated particulars think that events are causal relata. Some philosophers contend that causal relata are restricted to features of events (Dretske) or features of objects (Honderich).[8] In this section I will suggest that views of this sort do not necessarily mark an improvement over concrete events. That depends on whether "features" satisfy the in-virtue-of assumption. If features exemplify explanatory higher-order features, transitivity violations are possible. "Feature" views combined with the in-virtue-of assumption generate a position analogous to the concrete-event account, with the same kind of transitivity problem. I do not suggest, however, that this combination of views is held by any particular philosopher.

Before considering transitivity, however, we must first ask about the nature of features. More specifically, what must features be like to be consistent with the assumption that causal relata are dated particulars? There are three possible interpretations, one of which is not compatible with dated particulars: features are either universals, or exemplifications of universals, or tropes. Since universals are not particulars, this first gloss is incompatible with "event" causation. The other two ways of cashing out the feature view are consistent with treating causes as dated particulars. The second interpretation, for example, is consistent with both the existence of universals and the "dated particular" view of causal relata. If causal relata are *exemplifications* of universals, then they are dated particulars (since exemplifications are dated particulars). On the other hand, features may be interpreted as tropes, or properties that are by nature spatio-temporal particulars (since they cannot characterize more than one object at the same time). On the trope view, properties are just as much particulars as rocks and trees are. Honderich, for example, claims that causal relata are individual properties (tropes) of objects. In any case, for our immediate purpose of evaluating the feature view with respect to transitivity, we need not decide between the exemplification and trope accounts.

Whether there is a genuine contrast between the event theorist and the feature theorist will depend partly on which view of features (as well as of events) is adopted. If causal relata are features of *objects* (Honderich)—whether tropes or exemplifications of universals—the feature and the event views will differ, if events are Davidsonian. If events are Kimian and features are exemplifications of universals by objects, the feature view and event account will not differ. On the other hand, if individual properties (tropes) of objects are causal relata (as distinct from the *having* of a universal by an object), and the constitutive properties of Kimian events also are read as tropes rather than universals (which does not seem to be Kim's actual view), then causal relata will be constituted by the individual properties of which a "Kimian" event *in part* consists (or is a constituent of), in which case there will be a contrast between a "features-of-objects" view and an "event" view of causal relata. The second reading of the feature view is that causal relata are features of *events* (Dretske) rather than of objects. In that case, if events are Davidsonian, then these two views will differ: events are characterized by causal relata but are not themselves relata. And if events are Kimian, then causal relata will include only the exemplified properties of these events, not the constitutive properties.

Fortunately, for our purposes here we need not clear up these ambiguities. What I am concerned with is whether a feature view, however interpreted, is compatible with causal transitivity. Before considering this question, however, a prior issue must be mentioned. Do first-order features, in fact, have second-order features? Some philosophers argue that first-order features have no second-order features,[9] and some have argued that second-order features are limited to "formal" properties, which are not associated with any causal powers.[10] I will not try to decide this issue here. However, note that if either of these views is correct, then the "feature" view is incompatible with the in-virtue-of assumption. Since I am attempting to support a "feature" view without this assumption, that result would be welcome. Still, there is room for doubt here, so we should consider our question on the assumption that the feature view is compatible with the in-virtue-of assumption. For the sake of argument, then, assume that there are second-order properties (which are not just "formal").

I want to suggest that if the feature view is combined with the in-virtue-of assumption, violations of transitivity can be generated. *If* the features that play the role of causal relata themselves exemplify an indefinite number of higher-order properties, only some of which are explanatorily relevant to their causal relations, breakdowns in transitivity are possible, for much the same reasons as in the concrete-event case. As we shall see, however, the feature theorist has a response not open to the concrete-event proponent—to reject the in-virtue-of assumption.

Suppose that features are efficacious in virtue of their higher-order properties, of which they are characterized by an indefinitely large number (whether or not features are exemplifications of universals or tropes, characterizing either objects or events). Is the feature view compatible with causal transitivity, given this assumption that they are efficacious in virtue of their higher-order features? In effect, we are asking whether "concrete" features that satisfy this assumption are consistent with transitivity.

In order to answer this question, the nature of causal chains must be clarified. On a concrete-feature view, causal chains are structured analogously to causal chains for a concrete-event theorist. In the three-relata case, the first feature causes the second feature in virtue of higher-order features of each. And the same will hold of the second and third features. As on the concrete-event view, the higher-order property of the second feature, in virtue of which it is caused by the first feature, may not be the same higher-order property in virtue of which that second feature causes the third.

This schema does not guarantee transitivity. An example illustrates this lack of warranty:

> A ball is in motion. Suppose that the velocity-property of the ball itself has higher-order features, including a certain rate of change of speed (S_1) and a certain rate of change in direction (D_1).[11] Suppose that there is also a meter that measures only rates of change in *direction* of the ball by way of changes in direction (D_2) of the movement of the needle on the meter (which is already in motion). These changes in direction are higher-order features of a feature of the needle's movement, its velocity. The needle's velocity is also characterized by a certain rate of change of *speed* (S_2). Finally, there is another meter that measures only the rate of change of *speed* in the needle in the first meter. The rate of change of speed of the first needle is measured by changes in the rate of change in speed in the second needle. In short, the first meter registers the rate of change in direction in the ball's motion (by way of the needle's rate of change in direction), and the second meter measures the rate of change in speed in the first meter's needle (by way of the rate of change in speed in the second meter's needle).

Given the second meter's relation to the first meter, the rate of change in the speed of the first meter's needle is relevant to the rate of change in the speed of the second meter's needle. Hence, on the picture of causal chains under review, the velocity of the second meter's needle is caused by the velocity of the first meter's needle, since there is a feature of the velocity of the first needle that is relevant to a feature of the velocity of the second meter's needle. And we have supposed that the rate of change of the direction of the ball is relevant to the rate of change in direction of the first meter's needle. Thus we must say that the velocity of the ball is a cause of the velocity of the needle (since a feature of the first is relevant to a feature of the second). But then by transitivity we are forced to say that the velocity of the ball is an indirect cause of the velocity of the second meter's needle.

But this is false. The second meter's needle is not at all sensitive to the rate of change in direction in the ball's velocity. The velocity of the ball's motion is quite irrelevant, even indirectly, to the velocity of the second meter. Again, one test for a causal relation in a short chain with no preemption is to see what would have happened in the absence of the prospective cause: had the velocity of the ball been different, although the rate of change in direction in the *first* meter's needle may have been different, the rate of change in speed in the *second* meter's needle would have been the same (and so would every other aspect of the second needle's velocity).

The velocity of the ball is not a cause of the velocity in the second meter. Transitivity fails.

This breakdown of transitivity is the result not so much of adopting a "feature" view but of carrying over to the feature view an assumption from the concrete-event view—that relata stand in causal relations in virtue of the properties they exemplify. In effect, we have moved from a concrete-event view to a concrete-feature view. The "features" that play the role of causal relata are characterized in much the same way as Davidsonian events. Each exemplifies an indefinite number of properties, only some of which are explanatorily relevant with respect to any specific causal relation. Transitivity simply cannot be guaranteed under this kind of picture.[12]

Possible Responses

There are two responses available for defending a feature view. Either transitivity or the in-virtue-of assumption can be abandoned. The rejection of transitivity is the less attractive of the two, since transitivity is a fundamental logical feature of the causal relation, along with irreflexivity and perhaps asymmetry. Causal transitivity should be disavowed only as a last resort. The second option, if viable, should be preferred.

We should then discuss the rejection of the in-virtue-of assumption. What precisely does this rejection amount to? Thus far we have treated this assumption as equivalent to the assumption that causal relata have explanatory features; hence, the failure of this assumption is equivalent to saying that causal relata are in an explanatory sense fundamental—that is, that their causal efficacy is not explainable by reference to their features. Causal relata do not exemplify both explanatory and nonexplanatory features. Although this conception is correct as far as it goes, it has a serious limitation: an ontological notion, "causal relata," is too closely associated with an epistemological notion—that of explanation. At this point, a nonepistemological account would be preferable.

A possible ontological explication might make use of the lawful connections we have assumed between causes and effects. Perhaps causal relata include just those events or features that stand in lawful relations independently of their features. More precisely, we might say that f fails to satisfy the in-virtue-of assumption relative to h if and only if there is no higher-order feature F of f and higher-order feature H of h such that had f not been characterized by F or h not been characterized by H, f would not have been lawfully connected to h. This formulation captures the idea that the lawful relations in which causal relata stand do not depend on any of their (higher-order) features, and this independence is explicated by way of a lack of counterfactual dependence of the lawful connections of the causal relata on their features.

But this formulation is also problematic, since there can be lawful relations between causally unconnected events or features. Lawful connection is not sufficient for causation. A better characterization would make it clearer that the *causal relations* of the event or feature are not dependent on the event's or feature's features. However, in order to avoid circularity in an account of causal relata, we should not make reference to unanalyzed causal relations. So let us use a place-holder for causal relations. This place-holder will stand in for whatever relation or relations will serve to analyze the notion of "causal connection."[13] If the correct analysis of this latter notion is given by neo-Humeanism, manipulability theory, or counterfactual theory, this place-holder will alternatively stand in for "lawfully connected," "can bring about," or "is counterfactually dependent upon." If we use R for purposes of this place-holder, then the modified account is as follows. f fails to satisfy the in-virtue-of assumption relative to h if and only if:

(1) f stands in relation R to h, and
(2) there is no higher-order feature F of f and higher-order feature H of h such that had f not been characterized by F or h not been characterized by H, f would not have stood in relation R to h.

The basic idea is that causal relata are the types of things that stand in causal connections not in virtue of any of their features. Although such relata may possess (higher-order) features, these features are not necessary for that relata's actual causal connections.[14] Causal relata are just those "entities" that have no features on which their causal connections depend.

A feature view that rejects the in-virtue-of assumption eliminates the basis for violations of transitivity. A question remains, however, for the feature view. Can the in-virtue-of assumption be rejected without violating the feature-driven character of causation? Recall that in the case of Davidsonian events, that was not possible. The situation is quite different with features. If features are either exemplifications of universals or tropes, then even if their efficacy does not depend on their higher-order features, causation will be feature-driven. If relata are exemplifications of universals, then causal relata are constituted by property instances (which gives properties a central, though nonexplanatory, role in causation). The same is true if causal relata are tropes. The feature view minus the in-virtue-of assumption makes causation a relation between property instances.

Kim Again

I now return to Kimian events. Davidsonian events did not pass the test of transitivity. What about Kimian events? That depends on whether the Kimian accepts the in-virtue-of assumption. A Kimian certainly *could* adopt the in-virtue-of assumption. There is no logical inconsistency in holding Kimian events to be the sole causal relata and also supposing that Kimian events exemplify an indefinite number of properties and are efficacious with respect to any particular effect in virtue of some of these properties but not others. This combination of views, however, would be no better off with respect to transitivity. Fortunately, Kim *need not* and does not incorporate the in-virtue-of assumption into his view.

As we have seen, Kim associates with each event a unique constitutive property, and an event's causal relations to other events are determined by its unique constitutive property, not by its merely exemplified properties. Since the causal relations of a Kimian event are determined completely by the event's unique constitutive property, we cannot generate an example in the fashion of our earlier cases that violates transitivity with Kimian events. Our earlier cases depended on the fact that the second relatum, in a three-relata chain, exemplified distinct properties relevant to distinct causal relations. This configuration is incoherent when mimicked with Kimian events.

In a three-event chain d-c-e, the second Kimian event would have as its constitutive attribute at least two properties, H and R. H would be relevant to c's being caused by d (but not to e), and R would be relevant to c's causing e. Violations of transitivity might then be generated. But for the Kimian there is something incoherent in this description. H, one of c's constitutive properties, is irrelevant to c's causing e. On the Kimian model, however, any property that plays no role in any of an event's causal relations is not part of that event's constitution. The second event's constitution cannot include that property, H. And since R is irrelevant to c's being caused by d, R cannot be constitutive of c. There may be an event that is constituted by the exemplification of H and R, but c is not that event, given the causal facts. A property is constitutive of only those events for which that property has relevance. The constitution of an event is posterior to its causal relations. Our strategy for generating violations of transitivity does not work against Kim.

Kimian events are, hence, exempt from these transitivity problems because they do not satisfy the in-virtue-of assumption. Kimian events are not efficacious in virtue of their merely exemplified properties. None of the merely exemplified properties of a Kimian event go into an accounting of its causal relations.

Two Ways to Interpret Property Instances

Earlier I mentioned an ambiguity in the feature camp. Features that play the role of causal relata are either exemplifications of universals or individual properties. On the first reading, the feature view and the Kimian view are quite close. Indeed, the feature view is identical to the Kimian view if the relevant exemplifications of universals of the feature camp are restricted to exemplifications of universals by *objects* at a time. However, if these exemplifications also characterize *events*, then these views are not equivalent, since Kimian events are exemplifications of universals by objects. Nevertheless, if we allow into the class of "Kimian" events exemplifications of universals by events at a time, then again the views are equivalent. Let us call this the broad interpretation of Kimian relata.

On the second interpretation of the feature view, causal relata are tropes, properties that are themselves spatio-temporal particulars. Causal relata include, for example, the velocity of that ball and the whiteness of this page. And these expressions are understood not to refer to universals. Causal relata are individual properties of objects (and events), not the having of such particularized properties or the having of a universal by an object or an event. The cause of snow blindness is a particular whiteness, but not the exemplification of the universal "whiteness" by the snow. Causes are individual properties, not exemplifications of properties.

Recent philosophers who count themselves in the trope camp include Honderich, Bennett, and Campbell.[15] However, proponents of a so-called trope view of causal relata do not always adequately distinguish their position from that of an exemplification view. Of these three, only Campbell both makes this distinction and clearly associates himself with a trope view of causal relata.

As indicated earlier, Ted Honderich takes causal relata to consist in properties of ordinary objects: "the most natural and explicit answer to the question of what caused something, then, is simply a property or relation of an ordinary thing."[16] In fact, he has in mind specifically individual properties: "it is not the *general* property or *universal* of weighing two pounds, whatever it is, that is flattening the napkin.... what is flattening the napkin is *this bottle's weight*, an *individual or particular property* of this bottle of wine and nothing else whatsoever."[17] In that sense, he is in the "property instance" camp. However, a closer examination of his views makes it unclear whether these "individual properties" are tropes or exemplifications of a universal by an object. What makes for this lack of definiteness is the fact that he takes his "individual property" thesis to be compatible with, but not necessarily to imply, the idea that individual properties supervene on substances and universals.[18] In the event that individual properties do so supervene, it is perhaps most reasonable to construe them as exemplifications of universals by objects. In any case, we should at least leave it open whether Honderich would support tropes *as opposed to* exemplifications of universals.

Jonathan Bennett and Keith Campbell are primarily responsible for reintroducing the notion of tropes into contemporary discussions of metaphysics and causation. Bennett's main interest in tropes is in the context of a theory of events. Indeed, in his *Events and Their Names*, Bennett argues that events *are* tropes. But what then are tropes for Bennett? Tropes are instantiations of properties at a spatio-temporal zone. Tropes are property instances and as such are particulars, to be distinguished, strictly speaking, from facts.[19] What Bennett leaves purposely unclear, however, is whether tropes are distinct from exemplifications of universals: "events are supervenient on substances and properties, unless the supervenience runs the other way because tropes are more fundamental than substances and properties."[20] He is simply not interested in this metaphysical issue. His only concern is to deny that events are on the same level as substances and properties. Thus, by "trope" Bennett has in mind "property instance," where this is neutral between a genuine trope and an exemplification of a property by a space-time zone. Consequently, Bennett cannot be read as a straightforward proponent of a trope view of causal relata.

And, in fact, events qua tropes seem to play very little role in Bennett's actual analysis of "event causation." According to Bennett, roughly, each event name refers to an instance of a property that includes but may not be identical with the property expressed by the predicate in the event name.[21] Corresponding to every trope picked out by such an event name is a unique fact.[22] What Bennett then tells us is that "event e_1 causes x" means that some fact that is part of e_1's companion fact is a cause of x.[23] Event causation, then, in the final analysis, is not distinct from fact causation, except in being less fine-grained. Given this assimilation of event causation into fact causation, the role of property instances in event causation becomes even more unclear.[24]

Keith Campbell, on the other hand, is an unambiguous proponent of a trope view of causal relata.[25] Causes are property instances for Campbell, but these instances are tropes, not exemplifications of universals:[26] "the philosophy of cause calls for tropes."[27] Causes are either standing conditions or events. If a standing condition, then the cause is a trope: "the cause of the collapse is the weakness of this cable (and not any other), the whole weakness, and nothing but the weakness. It is a particular, a specific condition at a place and time: so it is an abstract particular. It is, in short, a trope."[28] If the cause is an event, then it is a change in abstract particulars: "[e]vents, the other protagonists in singular causal transactions, are ... best viewed as trope-sequences, in which one condition gives way to others."[29] Finally, since Campbell holds a trope-only ontology, there is no possibility of interpreting his tropes as exemplifications of universals (not that a trope-only ontology is a necessary condition for a genuine trope view of causal relata).

By a trope view I will have in mind an account of causal relata that is incompatible with exemplifications of universals as causal relata. At this point we can think of our alternatives as variations on the view that causal relata are property instances. The Kimian view, in some sense, takes causal relata to be property instances. And the two views we are considering can be read as two different ways of understanding property instances. For those who disfavor tropes, a property instance is the exemplification of a universal, and for those who disfavor universals, a property instance is a trope. Whether it is appropriate to characterize these views as variations on Kim is perhaps debatable. However, I find it useful to think of the differences here as variations on the thesis that causal relata are property instances.

In fact, the trope view requires a further qualification. There are two ways of thinking about tropes. Tropes are either capable of persistence or not capable of persistence. On the latter view, tropes are momentary entities. I will argue for trope persistence in the following chapter. As a consequence, the trope view of causal relata must be modified in anticipation of that result. Causal relata do not consist in tropes simpliciter but in tropes at a time.

The question that we must answer is which variation we should prefer. Are causal relata restricted to exemplifications of a universal at a time or to tropes at a time? The answer to this question would be straightforward if the trope account failed the transitivity test, since the exemplification account does not fail this test. But, in fact, whatever virtues the exemplification account has with respect to transitivity are also available to the trope view.

Recall that the exemplification view passes the transitivity test because it can and does reject the in-virtue-of assumption. Not surprisingly, the compatibility of the trope view with transitivity depends on whether it can be combined with the rejection of the in-virtue-of assumption. If tropes (at a time) can be efficacious only in virtue of their higher-order properties, violations of transitivity will be possible. If tropes have higher-order explanatory properties, it will be possible to generate chains in which causal transitivity breaks down. But the trope theorist need not affirm that tropes are efficacious in virtue of their higher-order properties. There is nothing in this account of causal relata that requires otherwise.

The reason that the trope theorist can reject the in-virtue-of assumption but the concrete-event theorist cannot is that the concrete-event theorist who abandons the in-virtue-of assumption will violate the feature-driven character of causation, but the trope theorist will not. Unlike with concrete events, when we abstract away from the (higher-order) features of tropes, we are left with an individual property. Independently of its higher-order features, this property may enter into causal relations. What this means is that the trope theorist can reject the assumption that causal relata exemplify explanatorily relevant properties. Causal relata are those individual properties of objects (or events or individual properties) that possess no higher-order features explanatorily relevant to their effects (except perhaps logically connected higher-order features). The denial of the in-virtue-of assumption does not entail that causally efficacious tropes lack properties (if that is even possible). The claim here is simply that a cause is just an individual property at a time which is causally relevant to its effect independently of any property it exemplifies. If trope c at t_1 is a cause of trope e at t_2, then c at t_1, although it may exemplify properties itself, exemplifies no properties that explain why it causes e at t_2. Without such explanatorily relevant higher-order properties, the trope view can avoid violations of transitivity.

Hence, transitivity cannot be the deciding factor between these two views. Additional considerations must be brought into play.

Exemplifications of Universals versus Tropes

A theory of causal relata should be consistent with one's account of causation. Hence, I need to anticipate a bit. In particular, we need to look ahead to how certain very simple cases of causation involving no change over time will be analyzed. We can then show that the exemplification view of causal relata is not congruent with the most basic component of our account of causation, or of causation's singularist component.

Suppose that an object in isolation from outside causal forces persists in a state P from t_1 to t_2. What is the cause of the state P at t_2? I would suggest that the answer is P at t_1. Others might suggest that there is no cause. P at t_2 is the "result" of an inertial process and hence uncaused. I reject this interpretation for two reasons. The first is that these cases have too much in common with more prototypical cases of causation to be treated separately. Many of the normal indicators of a causal connection are present. Most important, the later exemplification is counterfactually dependent on the earlier, and the later state is lawfully connected to the earlier. The presence of these fallible indicators signals a causal connection. Hence, we ought to assimilate these cases to the causal realm. My second reason for rejecting a noncausal description is more indirect. The inclusion of these cases will put us in a better position to understand causation in general. I will suggest, in chapter 5, that once we give an account of these simple cases of property persistence, we will then be able to build up from that simple analysis to a more complex theory on the basis of which we can handle more widely recognized causal phenomena. If this project is successful, that gives us reason to include this kind of "inertial" persistence in the class of causal phenomena.

Consider, then, a causally isolated object that is not changing with respect to property M, its mass. The object's mass M at t_2 causally depends on its mass M at t_1. I will suggest in chapter 5 that these states are causally connected in virtue of the fact that the same property persists over time. Salmon seems to say something like this in discussing causal processes. This characterization requires refinement, but for our purpose here the important point is that the theory of causation that will emerge begins with a notion of property persistence, and that notion will be used to analyze causation. Our question at this point is whether an exemplification view of relata is compatible with property persistence as a basis for a theory of causation. This question is importantly different from a similar-sounding question that is addressed in chapter 4. Among other issues, chapter 4 raises the question of whether property persistence can be understood without positing tropes. In particular, can property persistence be understood on the basis of the notions of "exemplifications of universals" and "causation"? The question we are addressing here is whether property persistence can be given a satisfactory characterization from within a Kimian framework relative to a theory of causation that makes use of the notion of property persistence. This latter qualification excludes the use of the concept of "causation" in giving such an account of property persistence in the context of this anticipated "property persistence" account of causation. No such restriction limits our discussion in chapter 4.

Can a persistence theory get a grip on this case given that causes and effects are exemplifications? Can we combine a persistence theory of causation with an exemplification view of causal relata to provide an account of causation that fits this case and is generally adequate? I would suggest that we cannot. If I am right, it will follow that given our commitment to persistence theory and the possibility of caused unchanges, we ought to reject the exemplification view.

As indicated, in these basic cases our persistence theory will analyze the causal situation as follows: the later incarnation of P being caused by the earlier incarnation is constituted by the fact that these are temporally distinct incarnations of the same property.

There are two ways the exemplification theorist might reconstruct this talk of a persisting property. The first option is to insist that the exemplification of P by the object at t_1 is the *same exemplification* as the exemplification of P by the object at t_2. But this first option is not coherent. Exemplifications are essentially momentary. Temporally distinct exemplifications are not identical.[30] In addition, I will argue in the next chapter that even if this option is not incoherent, the notion of a persisting exemplification cannot account for property persistence. The second option is to invoke some relation R that connects these exemplifications of P. The most obvious candidate for R is "causes." However, in the context of constructing an account of causation, that option is not open if circularity is to be avoided. (I discuss this interpretation of property persistence in the next chapter for independent reasons.) Since we are attempting to give the outlines of a persistence account of the causal connection between the exemplification of P at t_1 and the exemplification of P at t_2, the relation to which appeal is made cannot be causation itself.

What other possible relations might be utilized? The exemplification proponent might bring into play either a probabilistic relation, a legal relation, some spatio-temporal relation, or some combination of the three. In other words, the exemplification theorist may try to analyze property persistence (and hence causation given a persistence theory) by reference to any of these relations. The difficulty is that this approach will generate an account of causation that at a fundamental level is probabilistic, law-based, or spatio-temporalist. Property persistence will be a matter of some such relation. As a consequence, we will be returned to the preemption pairing problem, since as we have seen, theories of causation that primarily rest on these relations cannot resolve this problem. But that is just what we were trying to avoid by way of a persistence theory. In short, one is hard-pressed to formulate a persistence theory of causation that relies on the notion of property persistence within an exemplification framework without falling prey to circularity or the preemption pairing problem. This gives us a prima facie reason for rejecting the exemplification view of causal relata.

Whether this is also a reason for shifting to the trope view is yet undecided. If the trope view runs into the same difficulties with understanding property persistence—relative to a theory of causation that makes use of the notion of property persistence—then we have an equally good reason for rejecting the trope view of causal relata. In fact, these same kinds of difficulties will surface if we analyze property persistence in terms of some relation (other than causation) between trope stages or momentary tropes. Here, however, the trope theorist has an option not open to the exemplification theorist. In the next chapter I will argue that tropes are not essentially momentary and that there is room for a nonrelational account of trope persistence. With such an account in hand, a persistence theory of causation that makes use of the notion of property persistence will be able to avoid circularity as well as the preemption pairing problem.

Causal Inquiry and Causal Relata

Investigation of a causal question includes a process of eliminating irrelevancies. A particular causal question might initially receive a rough, approximate answer that includes irrelevancies. Further inquiry leads to refinement and elimination of irrelevancies, until we end up at the level of a property. But if properties are universals, this whittling process, it would seem, has gone too far, since causes are particulars.[31] Causal inquiry must be interpreted as ending with a particular. Universals will not do. But particularity is not enough. Just as universals cannot be causes, neither can bare particulars—particulars without a nature. Causes are particulars with a nature, with a character. This constraint, however, still leaves us with an interpretive choice. Both exemplifications of universals and tropes are particulars with a nature.

This choice, I have suggested, should be made in favor of tropes. Given the demands of a persistence theory, we ought to opt for tropes. If this is right, we can say that causal inquiry reveals the causal work done by individual properties. What we discover when we discover the cause of your seeing red is a particular instance of red, a trope.

If this conclusion is right, we can describe the process of causal inquiry as follows. In the process of identifying causes, we begin with some region. We identify a region that includes the cause. From the region we pick out some concrete event. The search for causes proceeds further by abstraction. We abstract away from various irrelevant properties (and objects) and focus on certain first-order individual properties that are realized in the region. We then turn our attention to the properties of this first-order property. We move up to its higher-order features. If none of these features is relevant, then we conclude that the first-order property is a cause (or effect). If one of the higher-order features is relevant, we move up to that level and abstract away from the first-order feature, as we did with objects. This procedure is repeated at the higher level with respect to even-higher-still features of features. Once we reach a level of irrelevancy, we settle on the next level down as the cause.

Summary

It is worthwhile summarizing the main points of these first three chapters. We began with an examination of the preemption pairing problem. A comparative analysis of various leading theories of causation in chapter 1 led to two conclusions in chapter 2: (1) an adequate theory of causation must provide a basis for answering the question of how causes give rise to their direct effects, and (2) this answer must invoke some persisting "entity." In the present chapter, consideration of causal transitivity led to the conclusion that a theory of causal relata should not provide an answer to the question of why c causes e—that is, should reject the assumption that causes must exemplify features which will help explain why they cause the effects they cause. Further discussion tentatively established the result (with a view to a persistence theory) that if there are tropes, then tropes rather than exemplifications of universals play the role of causal relata, at least given a persistence theory of causation.

In the following two chapters these two lines of reasoning will be further developed and brought together. I will suggest that the singularist component of causation is best understood as a matter of the persistence of tropes. Our first task, however, will be to demonstrate two things about tropes: first, that there are tropes, and second, that they can persist and hence really do provide the best candidate for causal relata in a theory of this sort.

4

Qualitative Persistence

The main conclusion of chapter 3 is that concrete events are not causal relata and that tropes are to be preferred over exemplifications of universals. This preference, however, is conditional on two further claims: that there are tropes and that tropes can persist over time. Given that the existence of tropes cannot be taken for granted, this conditional argument must be followed by an argument for tropes as such. And given that the preference for tropes is partly based on the anticipation of an account of causation in terms of persistence—specifically, of trope persistence—an argument for the possibility of trope persistence is called for. Fortunately, both of these argumentative requirements can be satisfied by a single argument.

The first task of this chapter is to demonstrate that there are tropes and that they can persist (and that exemplifications of universals cannot persist). The second task is dictated by the fact that for someone to make use of trope persistence in an account of causation, there must be some guarantee that trope persistence is not a matter of causal relations among trope stages. Without such a guarantee we risk circularity in giving a trope-persistence account of causation in chapter 5. In the second part of this chapter, I argue that a causal account of trope persistence is inadequate.

For the Existence and Persistence of Tropes

There is no general agreement on the existence of tropes. The lack of general agreement, however, does not mean that there have been no attempts to argue for tropes' existence. The problem is that these arguments have not been very convincing. I will very briefly mention two such arguments and certain criticisms that have been made of them. This short exercise will help determine just what an argument for tropes needs to do—that is, what sorts of objections must be overcome. As it will turn out, there is a very strong reason for believing in tropes, and this reason also supports the claim that they can sometimes persist.

Before considering efforts to demonstrate tropes, we should remind ourselves just what a trope is supposed to be and how it differs from universals. A universal is a property that can characterize more than one object at the same time. The universal "pale redness" may be exemplified by a rug at this end of the room, and that very same universal may be exemplified by a table at the other end of the room, at the exact same moment. A trope, on the other hand, is a property that cannot be an aspect of more than one object at a time. The blue color tropes of two different paintings, no matter how similar, are nonidentical. In that sense tropes cannot be shared. "Wisdom" is a universal, if there are universals, and "Socrates' wisdom" is a trope, if there are tropes. The absence of the possibility of multiple simultaneous instances makes tropes particulars—particularized properties.[1]

Arguments for tropes take the following form: some linguistic practice or metaphysical fact is cited, and it is claimed that only an ontology including tropes can account for this practice or fact. A common strategy for criticizing arguments of this form is to grant that *some* particular may be required to account for the cited practice or fact but to argue that a nontropic particular is sufficient for the explanatory task. By way of illustration, consider the following two fairly typical arguments and criticisms.

Wolterstorff suggests, in his "Qualities," that certain uses of expressions such as "the green in the lower-left-hand corner of Cezanne's *L'Estaque*" must be interpreted as referring to tropes rather than universals.[2] The way this expression is used on occasion is not consistent with reference to a universal but is consistent with reference to a trope. This linguistic justification, however, is questioned by Jerrold Levinson in his "The Particularisation of Attributes." Levinson claims that there are other readings of the reference of this expression, readings according to which the referent is neither a universal nor a trope. This expression may refer to the exemplification by that region of the painting of a certain universal color or to that area of the canvas itself:[3]

> by 'the green in the . . .' someone might mean on occasion: this painting's *having* that particular green, the phrase there being used to direct attention to a particular state of affairs. But exemplifications, although non-shareable entities, are not particularised attributes. So the attribute description Wolterstorff invites us to consider need not be construed as making reference to a particularised attribute; it may refer to a universal one, or, more obliquely, to a particular surface or a particular exemplification.[4]

On the metaphysical side, Charles Landesman, in his "Abstract Particulars," offers a similar criticism of an argument for tropes from Stout.[5] Stout gives the following argument:

> If substance is nothing apart from its qualities, to know the substance without knowing its qualities is to know nothing. It follows that we cannot distinguish substances from each other without discerning a corresponding distinction between their qualities. It follows also that if the distinction of the substances is not preconditioned by any discerned dissimilarity between their qualities, the qualities must be primarily known as separate particulars, not as universals.[6]

If substances are just bundles of qualities, then the possibility of exactly similar but numerically distinct substances can be accounted for only if qualities themselves are particulars.

Landesman rejects this argument. He applies what he takes to be Stout's argument to an example involving two qualitatively indistinguishable color patches, which he names "Left" and "Right." Stout's argument, if right, would entail that the color of

Left, which Landesman calls "a," is a different entity than the color of Right, which he calls "b." Landesman claims that the weakness of this argument is found in the fact that although the sum of a and the position of a is a different *color spot* than the sum of b and the position of b, this does not establish that a is different than b: "a and b are colors, not color spots; the two sums are color spots, not colors, though they contain colors as parts. Thus a positional difference, though it does lead to a difference in entity, fails to yield a difference in the required kind of entity."[7] The individuation of substances can be accounted for without tropes as long as we have positions summed with universals.

This extremely brief summary of these typical arguments and objections can provide guidance of a sort on the demands any argument for tropes must meet. Notice first that Landesman's criticism of Stout has an obvious parallel with Levinson's criticism of Wolterstorff. Wolterstorff argues that an account of the referential use of certain expressions demands tropes, and Levinson counters by claiming that exemplifications of universals (or regions) will do as well. Stout argues that certain facts of individuation are possible only if tropes exist, and Landesman counters by claiming that universals summed with regions are sufficient for individuation. Both critics say that the work done in these arguments by the postulation of tropes can be done either by positions, by positions together with universals, or by exemplifications of a universal. All we need from the particular side of the ledger in order to account for the cited linguistic practice or metaphysical fact are nontropic particulars. Wolterstorff and Stout at best establish the existence of some particular, but not necessarily a trope.

Two points relevant to the task of demonstrating the existence of tropes can be extracted from these criticisms. The first is that the existence of exemplifications of universals is not sufficient for the existence of tropes, since the antitrope theorist counts himself successful if he can show that exemplifications of universals can do the work that the trope theorist has set for tropes. That conclusion is in line with the fact that the existence of exemplifications of universals is independent of the existence of tropes. Second, the existence of tropes can be established if we can specify some metaphysical (or perhaps linguistic) fact that could be accounted for by reference to tropes, but not by way of any of these nontropic alternatives (exemplification of a universal, position, or position plus universal). What Landesman and Levinson show is that it is not enough to establish the need for some particular in order to demonstrate the existence of tropes. Other nontropic particulars also must be excluded. Although the arguments of Wolterstorff and Stout may not meet these two demands, there is an argument for tropes that does, as I will now try to show. More specifically, there is a metaphysical fact, in the form of qualitative persistence, which can be accounted for only by positing tropes. No other nontropic particular will work.

Nonsalient Qualitative Change and Property Persistence

The kind of phenomenon I have in mind, qualitative persistence, can be highlighted best through contrast with different forms of qualitative change.

Qualitative change divides into two kinds, one common and the other logically possible but definitely not common. The common form of qualitative change consists in the following pattern (described in the language of universals): an object o

exemplifies (or does not exemplify) a universal at t but fails to exemplify (or does exemplify) that universal at a later time t'. For example, a spherical object is flattened and as a result no longer possesses a spherical shape. The less common form of qualitative change does not fit this pattern. In this latter form of qualitative change, there is no kind of quality possessed by (or lacking in) the object at t which is lacking in (or possessed by) the object at t'. An object can, *in some sense*, lose a quality possessed at t without there being a later time t' at which point the object fails to exemplify any (at least nonrelational) universal exemplified by the object at t. In other words, an object can undergo qualitative change from t to t' without it being the case that that object is "qualitatively distinguishable" from t to t'. This possibility may sound paradoxical, especially if we have in mind universals and not individual properties, but I will now provide an example of this kind of change, which I call "nonsalient qualitative change."

Consider the following two situations:

> *Case 1.* There is a machine that eliminates all electrical charge from objects without a trace and with no other effect on the object.[8] A second machine instantly generates electrical charges in objects. Suppose that these two machines, directed at the same particle, are set to activate at just the same moment t'. The second machine is set to generate an electrical charge in the particle of exactly the same magnitude that the particle previously exhibited. As a result, there is no apparent shift in electrical charge in the particle from t to t'.
>
> *Case 2.* The particle undergoes no transformation by way of any machines but retains its electrical charge over this same time period.

I would suggest that there is a real difference between these cases. Although there is some sense in which the particle in the first case retains its electrical charge, there is another sense in which the particle's electrical charge changes. But there is no relevant sense in which the second particle's electrical charge changes. The phenomenon present in the second case, but not the first, I will refer to as "property persistence." I will argue that property persistence, as distinct from nonsalient qualitative change, is intelligible only as the persistence of tropes or individual properties.[9] In other words, we will be able to account for qualitative persistence and for the fact that such persistence is distinguishable from nonsalient qualitative change only if we posit the existence of tropes that can persist over time.

How might a trope theorist describe the difference between these two cases? In the language of tropes, the change in the first case consists in the replacement of an individual property with a new individual property, which happens to be very similar to the original. In the second case, the corresponding electrical charge trope persists over time. The particle in the second case, which is not interfered with by the machines, retains the individual property, a certain electrical charge, but the first particle loses the relevant individual property, which is replaced by a new individual property of the same level of electrical charge. So goes the trope-theoretic description of the difference between these cases.[10]

If this argument for tropes is to be convincing, a nontropic characterization of the difference between these cases must not also be possible. We must show that the antitrope theorist who admits the possibility of nonsalient qualitative change as well as qualitative persistence cannot provide an account for property persistence that both is generally adequate and provides a basis for distinguishing property persistence from nonsalient qualitative change.

Can nonsalient qualitative change be accounted for by reference to universals? It is easy to see that universals will not help to distinguish between these cases. Consider again case 2: there is no change at the level of universals whatsoever from t to t'. The universal "electrical charge of magnitude e" that characterizes the particle at t is the same universal that characterizes the particle at t'. But the same must be said of case 1: from t to t', by assumption, the particle does not take on a new magnitude of electrical charge but, rather, retains the same magnitude. Whatever change takes place in case 1 goes unrecognized, since the same universal "electrical charge e" is exemplified at t and at t'. The two cases are on a par with respect to universals.

But what this shows at most, if at all, is that some *particular* must be posited to account for property persistence. Universals are not enough. And as Landesman and Levinson argued earlier, there may be nontropic particulars to which the antitrope theorist can appeal. Of the realist's arsenal of concepts, the most likely candidate to which appeal can be made is that of the exemplification of a universal. Perhaps we can mark a difference in these cases as follows: in case 2, the exemplification of the universal "electrical charge e" at t persists until t', but in case 1, the exemplification of the universal "electrical charge e" does not persist until t' and is in fact replaced with a *new* exemplification of the same universal. Can the concept of a "persisting exemplification" provide an adequate basis for defining property persistence and for distinguishing these cases? The answer is definitely no. Either the notion of a persisting exemplification is incoherent or it is coherent yet does not determine a difference between these cases.

The notion of a persisting exemplification does seem to be incoherent. Exemplifications are individuated in part by reference to their time of realization. Hence, at least for many universals, persistence is ruled out. Consider monadic properties. We may reasonably assume that exemplification E is the same as an exemplification E' only if the E-object is identical to the E'-object, the E-universal is the same as the E'-universal, and the E-time is the same as the E'-time.[11] Hence, since an exemplification is the having of a universal by an object (or perhaps a spatial region) *at a time*, differences in time are sufficient for a difference in exemplifications. It follows that we *cannot* say in case 2 that the exemplification of electrical charge e at t' *is* the same as the exemplification of electrical charge e at t, but in case 1 the exemplification of electrical charge e at t is *not* the same as the exemplification of electrical charge e at t'. We cannot say this since the exemplification of electrical charge e at t, in case 2 (as well as case 1), involves a different time and, hence, is different than the exemplification of electrical charge e at t'. For universals such as "electrical charge of magnitude e," we can perhaps at best talk about a series of temporally distinct exemplifications.

The conclusion that there are no persisting exemplifications applies, however, only to certain universals, even if the identity conditions we have stated are granted. There still may be room for the notion of a persisting exemplification if we shift to other universals. Consider, for example, the universal of slowly raising an arm. Without violating these identity conditions, we can pick out an earlier and later part of this exemplification. But even if we accept that there are some persisting exemplifications, there are two difficulties in applying this claim to the cases at hand. The first, and most obvious, is that the universal in cases 1 and 2, "electrical charge of magnitude e," unlike the universal "slowly raising an arm," does not have duration built in. The exemplification of "electrical charge of magnitude e" does not necessarily have temporal duration. At each moment, we have a different exemplification of this property, which cannot easily be construed as a temporal part of a longer-running exemplification.

Second, even if it is granted that the exemplification of electrical charge e can have temporal duration, there is reason to question whether these two cases can be distinguished on this basis. An exemplification will consist of three terms—the object, the universal, and a time along with a "relation," "exemplification of U by x at t" (restricting our attention to monadic properties).[12] Comparing these two cases gives the same result: in each case at t there obtains the exemplification of the universal "electrical charge e" and at t' the exemplification of the same universal "electrical charge e" by the same object. The cases are parallel with regard to objects, times, and universals; hence, there is no room for describing one as involving a persisting exemplification and the other as not. The symmetry of the cases requires the same assessment, either positive or negative, with respect to the question of whether the exemplification persists. Hence, even if there is sense to be made of persisting exemplifications (of universals such as "electrical charge of magnitude e"), qualitative persistence cannot be distinguished from nonsalient qualitative change on the basis of this notion.

However, to demonstrate the need for tropes we must also show that other nontropic particulars will not help us account for qualitative persistence and for the distinction between such persistence and nonsalient qualitative change. In fact, we are brought no closer to an adequate account of this distinction if we shift our attention from exemplifications to nontropic particulars such as positions or positions in combination with universals. Consider position. Although nothing was explicitly said about the positions of the objects or their electrical charges in our examples, let us now suppose that there is no change in position in either case. If there are no positional differences from case 1 to case 2, then no basis exists, as far as position goes, to demonstrate change in the first case but not in the second case. In addition, since, as we have seen, there is no relevant difference in universals, summing positions and universals will provide no grounds for finding change in case 1 but no change in case 2. The relevant nontropic particulars that might be invoked by the antitrope theorist can safely be excluded.

The resources of the antitrope theorist, however, are not yet exhausted. There may still be a way of accounting for property persistence and for distinguishing between these cases by reference to exemplifications of universals, if we bring into play causal relations between exemplifications. Qualitative persistence may be a matter of a series of causally connected exemplifications of the same universal—causal connections that are present in the second case but not the first. More specifically, in case 2 but not case 1, there is a causal connection between the exemplifications of electrical charge e just before and just after t (let us call these exemplifications E and E'). In case 2, the object exemplifies electrical charge e at the later time in part *because* the object exemplifies electrical charge e at that earlier time, but in the first case the earlier exemplification plays no part in the causal explanation of the later exemplification, since the activities of the creator machine are not affected by the earlier exemplification. We can then generalize this observation as follows: property P persists in object o from t to t' just in case the exemplification of P by o at t' is caused by the exemplification of P by o at t.

This latest strategy, which notes a causal difference, is certainly sufficient to distinguish between these cases without bringing tropes into play. However, we can quickly detect the weakness of this approach by slightly modifying case 1: imagine that the destroyer machine is set to activate if electrical charge e is detected, and the creator machine is set to activate if the destroyer machine is activated. If these machines are set up in this way, then upon activation, part of the causal explanation of the object's exemplifying electrical charge e at t' is that the object exemplified electrical charge e at t. The later exemplification is caused by the creator machine, which is caused to operate by the destroyer machine, and the destroyer machine's operation traces back causally to the earlier exemplification.

Nevertheless, there may remain a causal basis for distinguishing between case 1 as modified and case 2 without positing tropes: there remains a causal difference between case 2 and case 1 as modified. The causal chain running from E to E' runs *outside* of the object in the modified version of the first case, but not the second. And perhaps we can make use of this fact in giving an account of qualitative persistence as follows: property P persists in object o from t to t' just in case (1) there is no causal chain that runs outside of o such that the exemplification of P by o at t' is caused by the exemplification of P by o at t by way of that chain, and (2) these two exemplifications are causally connected. Qualitative persistence then is still a matter of certain kinds of causal chains connecting exemplifications of the same universal.

Unfortunately for the antitrope theorist, this characterization of property persistence is too strong. Properties may persist even if there are such operative external causal chains. We may suppose, for example, that the electrical charge of the object at t has an effect on some external condition, such as a magnetic field, which in turn has some partial influence on whether the object retains its electrical charge until t'. In that case, the electrical charge of o at t' depends on the electrical charge of o at t in part in virtue of a causal chain that runs outside the object.

This analysis may, however, be weakened. We need only require that there be some *internal* causal dependence, without excluding external causal chains. Let us then say that property P persists in object o from t to t' just in case the exemplification of P by o at t' is caused by the exemplification of P by o at t by way of a causal chain that runs inside of o. This account is compatible with our last example, which partly depends on an external chain, given the reasonable assumption that part of the causal story is an internal one. But even in this weakened form such an analysis is too strong. Imagine, for example, that the destroyer/creator machines are somehow placed internally in the object. In that event, all the relevant causal chains will be internal, but the charge will not persist if the machines are activated.

A different strategy for a causal analysis would involve the distinction between direct and indirect causation. One causal difference between case 2 and all the various versions of case 1 thus far is this: in the latter but not the former case, there is a segment of the causal chain connecting exemplifications of "electrical charge of magnitude e" that does not contain an exemplification of charge. The exemplification of charge just prior to t does not directly cause the exemplification of charge just after t. The earlier charge exemplification is only indirectly linked, through the operation of the machines, with this later charge exemplification. We might then analyze qualitative persistence as follows: property P persists in object o from t to t' just in case there is a chain of P exemplifications in o, starting with P at t and ending with P at t', such that each exemplification of P by o *directly* causes its immediate successor.

This variation, however, will also fail. Case 1, involving the destroyer/creator machines, can be modified further to take into account this analysis. Suppose that the creator machine is effective only if there is an immediately preceding instance of that same magnitude of charge. In that case, the preceding charge will be a direct cause of the next charge instance. However, given the operation of the destroyer machine, there is no property persistence.

Given the failure of these variations, one begins to lose confidence in the possibility of generating a substantial account of qualitative persistence along these lines. Perhaps the best that can be done for a causal analysis is to identify the causal route with less specificity: property P persists in object o from t to t' just in case the exemplification of P by o at t' is caused by the exemplification of P by o at t by way of a causal chain *of an appropriate kind*. Indeed, if the fate of causal theories in other domains is any guide, there is reason to think we can do no better. Causal theories are typically forced to make use of the notion of an "appropriate causal chain" to address the problem of "deviant causal chains." Although it is possible that "appropriate" can eventually be replaced with some more substantial specification of the nature of these chains, our review makes that an unlikely prospect. Without any real possibility of such a replacement, we must ask whether this analysis is adequate.

The answer to this question is negative. Consider that things are appropriate only relative to some standard or situation. What role does "appropriate" play here? Appropriate to what? This analysis in effect tells us that the relevant causal chains must be of a type that is typical of or compatible with property persistence. But it is just property persistence we have been trying to characterize. This characterization (if it is not just a place-holder) ends up being circular.[13] The notion of property persistence is used to give an account of property persistence. The point about circularity can be put more generally still: any attempt to analyze property persistence in terms of a relation between temporally distinct exemplifications of the same universal will be either clearly inadequate or circular. Suppose, for example, that the antitrope theorist proposes that property persistence consists in some primitive (unanalyzable) relation R among exemplifications of the same universal. Either relation R will contain a causal component (R may still be unanalyzable just so long as the causal component does not exhaust R) or it will not contain such a causal component. If R does not entail that a necessary condition of property persistence is that the relevant exemplifications be causally connected, then the analysis will be vulnerable to easy counterexample. But if R does contain a causal component, that component, as we have seen, must in part specify what are to count as appropriate causal connections by reference to the notion of a persisting property, which will lead to circularity.

Although circularity is not always objectionable, in this case it is, for two reasons. The first is that this is a very small circle, so the analysis is not particularly informative. The second reason is that the analysis does not put us in a position to do one of the things we wanted an account to do: distinguish between cases of genuine property persistence and cases of nonsalient qualitative change. Unless we have already distinguished between these cases on some other ground, this analysis will not improve our chances of making these distinctions. Neither of these reasons for rejecting this version of the causal analysis is completely conclusive. However, each of them provides a prima facie case against the causal/exemplification approach to property persistence. If there is another way of analyzing property persistence and for distinguishing property persistence from nonsalient qualitative change, we ought to opt for it.

Trope Persistence

Let us thus return to the trope-theoretic account of property persistence. The proponent of tropes claims that qualitative persistence is simply trope persistence. And again, in our examples, the difference between cases 1 and 2 is that in the second case, but not in the first, a charge trope persists over t. This account of the distinction between qualitative persistence and nonsalient qualitative change raises the question of how trope persistence is to be understood.

Before addressing this question, I need to clear up a possible confusion about the conclusion of the discussion thus far: I am not suggesting that all tropes persist. The conclusion of my argument at this point is that some tropes persist over time. There may be tropes that do not persist—momentary tropes. Consider, for example, the shape of a square projected on a screen. The shape of that projected image at any moment is an individual property. However, from one moment to the next the images are eliminated and replaced with new, exactly similar images. Here we have a series of distinct trope shapes that do not constitute a persisting trope. There are two possible causal stories that correspond to series of exactly similar but nonpersisting tropes. The first is illustrated by the example of the projected image. Here the various momentary images are successive effects of a series of similar causes. The second, at least possible causal story is illustrated by a series of objects that pop into existence uncaused, only to disappear immediately and be replaced with an uncaused but qualitatively similar object. Here the various tropes are nonpersisting, and each momentary trope is uncaused. In any case, there are both momentary and persisting tropes.

There are two possible ways of understanding trope persistence, either relationally or nonrelationally. On a relational characterization, tropes have temporal stages, and distinct temporal trope stages are stages of the same trope just in case they stand in some relation R to each other. The second possibility is that tropes lack temporal stages: tropes are wholly present at each moment of their existence. This second view is the one I will adopt after briefly discussing the relational view.

On a relational view, tropes have temporal parts, and trope stages are gen-identical just in case they are connected by a certain relation or relations R. Now either R can be fully analyzed or it cannot be. In either case, part of the correct analysis of R will include a causal component. Stages of the same trope must be suitably causally connected. But the attempt to substitute a more telling characterization of the nature of such chains will lead us down the same road we have just abandoned, presumably with the same result—an implicitly circular account of property persistence.

There is, however, an alternative account of trope identity that cannot be similarly criticized: the nonrelational view.[14] On this view, tropes do not have temporal parts, and their persistence from t to t' consists in their existing wholly at t and t'. This position has similarities to nonrelational views of physical object identity over time, according to which physical objects do not have temporal stages (are not four-dimensional space-time worms) and are wholly present at each moment of their existence. I will understand trope persistence on analogy with such views.[15]

Before considering objections to this claim, it is worth repeating in brief the argument that has brought us to this conclusion. It was argued that property persistence cannot be analyzed in terms of a relation between either exemplifications or trope stages without circularity. It was then suggested that property persistence can be understood as trope persistence if the latter is construed nonrelationally. With a workable notion of trope persistence, we can also account for the difference between case 1 and case 2. In case 2, but not in case 1, the electrical charge trope persists over t'. We may then conclude that the best way to account for the phenomenon of property persistence is to posit the existence of tropes that can persist.

I now consider four objections to this argument for the existence of persisting tropes.

Objection 1

The first objection is this: if the trope theorist can make use of a nonrelational view of trope persistence, an antitrope theorist also should be able to distinguish between qualitative persistence and nonsalient qualitative change by making use of a nonrelational view of "persisting exemplifications." On such a view, there are persisting exemplifications, and their persistence is a matter of the exemplification's being wholly present at each moment it is realized. The antitrope theorist can then say that there is such a persisting exemplification in case 2 but not in case 1.

I have already raised doubts about the possibility of persisting exemplifications. However, even if there are persisting exemplifications and they are interpreted nonrelationally, there is reason to doubt that nonsalient qualitative change can be distinguished from property persistence on this basis. Consider that an exemplification has various "components," including the exemplification relation—if it is a relation—(a universal on this view), the object and the relevant universal that is exemplified. In order to distinguish between cases 1 and 2, some difference must be found at the level of these "components." The difficulty, as we have seen earlier, is that in each case these components remain constant through t'. There is no new object, new universal, or a new exemplification relation (since this is a universal) that comes into existence during the period that spans t' in case 1. There is no basis for thinking that these cases differ in any way with respect to objects and universals, hence there is no room for finding a persisting exemplification in one case but not the other, even if we grant a nonrelationally characterized persisting exemplification.

Objection 2

The second objection plays on the fact that tropes are particulars rather than universals and questions the claim that tropes both persist and are wholly present at each moment of their existence. Since tropes are not universals, this objection argues, they are not repeatable and hence cannot be strictly identical in their various instances, including at various times. Only a universal could be wholly present in each object it characterizes. If this objection were sound and properties were tropes, then there would be no qualitative persistence whatsoever. An object would have to change in all respects from each moment to the next. Given that tropes are particulars, there is too much room for change and none for property persistence. And, the objection continues, if we repair this defect by perhaps defining property persistence in terms of the resemblance of the successive tropes (returning to some kind of relational but noncausal theory of trope persistence), we will end up ruling out nonsalient qualitative change, since in those cases there is the same degree of similarity across time as in the cases without qualitative change of any kind.

This objection rests on the assumption that properties that are not universals cannot be strictly identical in their different instances, even at different times. But this assumption is simply false. The denial that property *P* is a universal does not entail that that same property cannot occur at two different times. The denial that *P* is a universal at most entails that *P* cannot be strictly identical in its different instances *at the same time*. Physical objects, for example, since they are not universals, cannot occupy different spatial locations at the same time but can occupy more than one temporal location. The point is that denying that a property is a universal does not entail that that same property cannot be instanced at two different times.

Objection 3

My argument for tropes depends crucially on case 1, as contrasted with case 2. A third line of attack is simply to deny that case 1 is logically possible. If case 1 describes an impossible situation, then we need not consider the contrast between cases 1 and 2.

Unless we are given some reason for this denial, this objection is wholly unpersuasive. What is supposed to be impossible here? An electrical charge creator machine is logically possible, as is an electrical charge destroyer machine, and there seems to be nothing that would exclude their simultaneous operation.

Objection 4

There is a more serious challenge, however, which can be brought against case 1. On my reading of these cases there is a significant contrast between case 1 and case 2. In case 1 there is a qualitative change that is absent in case 2. But, says this objection, there really is no such change in the first case for which we need to account. There is no such thing as nonsalient qualitative change. In case 1 the two machines simply cancel one another out, with no net effect. The particle in case 1 is analogous to a projectile in free fall, with a constant velocity, to which two forces are simultaneously applied that exactly cancel out, with no change in velocity. We need not and should not say that the projectile undergoes a nonsalient change in velocity. Similarly, in case 1 we ought to say that the two machines cancel each other out with no nonsalient change in charge. The machines produce no difference internal to the particle, but only a strictly external difference in the cases.

Certainly there are ways of specifying the details of case 1 such that this alternate interpretation is more natural. Suppose that the destroyer machine is set to destroy the charge but that in place of a creator machine there is a second destroyer machine directed toward the first destroyer machine. The result is that the first machine is destroyed and never activated. There is no nonsalient change in the particle, since the first destroyer machine itself was destroyed before it could be effective. Or we can suppose that both machines act by sending out a "ray" and that these rays cross paths and cancel each other out before reaching the particle. In that case, there is no nonsalient qualitative change in the particle. But the fact that there are ways to fill out case 1 that do not involve nonsalient qualitative change does not mean that there are no versions of this case in which the machines do not cancel each other out.[16] Here are some circumstances in which we would have good reason for rejecting the "canceling-out" interpretation.

First, there are circumstances in which we could test whether there is canceling out. Suppose that the creator machine is set to generate a charge *twice* as great as that which the particle currently possesses. The destroyer is set to eliminate a charge equal in magnitude to that which the particle currently exhibits. Suppose also that charges are not physically divisible or addable.

There are two relevant possible outcomes to running these machines, one of which is consistent with the canceling-out hypothesis and the other of which is inconsistent with that hypothesis: (1) the particle's charge retains the same magnitude and (2) the particle's charge is doubled in magnitude.

If the charge's magnitude after activation stays the same, then the best explanation may be that the machines canceled each other out. If the machines operated by canceling out, we would expect that the particle would retain a magnitude of charge equal to that with which it began rather than doubling. But suppose we do get doubling. If the particle's charge doubles, we cannot explain this result by "partial" canceling out. Even if the destroyer machine in the canceling-out process halved the effectiveness of the creator machine (so that it produced a charge of only half the magnitude it was set to produce), we could not assume that the doubled charge of the particle was the result of addition of that charge from the creator machine. That would be out of line with the laws excluding addition. The best explanation, given doubling, is that the destroyer machine eliminated the original charge of the particle and the creator machine replaced that charge with a new, greater charge.

What does that say about the interpretation of case 1 in which both machines are set to the *same* magnitude? If the machines are operated in the same way as in the doubling case, with the exception of a different setting on the creator machine, we then have reason to think that in case 1, there is also no canceling out.

We may have other evidence to support the "no-canceling-out" hypothesis. We may, for example, know about certain obvious side-effects when canceling out occurs and know that those effects are absent when the machines are activated in case 1. Or, from experimenting, we may know that whenever the rays from each machine cross paths, there is canceling out. Mutual interference leads to complete ineffectiveness. And on a particular occasion of our test, when the machines are arranged in a certain fashion and the creator is set to double the charge and the destroyer is set to destroy only the present magnitude of charge, we find that the charge is doubled. We now have even more reason to conclude that the new, higher charge is a result of the creator machine and that the original charge has been eliminated by the destroyer machine. Had there been canceling out, we would expect to see no net change in magnitude (since any canceling leads to the total ineffectiveness of both machines). We can conclude that when the machines are arranged in this same fashion in case 1, but both are set to the actual magnitude of the particle's charge, there is also no canceling out.

Next consider another case that is best interpreted as involving nonsalient qualitative change, for which canceling out is not a reasonable hypothesis:

> a creator machine is activated so as to double the charge of a particle (to the level of twice the minimum), and a destroyer machine *sometime later* halves the charge of this same particle.

As part of the background to this case, suppose that there is a law that prevents the division of a minimum charge quantum, and that any particle with twice the minimum charge possesses two different charges (quanta) rather than a single charge of double the magnitude. Also assume that on some occasions when the machines are activated (1) the destroyer machine destroys the original charge, leaving in place the new charge generated by the creator machine, but on other occasions (2) the destroyer machine destroys the new charge generated by the creator machine, leaving in place the original charge. However, what we observe does not vary from one occasion to the other: the initial minimum charge is doubled, then that doubled charge is halved.

There is a difference between what happens on these different occasions. In scenario (1), before the doubling, the particle is characterized by a certain charge, which continues to characterize the particle after the doubling but which no longer characterizes the particle after the halving. In this case, the charge after the halving is not identical to the charge before the doubling, although it is of the same magnitude. In the second case there is no change over this entire sequence with respect to the original charge quantum; it is retained throughout. But in the first case the original charge property is destroyed by the destroyer machine during the halving. Even though these particles match perfectly at the level of charge universals, there is a change in the first case at the properties level that is missing from the second case. This difference can be accounted for by the trope theorist: in the second case, the original charge trope persists through the halving process, but not so in the first case. There is a form of property persistence which is absent in the first case.

Most important, the details of this example leave no room for the canceling-out interpretation. The machines operate at *different times*. Hence, there is no way for the machines simply to cancel each other out. This objection cannot get a grip on this variation of nonsalient qualitative change.[17]

Finally, a more indirect response to the canceling-out objection is to take note of well-accepted examples from the literature on physical-object identity which, although not ostensibly about nonsalient qualitative change, entail such change. In particular, Shoemaker describes a case in which a destroyer machine is set to eliminate without a trace a table and, coincidentally, a creator machine is set to create a qualitatively indistinguishable table at the location of the original table at the same time. There is general agreement that this example is possible and that it involves nonsalient *object* change. The original table goes out of existence and is replaced with a new, qualitatively indistinguishable table. This is not simply a matter of the machines canceling each other out. But if this description is acceptable, as it should be, we must also admit nonsalient *property* change. The original color of the table, for example, is destroyed with the original table and replaced with a new, exactly similar color instance. "Immaculate replacement" of physical objects *includes* nonsalient property change. Given that the former has been generally accepted as possible, so ought the latter.[18]

Summary

In this first part, I have argued for the existence of persisting tropes. I have pointed to two metaphysical facts in support of this conclusion: property persistence and the fact that it is logically possible for objects to undergo nonsalient qualitative change. A theory of property persistence should be noncircular and should provide a basis for distinguishing cases of property persistence from cases of nonsalient qualitative change. Only a theory positing tropes can accomplish both of these tasks. We thus have reason to believe that tropes exist and that some tropes persist. The argument of this first part also demonstrates that exemplifications are not the sorts of things which persist; hence, by themselves they bring us no closer to a persistence-based account of causation. The fact that tropes can persist, but exemplifications cannot, provides a partial basis for preferring tropes as causal relata, given the requirement that the singularist component in a theory of causation be persistence-based.[19] In the next chapter the persistence of tropes will provide the core of such an account.

Against a Causal Account of Trope Persistence

I have suggested that any relational account of property persistence, including a relational-trope account, will face a problem of circularity. The trope view will be no better off than the exemplification view (of property persistence) if the trope theory goes relational. I have thus opted for a nonrelational conception of trope persistence, an option not open to the exemplification proponent. In this section I seek to reinforce this resistance to relational accounts of trope persistence. I focus on causal-relational theories.

There are two reasons for this focus. First, any relational account of trope persistence that has a chance of success must include a causal component. Hence, in order to undermine relational accounts it is enough to disable causal accounts. Second, if trope persistence is a matter of causally connected trope stages, then the concept of trope persistence cannot provide a basis for analyzing causation. A trope-persistence theory of causation is viable only if there are reasons for forswearing a causal theory of trope persistence.

There are indeed such reasons. A causal theory of trope persistence will face a problem—that of accounting for trope motion, which is a variation of the problem of nonsalient qualitative change. In our earlier discussion, the question was raised as to how to distinguish between nonsalient qualitative change and qualitative persistence. This question was raised relative to an *object*: how do we distinguish the *particle*'s undergoing such change from simple qualitative persistence? The present problem in effect asks how to distinguish between nonsalient qualitative change and qualitative persistence relative to a *position* rather than an object. As we shall see, a causal theory of trope persistence cannot always distinguish positional qualitative persistence from positional nonsalient qualitative change.

What then is the problem of trope motion? Tropes are spatio-temporal particulars that can persist and, like some other persisting particulars, move. The color trope on one part of a color wheel, for example, changes location as the wheel rotates. According to causal-relational accounts of tropes, the same trope changes locations over time just in case the relevant trope stages that occupy different spatial locations are appropriately causally related. The difficulty with this account is that there are circumstances in which a causal theory fails to track moving tropes and, hence, fails to determine all questions of trope identity.

In order to get at these circumstances, I will consider a kind of example that has appeared in the literature on physical-object identity. Although these examples originally were meant to undermine relational accounts of object persistence (for Armstrong, continuity accounts, and for Kripke, any relational account including the causal view), they can be readily adapted to the causal theory of trope persistence. Consider Armstrong's variant: a perfectly homogeneous sphere in an otherwise empty universe.[20] This sphere is either rotating or stationary. At any moment in its history, however, the sphere's properties (understood as universals) and its relations to other objects at that time will not vary whether or not it is rotating. The question Armstrong raises is whether a continuity theory of object identity can discriminate motion or stasis of the sphere and hence determine, for example, to which later quadrant stage (the northwest or southwest, for instance) the current northwest quadrant of the sphere is gen-identical. The question I will ask is whether a causal theory of trope persistence can discriminate between motion and stasis of the *tropes* that characterize the sphere.

Consider the color trope of the northwest quadrant of the sphere. Can a causal theory discriminate between these two possibilities (is this trope in motion or is it stationary)? A causal account will be able to carry out this task just in case it can distinguish between hypotheses like the following:

(1) the color trope that characterizes the northwestern portion of the sphere at t_1 characterizes the southwestern portion of the sphere at t_2, and

(2) the color trope that characterizes the northwestern portion of the sphere at t_1 characterizes the northwestern portion of the sphere at t_2.

This particular problem is, in fact, a species of the problem of nonsalient qualitative change. But here the possibility of nonsalient qualitative change is relative to a *position* rather than an object. If the sphere is not rotating, then the position of the northwest quadrant is characterized by the same color over time, but if the sphere is rotating, that position is characterized by different (but indistinguishable) colors over time. If the sphere is rotating, there is nonsalient qualitative change relative to a particular position. The question as to whether a causal-relational theory of trope persistence can distinguish between the situation described in (1) and that described in (2) is in effect the question of whether a causal theory can distinguish between nonsalient qualitative change and qualitative persistence relative to a position.

The causal theorist says there will be a causal difference that determines whether the color trope is moving. If the color trope is stationary, the color stages that characterize the northwestern portion of the sphere over time are causally connected, but this is not so if the trope is moving. If the color trope is stationary, then the color trope stages of the northwestern portion from t_1 to t_2 will bear to each other the particular causal relationship that is required for trope phases to constitute phases of the same trope, and if the color is rotating, the earlier northwestern color trope stage will be causally connected in a similar way to the later southwestern color trope stage.

The claim that to the two possibilities, trope motion and stasis, there correspond very different intertrope-stage causal relations has strong initial intuitive appeal. However, this initial appeal is misleading and cannot be sustained on closer examination. In fact, the causal analysis does not provide a basis for distinguishing nonsalient qualitative change from qualitative persistence in these cases.

My argument for this negative thesis has the following structure. A causal theory of trope persistence will rest on one of three bases: either (1) causation is nonreducible, (2) the notion of causation is to be analyzed in terms of trope persistence, or (3) causation is to be understood in terms of one of the leading reductionist theories of causation. If causation is interpreted nonreductively and realistically, then there will be a nonreducible causal difference between the rotating and stationary cases. Are there independent reasons for believing that causation is nonreducible? I have already addressed this question in chapter 2, where the best arguments for nonreductionism were examined and found to be inadequate. The second gloss on causation, which analyzes causation in terms of trope persistence, will be circular in this context of attempting to decide questions of trope identity. I therefore focus on the third option. I suggest that the causal analysis of trope persistence, as applied to the sphere case, falters no matter which of these contemporary theories of causation we plug in. The causal treatment of the problem of trope motion can be demonstrated not to work when the concept of causation is spelled out within any of the traditional nonpersistence theories of causation. Once these substitutions are made into the causal theory, the problem of trope motion goes unresolved. I consider the causal theory in the context of the neo-Humean theory, counterfactual theory, and probabilistic theory of causation.

The Neo-Humean View

On a neo-Humean-based causal theory of trope persistence, trope stages are causally connected just in case they are connected by causal laws. In the case at hand, then, the main difference between a stationary and a rotating color trope consists in the difference between a lawful connection between northwestern trope stages at t_1 and t_2 and a lawful connection between the northwestern trope stage at t_1 and the southwestern trope stage at t_2.

According to the neo-Humean theory of causation, the causal facts about a given sequence S supervene on the laws that govern that sequence. If two sequences share all nonrelational properties stage for stage and all noncausal relations among stages, and they instantiate the same laws, then each sequence will have all the same causal relations among these stages. The causal theory of trope identity, interpreted as a supervenience thesis, states that the facts of identity of a given sequence supervene on the causal relations that characterize that sequence of trope stages. For these two theses to be compatible, it must not be true that what causal laws are true of a sequence in part depends on the facts of identity. In particular, it should not be the case that whether this or that possible law holds of a sequence S depends on whether the stages of that sequence are stages of the same trope—that is, whether they are gen-identical. Facts of identity are not admissible for purposes of determining whether stages are lawfully connected or of determining which laws connect these stages, since it is just these facts that the causal theory is supposed to determine *after* determining the laws.

The first problem with a neo-Humean account of trope persistence comes in the form of a dilemma: either the laws do not make reference to facts of persistence and are of no use in deciding questions of identity, or the laws do make such references but a determination of which lawful statement is true depends on facts of identity, rather than the other way around. This dilemma requires elaboration.

Consider a lawlike statement, L_1, and a sequence of trope stages, S. Suppose that L_1 does not entail any fact of identity about S. L_1 states that if a trope which is of kind P exists at t_1, then there will exist a trope at t_2 that will be of kind P. Assume that the sequence S begins with a trope stage that is of kind P and that this stage is followed by a trope stage that also is of kind P. L_1 is compatible with *either* (a) these two trope stages of S being gen-identical or (b) these two trope stages not being gen-identical. Reference to L_1 will not resolve the question of the gen-identity of the stages of S. In the sphere case, the neo-Humean theory tells us that if the color trope is stationary, then the color trope that is in the northwest position at t_1 will be lawfully connected to the color trope that is in the northwest position at t_2, but if the color trope is rotating, then the color trope in the northwest position at t_1 will be lawfully connected to the color trope in the southwest position at t_2. Suppose that the relevant laws do not include reference to cross-temporal trope identities. The laws, like L_1, state that if certain types of properties are instantiated at a time t, then certain types of properties will be instantiated at another time t'. Laws of this type do not make it possible to distinguish between trope rotation and stasis in the sphere case. Since the sphere is qualitatively homogeneous, any property type that is instantiated on one part of the sphere will also be instantiated at all other locations on the sphere.[21] The law will state that given that the sphere displays a certain configuration of property types at t_1, it will display that same configuration of properties types at t_2, since the sphere is qualitatively homogeneous. The configuration of property types at t_2 will be the same whether or not the color trope is rotating. And since the law does not contain information about cross-temporal identities, we will not be able to read off from the law whether or not the sequence it describes involves a moving or stationary color trope.

The other half of the dilemma is predicated on the assumption that the relevant, possible laws do make reference to trope identity facts. Suppose, for example, that L_1 and L_2 are not neutral with respect to identity facts about S. L_1 states that if a trope x of kind P is realized at t_1, then x will be realized at t_2. Now if this law is true and applies to sequence S, then it entails that at least the initial stages of S are stages of the same trope. Another possible law, L_2, states that if a trope x of kind P is realized at t_1, x will go out of existence and be replaced with a qualitatively similar trope, y, at t_2, which is also of kind P. If this law is true and applies to sequence S, then the initial stages of S will *not* be gen-identical. Now assume that the first stage of S consists in a trope stage of type P and the next stage consists of a qualitatively similar trope stage of type P. Which of these lawlike statements is true of S—L_1 or L_2? Without further information this issue cannot be decided. Indeed, without a specification of the facts of identity about S, this determination cannot be made. What we must know is whether the first and second stages of S are or are not stages of the same trope. If the former is true, then L_1 is true and applies to S, and if the latter is true, then L_2 is true and applies to S, if all other facts are equal and in favor of either L_1 or L_2. The point is that appealing to laws to decide identity questions will in some cases at least misrepresent the relation between the laws and what makes the laws true. Facts of identity will in some cases help determine which of a set of possible laws is actual. The supervenience base of laws includes facts of identity; hence, the neo-Humean causal theory of identity, understood as a supervenience thesis, cannot be accepted.[22] This conclusion will have implications for the question of whether a neo-Humean causal theory of identity can determine whether the color trope of the northwestern portion of the sphere at t_1 is rotating or not. Suppose there are two possible laws, one of which dictates trope rotation and the other of which entails that the color trope is stationary. What sorts of facts would make the difference between the holding of one of these laws rather than the other? The answer to this question, as we have seen, may be facts of cross-temporal identity. If the sphere is such that the color trope at the northwest location at t_1 remains at that same location at t_2, then the law specifying no rotation holds, and there is no rotation. On the other hand, if that color trope shifts to the southwest position at t_2, the law specifying rotation applies, and the trope is moving. Both laws are compatible with a description of the case that leaves out all reference to cross-temporal identities. Which law is true itself depends on facts of identity and, hence, on whether or not the color trope is in motion.[23]

There is one other possibility we should consider: suppose the laws make reference not to trope persistence but to object identity over time. Suppose, for example, that the relevant laws dictate that the northwest quadrant of the sphere at t_1 is identical to the northwest quadrant at t_2. Will we not then be able to conclude that the color trope that characterizes the northwest quadrant at t_1 is the same color trope that characterizes the northwest quadrant at t_2? The answer is no. Even if the laws determine object identity, that will not be enough to read off property identity. The reason is that as we have seen earlier, object identity does not guarantee trope identity. Recall that in the first part of this chapter we explored cases in which the same object over time is characterized by different tropes of the same type. The general possibility of nonsalient qualitative change means that we cannot in all cases infer trope persistence from object persistence.

In the preceding argument I claimed that which possible law is actual will in some cases depend on facts of identity. However, I took it for granted that if the law made reference to trope identity, then we could at least read off the facts of trope identity from the law and on that basis make a determination as to whether the trope was rotating or stationary. But even that much may not always be true. In particular, given certain forms of indeterminism, even if the law makes reference to trope identity and even if we know which of the possible laws is true, we still will not be in a position to resolve some trope identity and motion questions. There exist indeterministic worlds in which the laws and noncausal facts determine that a trope at a time t_1 continues to exist to a time t_2 without determining to which trope stage the t_1-stage is gen-identical. For example, suppose that there is a law that entails that:

> there is a 50% chance that the color trope in the northwest location at t_1 will relocate to the southwest location at t_2, and there is a 50% chance that the northwest color trope at t_1 will remain at the northwest location at t_2.

This law guarantees that the color trope at the northwest location at t_1 will persist to t_2 but does not determine which color trope at t_2—the color trope at the northwest location or the one at the southwest location—that color trope is identical to.[24] Hence, on the basis of this law we cannot infer whether or not the color trope is rotating.

Counterfactual Theory

This same indeterministic case undermines a causal theory of trope persistence based on a counterfactual theory of causation. Recall that the counterfactual theory states that an effect is counterfactually dependent on its immediate cause.[25] Events that are indirectly causally connected are connected by a chain of events such that each member of the chain is counterfactually dependent on its immediate predecessor. Different versions of the counterfactual theory spell out varying accounts of the truth conditions for counterfactuals.

Again suppose that there is a certain probability that the sphere will rotate and a certain probability that the sphere will remain stationary. Under these conditions, it will not be true that had an earlier color trope stage not been realized, some successor trope stage would not have been realized. Consider the case where the sphere is stationary. The appropriate counterfactual that should be true is (C'): had the northwest color trope at t_1 not existed, the northwest color trope at t_2 would not have existed. But given these indeterministic assumptions, (C') will be false. Even if the northwest color trope at t_1 had not existed, the northwest color trope at t_2 might still have existed, since there was some chance that the sphere would have rotated. Put in the language of Lewis's semantics for counterfactuals, (C') is true just in case there is some world in which the northwest color trope at t_1 is not realized and the northwest color trope at t_2 is not realized that is closer to the actual world w than all worlds in which the northwest color trope at t_1 is not realized but the northwest color trope at t_2 is realized. But if we compare worlds in which the northwest color trope at t_1 is not realized, we do not find this to be true. In some of those worlds (those in which the sphere is stationary), the northwest color trope at t_2 is not realized but the southwest color trope at t_2 is realized, and in others (worlds in which the sphere is rotating), the northwest color trope at t_2 is realized but the southwest color trope at t_2 is not realized. In neither of these worlds need there be a law violation, since the laws governing the motion of this sphere are indeterministic. Worlds of both descriptions are compatible with the indeterministic laws and the earlier facts of our world. In addition, neither world counts as closer to *w* in virtue of the nonlaw facts. Both worlds differ from the actual world to the same degree along this dimension—both are missing a single color trope.

The prospects for a causal theory do not change significantly if we switch to a probabilistic version of counterfactual theory. Recall that the basic idea is that if the cause had not occurred, the *probability* of the effect would have been different. If we use the probabilistic version of counterfactual theory to back up a causal theory of trope identity, we then have two possible counterfactuals, one of which a causal theory will presumably associate with trope motion and the other with stasis (given the simplifying assumptions made above):

(*P*) had the northwest trope at t_1 not been realized, the probability of the northwest trope at t_2 being realized would have been different.
(*P'*) had the northwest trope at t_1 not been realized, the probability of the southwest trope at t_2 being realized would have been different.

This theory may provide a correct guide to motion and identity in some indeterministic worlds, but the following example shows that this theory will not help in all indeterministic worlds. Suppose that w_1 is largely deterministic except in the following respect: the rotational motion of spheres made out of a certain substance is an indeterministic matter. In particular, given a set of circumstances at t_1, although most of the properties of the sphere at a later time t_2 are deterministically fixed, whether the sphere rotates or remains stationary from t_1 to t_2 is indeterministic. In such a world both *P* and *P'* will be true. Suppose that the northwest trope at t_1 had not been realized but that things had otherwise been as much like the w_1 world up to t_1 as possible. Would this absence of color at the northwest location at t_1 have increased the probability of an absence of color at the northwest location at t_2? The answer is that the latter probability *would* have increased, since at t_1, given the circumstances, there was a certain probability that the sphere would remain stationary. The introduction of an absence of color at that location at t_1 would increase the chance of an absence of color at that location at t_2. But it is also true that the introduction of an absence of color at the northwest location at t_1 would increase the chance of an absence of color at the southwest location at t_2, since there is some chance that the sphere will rotate. The probability of an absence of color at the northwest location at t_2 and the probability of an absence of color at the southwest location at t_2 are both greater given an absence of color at the northwest location at t_1 than they are given the actual facts at t_1 (including no gap). But since both *P* and *P'* are true, the causal theory, given this probabilistic counterfactual theory of causation, will not be able to determine whether the color trope is rotating or not rotating.

Probabilistic Theory

What about the more traditional probabilistic theory of causation? Again, recall that the basic idea behind probabilistic theories of causation is that causes increase the probability of their effects.

Suppose again that there is a certain probability that the color trope will rotate given the state of the sphere at t_1 and a certain probability that it will not rotate. Given this assumption, a probabilistic theory will not be able to distinguish between movement and stasis of the color trope.

Either the relevant conditional probabilities will be free of any reference to cross-temporal identities or there will be such references. If these conditional probabilities are not stated in terms of cross-temporal trope identities, no determination can be made as to whether the color trope is rotating. Conditional probabilities that did not mention identities would state, for example, that there is a certain probability that if a certain type of color trope is displayed at t_1, then the same type of color trope will be displayed at t_2. But the type of color trope displayed at t_2 will be the same whether the specific color trope is rotating or not, given that the sphere is perfectly homogeneous. Hence, we will not be in a position to determine whether or not the color trope is in motion.

If these conditional probabilities *do* include reference to cross-temporal identities, it will still be the case that no determination of the question of trope motion can be made. Suppose, for example, that the probability that the color trope P will occupy the southwest position at t_2 given that it occupies the northwest position at t_1 is greater than the probability that P will occupy the southwest position at t_2. Assume also that no earlier circumstance screens off this probabilistic relation. On the assumption that none of these probabilities is 1 or 0, we will not be able to infer whether the color trope is stationary or whether it is moving. All we can infer is that there is some probability that the color trope is moving and some probability that it is stationary.[26]

Finally, I consider two objections to the sphere cases that question the assumption that the spheres are qualitatively indistinguishable.

Objection 1

Denis Robinson holds a causal account of motion that appeals to the law-governed nature of motion, and he proposes that the qualities of matter are "self-propagating"— that is, that they undergo a process of propagation that is law-governed.[27] The difference between the stationary sphere and the rotating sphere is that "the process of material propagation heads off in different spatio-temporal directions in the two cases."[28] This difference is due not to a difference in the antecedent distribution of first-order material properties but to a difference in "second-order quasi-qualities." The latter are correlated with but do not represent the velocity of material motion. These "quasi-qualities," or vectors, are causally responsible for the propagation of the first-order qualities and hence for the velocity of the sphere. The stationary and rotating spheres differ with respect to these second-order properties.

I have four worries about Robinson's approach to the sphere case. (1) Robinson says these second-order properties are also self-propagating, although their distribution may be causally influenced. But if we need second-order properties to explain the direction of the propagation of first-order properties, will we not need third-order properties to help explain the direction of the propagation of second-order properties? This possibility seems to threaten an infinite regress. And if second-order properties do not require third-order properties to determine the direction of their own propagation, why should we think that first-order properties require second-order properties to determine the direction of their propagation? (2) We are told that "these vectors are not to be seen as simply representations of the velocity of material motion,"[29] and there are supposed to be lawful causal relations between these second-order and first-order properties. But our only access to these second-order properties is through the direction of the propagation of first-order properties, since these vectors, it would seem, have no other effects. And then one wonders how any particular law concerning the connection of second-order and first-order properties could be tested, since the second-order properties cannot be picked out independently of the first-order properties. (3) But if these vectors are distinct from the velocity and in fact cause the velocity, then it should be logically possible for two objects to agree on their first-order properties and their velocities but disagree on their second-order properties. But given that our only access to the former is through the latter, it is at least difficult to envision this possibility. On the other hand, if these second-order properties are "simply representations of the velocity of material motion," then we cannot use these second-order properties to resolve the sphere case, since in this case, which of these properties are present would logically depend on whether the sphere was rotating or stationary. (4) Finally, and most important, as we have seen, these quasi-qualities "figure causally in determining the direction of propagation of the other material properties."[30] But suppose that the only causal links are probabilistic, including those that hold between these second-order properties and the first-order properties. Then two spheres that agree on all of their properties at a time, including their second-order properties, may differ with respect to motion. For example, we may suppose that the second-order properties of both spheres favor motion but that this second-order property is efficacious in one case but not in the other.

Objection 2

Even if Robinson's appeal to "second-order quasi-properties" is misguided, there still may be a way to challenge the sphere argument by reference to a conception of velocity as a first-order property, but not as a relational property. It might be suggested that the sphere argument rests on the assumption that velocity is not an intrinsic property of an object at an instant, but rather a property that is a relation between an object's positions at various times. But if, contrary to this assumption, velocity is an *intrinsic* property of an object at a time, then (1) the spheres' velocities will certainly differ in the cases of rotation and stasis and (2) the rotating sphere will not be qualitatively homogeneous, since not every property instantiated in one part of the sphere will be instantiated in other parts of the sphere—different parts will have different velocities (differing in either magnitude or direction or both). In short, if velocity is an intrinsic property, the spheres will differ in velocity at each moment, and the rotating sphere will not be qualitatively homogeneous. Finally, there may be good reasons for taking velocity to be an intrinsic property at a time. So says Michael Tooley in his "In Defense of the Existence of States of Motion," where he argues that velocity is not logically supervenient on facts about position over time but is an intrinsic theoretical property, which *explains* change in position.[31] His argument includes a series of cases to support this nonsupervenience claim.

In fact, though, this objection fails. Even if velocity is an intrinsic property of an object at a time, the sphere argument goes through. Consider a modified version of a case developed by Tooley. Imagine a two-sphere world in which motion is probabilistic and sometimes discontinuous: for each sphere, there are a number of possible positions (rotate left or right or remain at rest), but even complete information about its present state generates only probabilities of its being in different positions later. The position of this trope at a time depends solely and probabilistically on its immediately preceding position. The locations over time of the color tropes of these spheres will generally be discontinuous. However, on this occasion, suppose that improbably, the positions of the color trope on one of the spheres, which initially characterizes the northwest quadrant, happen to correspond to a continuous curve that is differentiable at every point. What Tooley suggests about such sequences is that the object in motion (here, the color trope) "would not have a velocity at any time, even if all its positions happened to fall along a curve describable by some continuous, differentiable function."[32] Applied to the northwest trope, which happens by chance to display such movements, we must say that even though this trope changes position over time and even does so continuously, at no point does it have an intrinsic velocity.[33]

Now let us return to the comparison of the two spheres, one of which is, by chance, "rotating" (either in a continuous fashion or discontinuously) and the other of which is stationary over the same period by chance. In that case, if we follow Tooley, we *cannot* say that the rotating sphere and nonrotating sphere differ with respect to velocities. Even if velocity is an intrinsic property, the quadrants of the sphere in the rotating case have no velocity at any point. This holds whether or not the movements of the sphere happen to fit a continuous curve. And when we focus just on the "rotating" sphere, there is no room to claim that the different parts of the rotating sphere have different velocities. That is what Tooley's assessment dictates: those parts have no velocity at all at any time, since an object whose movements only happen by chance to fit a continous curve has no momentary states of velocity, according to Tooley. In short, even if velocity is intrinsic, there is no difference in velocity between the spheres, and there would be no difference in velocity among the parts of such a "rotating" sphere. More generally, if there are worlds in which there is movement but no velocity, then appeals to velocity (as an intrinsic property) cannot serve to undermine all versions of the sphere case.

Second, the states of motion and velocity of an object at a time, according to Tooley, are logically independent from the later states and positions of an object. For the same object with the same position and state of motion on different occasions, it is logically possible for that object to be in different positions after the same interval of time. Indeed, this must be so if the states of motion are to causally explain changes in position. The state of motion does not logically guarantee future positions. However, it might be suggested that the states of motion and velocity at t_1 will fix later positions if the relevant laws (which refer to states of motion and velocity) and forces are given. So, on this suggestion, given the relevant laws that make reference to states of motion (not cross-temporal identities), we will be able to trace the movement of the color trope of the northwest quadrant.

In fact, however, even if we include the relevant laws/forces, that does not automatically guarantee the same later positions. The laws of motion may be probabilistic. If so, even if states of motion are intrinsic, we will not be able to distinguish between stasis and rotation. If probabilistic in the right way, the laws will be compatible with different possible later positions for the color trope—say, either the southwest quadrant or the northwest quadrant—and hence with motion or stasis. The laws may dictate at best probabilities of less than 1 to each of these outcomes. Hence, even if states of motion/velocity are intrinsic properties of an object at a time, that by itself does not entail that the rotating sphere can be distinguished from the nonrotating sphere in any given period. Furthermore, this means that even if we can determine that the spheres are not qualitatively homogeneous because we can attribute different velocities at t_1, that does not determine which sphere is rotating, if the laws are probabilistic.

Summary

In general terms, we can say that a causal theory of trope identity, when conjoined with a theory of causation, will face the following pattern of difficulties in accounting for trope identity and, hence, trope motion. If indeterminism is true, then even if the theory, at some level, makes noncircular reference to trope identity, the theory will not fix a unique set of trope identity facts in indeterministic versions of the sphere case and, hence, will not fix the fact of trope rotation or stasis. If determinism is assumed, then if the theory does *not* invoke trope identity, application of the theory will be compatible with more than one set of facts of identity and will be compatible with either trope motion or stasis. On the other hand, under the assumption of determinism, even if the theory includes some noncircular reference to trope identity, there will be more than one way for the theory to be applied, each of which will give a different verdict to the question of trope identity. Which of these ways is the correct way will depend on a prior determination of the facts of trope identity.

The main conclusions of this chapter are as follows.

(1)   Property persistence can be accounted for only by reference to trope persistence. An ontology that includes exemplifications of universals instead of tropes cannot account for property persistence. There are both tropes and tropes are capable of persistence.

(2)   Trope persistence cannot be analyzed relationally. In particular, trope persistence is not a matter of causal relations among temporal parts of tropes. A causal theory that does not make use of a theory of causation will end up being circular. And a causal theory that makes use of one of the

leading reductionist theories of causation will be inadequate to the problem of positional nonsalient qualitative change.

With these conclusions in mind, we may now finally return to the issue of the nature of causal relata. It was argued in the last chapter that causal relata are tropes, or at the least that it is the most reasonable view, if we can demonstrate the existence of persisting tropes. We have accomplished that task in this chapter. But a few more words need to be said about tropes as relata.

We have concluded that tropes are spatio-temporal particulars that exist wholly at each moment of their realization. Tropes do not have temporal parts. This conclusion creates a difficulty for the view that tropes are causal relata. Causal relata do not generally occur at more than one temporal point, but persisting tropes do. In order to rectify this discrepancy, we should say not that tropes as such are causal relata but that a causal relatum is the realization of a trope at a time. A cause is a trope at a time. This conclusion brings us very close to the view that relata are events, if events are understood to be the realization of an individual property at a time. This is not the Kimian view, however, according to which relata are exemplifications of universals by an object at a time. However, this view is close enough to that kind of view that we can speak of relata as "events" as long as we keep in mind that here we have not provided an account of events, only an account of causal relata. Nevertheless, for the remainder of this study I will use the word "event" to refer to the realization of a trope at a time.

The main burden of the next chapter will be to show that the persistence of tropes can provide the basis for an adequate persistence-based account of causation. Part of this burden requires showing that a trope-persistence account of causation can, in principle, solve the preemption pairing problem with which we began.

5

The Alphabet of Causation

As we have seen, the preemption pairing problem demands a singularist component in a theory of causation. Causes and their direct effects must be connected by a process or relation the realization of which does not depend on what happens in other regions or on how other token events of the same type are related. Spatio-temporalism furnishes a singularist component, but spatio-temporalism cannot handle the preemption pairing problem. A non-spatio-temporalist persistence-based account is needed. But transference theory is not sufficiently general, tied as it is to certain empirical assumptions, and Castañeda's theory, although less empirically based, is too vague. There is, however, another way of working up a persistence view. The results of chapter 4 provide a basis for exploring a theory based on trope persistence.

The main thesis of this chapter is that causation, or causation's singularist component, is a matter of different forms of property persistence. The singularist process that connects causes with their direct effects consists in the persistence or partial persistence of tropes over time. Before developing this view in detail, I want to cite one major historical precedent for this kind of view and say more about tropes and their persistence.

Mackie on Qualitative Persistence

The position developed in this chapter originates partly from an agenda set by Mackie's quite suggestive remarks about causation and qualitative persistence in *The Cement of the Universe*.[1] In chapter 8, "The Necessity of Causes," Mackie raises the question of whether there is anything more to causation than regularity and the direction of causation. More specifically, he wonders whether there is some "causal mechanism" underlying mere regular succession.[2] His interest is partly epistemological—to determine whether there is some element to causation that might license certain kinds of probabilistic a priori inference from cause to effect.[3] However, his ontological concern is more relevant to our discussion here. He is pursuing "the long-searched-for link between individual cause and effect which a pure regularity theory fails, or refuses, to find."[4] He suggests that certain forms of persistence constitute such a link and form a kind of causal mechanism. What does he have in mind?

First, he extends the concept of causation to certain forms of persistence: an earlier phase of a persisting object or self-maintaining process should be regarded as a cause of the later phases.[5] Then he speculates that this kind of causation is more widespread than it might seem. "This sort of causing plays a larger part, underlying processes that at a perceptual level are cases of unrelieved change."[6] Striking and lighting a match is a case in point: "on the face of it this effect has nothing in common with its cause. But if we were to replace the macroscopic picture with a detailed description of the molecular and atomic movements with which the perceived processes are identified by an adequate physico-chemical theory, we should find far more continuity and persistence."[7] The heterogeneity of macroscopic cause and effect disappears when these events are examined at a microscopic level. At the microscopic level there is a process "each phase in which exhibits qualitative as well as spatio-temporal continuity."[8] Such underlying processes exhibiting qualitative and spatio-temporal continuity Mackie calls "causal mechanisms," and these mechanisms are widespread in sequences that fall under basic "laws of working." Qualitative or structural continuity constitutes something "over and above complex regularity," and these mechanisms are the "long-searched-for link" between cause and effect.[9]

At least at the microscopic level, cause and effect display either complete or partial qualitative persistence (and spatio-temporal continuity). Qualitative persistence and spatio-temporal continuity make up "a general characteristic of causal processes, sometimes observable, sometimes not, which constitutes a link between cause-events and effect-events similar to but more selective than the relation defined by Ducasse, since it relates specifically relevant causal features to those features which constitute the result."[10] Mackie stops short of claiming a complete reduction of all causal processes to qualitative and spatio-temporal persistence. Interaction is the exception.[11]

It is also worth noting a further point of inspiration in Mackie for the argument of this study. Mackie cites preemption in support of the role of persistence in causation. Qualitative persistence (and spatio-temporal continuity) provide a basis for sorting through the causal facts in cases of preemption: "those cases of alternative overdetermination which nevertheless allowed us to pick out one rather than another of the over-determining factors as the cause were ones in which we could tell some more detailed causal story, in which we could find links in a continuous chain connecting the preferred factor, but not its rivals, with the result."[12] I am interested in developing the broad claim that qualitative persistence constitutes the singularist component of causation, although I abandon any requirement of spatio-temporal continuity. I now return to the topic of trope persistence.

Partial Trope Persistence

Tropes, as we have said, are properties *and* particulars. Unlike universals, tropes cannot characterize more than one object at the same time, but tropes can persist over time. We may now add that tropes will either be simple or compound. A simple trope does not have tropes as proper parts. A minimum-charge trope, if there are such minimums, is an example of a simple trope. A compound trope includes another trope as a proper part.

We may further distinguish among compound tropes. Compound tropes, I will say, are either conjunctive or structural. A compound conjunctive trope consists in the conjunctive compresence of more than one trope. Keith Campbell, the leading proponent of tropes, gives as an example of a conjunctive trope some nonminimum electrical-charge tropes, which he says are qualitatively simple but quantitatively conjunctive: "a case of charge of 200e is the same as the conjunctive compresence of two discrete 100e charges."[13] More generally, every case of an amount of a quantity above any minimum amount has smaller amounts as parts.

Structural tropes may be introduced by way of a momentary detour into the theory of universals. A structural trope is the trope-analogue to Armstrong's structural universal—a complex universal that is not conjunctive.[14] A universal's being structural is a matter of "something F standing in the relation R to something which is G."[15] "Being one meter in length" is a structural universal: for something to be one meter long is for it to be composed of two half-meter lengths adjacent to each other. The instantiation of a structural universal requires the instantiation of various universals, along with the instantiation of a relation between those instantiations. Structural tropes are analogous to Armstrong's structural universals. A structural trope consists in a trope F standing in a relation R (also a trope) to a trope G. The length of this particular ruler is a structural trope composed of length tropes adjacent to each other.

There is another important fact about tropes that can be brought out by comparison to Armstrong's theory of universals. According to Armstrong, complex universals sometimes overlap.[16] This consequence follows from Armstrong's view that complex universals have constituents that are also universals: complex universals sometimes will share a constituent-universal in common. This thesis about incomplete identity does not apply directly to tropes. Although complex tropes have tropes as parts, a complex trope will not necessarily overlap with another complex trope that characterizes a distinct object at the same time, no matter what the similarities. Tropes are particulars, and even if they have parts, partial identity will require more than similarity. The lengths of wholly distinct objects, for example, understood as tropes, are nonoverlapping particulars.

Nevertheless, there are analogous consequences of partial identity for tropes. First there is partial trope identity at a time. Consider a ruler that is a foot in length. The foot-length trope is composed of lesser-length tropes, and there is partial overlap between the whole length of the ruler and the lengths of its parts.

Second, there is also partial trope overlap over time. This possibility does not follow automatically from the fact that tropes can persist. However, closely parallelling the argument for trope persistence is an argument that supports partial persistence. And given the importance that partial trope persistence over time will have for us in an account of causation, we should briefly rehearse this argument.

Consider the following pair of cases:

> *Case 3.* The destroyer machine instantly eliminates a particle's charge, and the creator machine instantly restores, at the same time t, the particle's charge, but to a *lower* magnitude.

Case 4. The particle undergoes no transformation by way of any machines, but its charge changes over that same time period to that same lower magnitude.

In both cases the particular charge trope possessed by the particle does not persist wholly through *t*. However, there is still an important difference between these cases. There is some degree of qualitative persistence in case 4 that is missing in case 3. What is it that persists in case 4? The difference in persistence between the two cases can be captured as follows: in the second case but not the first, part of the charge trope persists. A trope that is qualitatively simple but quantitatively conjunctive may display partial persistence over time if one of its conjuncts persists without the other conjuncts. So if the charge of this particle is the conjunction of three charges of total value $3c$, for example, then that charge may partially persist if one of these three charges persists. In case 3, unlike case 4, although the total amount of charge present after the intervention is equal to that present in the second case at that same time, there is no persistence, since all of the quantity tropes that conjunctively make it up were destroyed and replaced with new tropes.

Partial trope persistence can be further illustrated as follows. One half of a twenty-foot ladder is destroyed, but the other half survives. At the level of properties we should say that part but not all of the original twenty-foot-length trope persists. The original twenty-foot length is a structural trope, composed of two ten-foot-length tropes adjacent to each other, and there is partial identity over time between this twenty-foot structural trope and the later ten-foot trope, which earlier was part of the twenty-foot trope. Some part of a compound trope persists in the wake of the destruction of another part of the same compound trope. There are two other distinct patterns of partial persistence.

Trope Fission and Fusion

Complex tropes also can come to form simpler tropes by fissioning: tropes that are parts of the same complex trope either cease to be compresent or cease to stand in a relation that is partly constitutive of a structural trope. The fissioning trope is partially identical to the simpler tropes that were its constituents. Tropes may sometimes persist partially through fission.[17]

Tropes may also fuse to form a complex trope. Distinct tropes can come to form a complex trope, either conjunctive or structural, when tropes either come to be compresent or come to stand in a relation that is partly constitutive of a structural trope. The fusing tropes are partially identical to the complex trope in which they come to be constituents.[18]

There are two different forms of trope fusion: stable and unstable. A stable fusion is a fusion of tropes into a single compound trope that will remain intact unless disturbed by some outside influence. An unstable fusion is a fusion that the laws of nature dictate will eventually, on its own, break up by way of fission. More specifically, if tropes form an unstable fusion, there are laws which dictate that it will fission at some point in time, or at least that fission is likely.

In addition to these basic patterns of partial trope persistence, there are combinations of these patterns. The most important combination is this: an unstable fusion followed by fission. In this case, two or more tropes, either simple or complex, fuse to form an unstable complex trope, either conjunctive or structural, and this complex trope then fissions into either the original fusing tropes or tropes that are constitutive of one of these fusing tropes or of the fused trope. A simple example of this combination is this: two charges of $2c$ fuse to form a conjunctive trope of $4c$, and this conjunctive trope then fissions to form four tropes of $1c$ each.

If there are simple tropes in the form of persisting point-tropes, then trope fusion can be understood as the combination over time of point-tropes to form complex tropes. Two point-tropes that are spatially separate may come to be compresent, thereby forming a conjunctive trope. And fission will consist in two or more point-tropes' ceasing to be compresent.

More could be said about partial trope persistence, but we have said enough to discuss the singularist component of causation in positive terms.

A Theory of Causation

The singularist component of causation is some local process that connects causes with their direct effects. Not just any process linking events (again read "tropes at a time") is suitable: this process must be characterized in terms of persistence. But what exactly is this singularist process? I think we can get at the answer to this question by briefly recalling Salmon's treatment of causal processes. This provides a jumping-off point.

Salmon gives at least two characterizations of a causal process. On the first, a causal process is a process capable of transmitting a mark, but a pseudo-process is a process that lacks this capacity. A moving ball is a causal process. We can mark the ball with a pen, and the ball will retain the pen mark without further interactions. But a shadow of a moving ball cannot transmit a mark. Although I can distort the shadow's shape by holding my hand on the shadow at a certain point, that distortion will not continue to characterize the shadow unless I move my hand in contact with the shadow, which constitutes further interactions. Salmon's second characterization of causal processes is importantly different than the first: "the difference between a causal process and a pseudo-process . . . is that the causal process transmits its own structure, while the pseudo-process does not."[19] The ability to transmit a mark, emphasized in the first characterization, is said to be an empirical criterion for this second feature, the actual transmission of structure. Although he gives both characterizations, his discussion is largely taken up with the ability to transmit a mark. Nevertheless, although Salmon does not develop his second characterization, I would suggest that it is more likely to lead us in the right direction. I want to take more seriously the notion of the actual transmission of "structures" in constructing a theory of causation.

I will not pursue the question of what "structures" is supposed to refer to. I will replace that notion with that of a property. The second characterization of a causal process then becomes: a process that extends from point A to point B such that there is some property P which characterizes this process at every point between and including A and B. Constancy of some properties is the defining characteristic of a causal process. Pseudo-processes lack any persisting properties whatsoever.

But this characterization is problematic, depending on how "properties" is understood. If we have in mind universals, this characterization is too weak. On this interpretation, some pseudo-processes will qualify as causal. Some pseudo-processes will instantiate the same universal throughout their duration. The moving shadow, for example—a pseudo-process—may display the same shape-universal over time. And if "property" is read as "exemplification of a universal," this characterization is too strong. No genuine causal process will display the necessary constancy. No two points in the history of a causal process will display the same exemplification, since exemplifications are distinct if their times are distinct.

We should reject any reading of "properties" in this context as universals or exemplifications of universals. Instead, we should read the transmitted properties as tropes. Causal processes are characterized by some tropes that persist throughout the duration of the process, but pseudo-processes are not so characterized. This brings us back nicely to what we take to be causal relata: tropes at a time.

On this criterion, shadows and the like are arguably pseudo-processes. There are two reasons for thinking that shadows do not embody persisting properties. The first is that generally there is no counterfactual dependence between successive instances of the properties of the shadow. For example, there is no clear counterfactual dependence between successive instances of the shape of the shadow. Second, and perhaps more clearly, Salmon's criterion of "markability" does not apply to the properties of shadows. It is not possible to transmit modifications in the shape of the shadow by acting on the shape at only one point. These considerations are not conclusive but are fairly persuasive. Neither counterfactual dependence nor "markability" is constitutive of trope persistence, but each provides good empirical grounds for assessing the question of trope persistence. Hence, we are safe in thinking that pseudo-processes are characterized by momentary tropes rather than persisting tropes and that the constancy of shape of a moving shadow does not correspond to a persisting trope. (Nor do any of the other properties of the shadow.)

This makes pseudo-processes somewhat analogous to our earlier cases involving creator/destroyer machines, in which there was a one-time intervention directed to the charge of the particle. In fact, shadows are more closely analogous to cases involving the continuous intervention of such machines, the intervention of which would generate a series of momentary tropes.

This conception of causal processes, however, requires further refinement. Causal processes are more fine-grained than this picture allows. Causally unrelated "events" (read "tropes at a time") will in some cases satisfy this definition. On this view, physical objects are causal processes. A ball is a causal process, since it is characterized by persisting tropes. It follows that the *shape* of the ball at one moment will be causally connected to the later *color* of the ball, since these tropes are linked by a causal process—the ball itself. In fact, these features of the ball may very well be causally independent. This conception of a causal process casts too wide a net. Various properties that happen, so to speak, to run side-by-side are wrongly paired causally in the same causal process. Causal processes should not include things as "fat" as physical objects.

This difficulty stems from the fact that as the definition stands now, its focus is on that which the persisting trope characterizes, typically an object. We can, however, readjust this focus. We can move from the level of the object to the level of the tropes themselves. A causal process is the persisting trope itself, rather than that which the persisting trope characterizes. The ball is not a causal process but merely the vehicle of such processes. And since the earlier shape of the ball does not persist as the ball's later color, these tropes are not connected by a causal process. The proper "level" for causation, and hence causal processes, is the level of properties. A causal process is a persisting trope.

Different Forms of Causal Processes

Causal processes may take a variety of forms, which I will now outline.

The most basic form is that of an individual property that persists unchanged. Tropes at different times that are linked by such a process are causally connected. The redness of a chair at t' is causally connected to the redness of the chair at t if the redness of the chair at t' is the same trope as the redness of the chair at t. Unchange as well as change falls within the causal structure of the world. Unchanging persisting tropes are no less important as causal processes because of their simplicity. Indeed, this form of causal process is pervasive. Property constancy supplies one of the most fundamental patterns that causal connections among events may take.

Causal processes, however, can take on other forms corresponding to different patterns of partial trope persistence. For example, parts of a complex trope may survive the destruction of other parts of that same trope. Part of the charge of a particle may be destroyed while another part remains intact. In that case, there is partial persistence of the original charge. We now add that this pattern of trope persistence corresponds to a causal process. The later, lesser charge is causally connected to the earlier charge in virtue of the fact that the earlier charge is partially identical to the later charge.[20] This kind of causal process is characterized by the partial but not complete destruction of a trope over time.

There are also causal processes corresponding to trope fission. Trope fission is illustrated by the division of a particle into two particles, each with charges less than that of the dividing particle. Here we can trace a causal process from the original charge to the emerging, lesser charges. The charge of the dividing particle is a cause of the later, smaller charges in virtue of the fact that the earlier charge was in part constituted by the charges that emerge in the process.

A fourth kind of causal process is trope fusion. Trope fusion is illustrated by the collision of two particles that come to form a new particle with a charge equal to the combined charges of the colliding particles. We can trace a causal process from the original charges to the emerging, greater charge. The charges of the colliding particles are causes of the later, greater charge in virtue of the fact that the later charge is in part constituted by the fusion of the charges of the colliding particles.

Fusion-based causal processes can be divided between stable and unstable fusions. In the case of unstable fusion, two or more tropes fuse to form an unstable compound trope, unstable by law, and that compound trope eventually fissions. We can trace a causal process back from the emerging fission products to the complex trope and then from that complex trope to the original fusing tropes.

Some constraints, however, must be set up on compound tropes. Under what conditions do two tropes at a time form a compound trope? The answer to this question will determine when causal processes fuse. I would suggest that the answer to this question is the following. Trope a at t_1 and trope b at t_1 form a compound trope just in case there is a relation R between a and b at t_1 such that the legal consequences of Rab and the fact that a and b are both realized are different from the legal consequences of not-Rab and a and b. An example will help. Suppose that two molecules come to form a common bond. The resultant molecule will have different law-governed consequences than the law-governed consequences of the unbonded molecules.

We must take care in reading this constraint. Suppose there are two tropes that are realized in widely separated regions and intuitively don't form a compound trope. The laws might be such that the sum of the legal consequences of a and the legal consequences of b differs from the legal consequences of the sum of a and b.[21] If we then take "conjunction" or "coexistence" as relation R, then it may turn out, given the laws, that the sum of the separate legal consequences of a and b coupled with the fact that a and b are not both realized differs from the legal consequences of the joint realization (conjunction or coexistence) of a and b. This difference might then be cited to support wrongly that a and b form a compound trope. This conclusion, however, is based on a misreading of the constraint. The constraint requires us to compare the cases in which both a and b are realized and Rab holds with cases in which both a and b are realized and not-Rab. If, however, R is coexistence or conjunction, then the second case is incoherent. We cannot consider the sum of the legal consequences of a and b if Rab does not hold—that is, if R is coexistence.

This characterization of compound tropes might appear to give rise to circularity. And, indeed, if appeal were made to the causal consequences of the trope combination, that would be true. But appeal here is to the legal consequences in general of a certain type of trope configuration. We are not referring to the actual causal consequences, nor even necessarily to the causal consequences of the configuration in general. Circularity is avoided, since the legal and the causal are not the same.

It is also worth noting that if the simplest tropes are point-tropes, fission consists in point-tropes' ceasing to be compresent, and fusion consists in point-tropes' coming to be compresent. The laws of nature could then be interpreted as constraints on the decombination and combination of point-tropes—a kind of causal combinatorialism.

To summarize thus far: the singularist component in causation consists in the persistence of tropes. Causes are connected to their direct effects in virtue of the fact that both are tropes and direct effects are identical or partially identical to their causes. The clearest case is that of an unchanging trope over time. In cases of unchange, the persistence of a trope is what constitutes the singularist causal connection among temporally distinct incarnations of that trope. We now must consider more complicated cases that will provide both a basis for illustrating causal processes consisting in fission and fusion and a basis for refining this account of the singularist component of causation.

Example 1

Consider a simple causal process that involves some change. Two atoms collide, and there is a one-way transfer of electrical charge by way of the transfer of an electron. The cause, on a trope model, is the charge characteristic of the sending atom, and the effect is the later charge characteristic of the receiving atom. The causal process connecting these events is the persisting charge trope, which gets transferred. The charge characteristic of the second atom is a later incarnation of the charge trope of the first atom.[22]

This picture is correct as far as it goes. However, certain complexities are omitted. A middle step has been left out. At the moment of impact, a short-lived compound trope is formed. This compound trope characterizes the atom pair. The property itself is complex. It includes the charges of each atom. But it also includes the "contact" relation between the atoms. There is no natural way to describe this complex property. Perhaps "the property of having two parts in contact such that each part has a certain charge" might come close. This compound property is a fusion of the charges of the two atoms, along with the contact relation that comes to hold between the atoms. This fusion product quickly fissions. One of this trope's constituents, the charge trope of the first atom, is transferred to the other atom. The contact relation ceases to hold. The causal process is thus more complicated than it appeared at first. We can trace back from the charge trope, of the second atom after the collision, to this short-lived complex trope, and then from that complex trope back to the charge trope of the first atom, which comes to form a part of this complex trope at the point of contact.[23]

Example 2
The second example illustrates two-way transfers of tropes. Two atoms collide, and there is a two-way transfer of electrons and charges. What is the causal process that links the later charges to the earlier charges? The causal process parallels the causal process in our first example up until the final point. At impact, a compound trope is formed, consisting in "the property of having two parts in contact such that each part has a certain charge." The charges of each atom at the point of contact become part of this compound trope, which also includes the contact relation between the atoms. The two "parts" are the atoms. This compound property is in part the outcome of fusion. The charges of the atoms come to form property parts of this structural trope at the point of collision. This compound trope quickly fissions. At the point of breakup, something happens that is more complicated than in example 1. There is fission, transference, and fusion: the charge of each atom fissions, and some of that charge is transferred to the other atom, which then fuses with whatever remains of that atom's original charge to form a new charge trope. The end result is that each of the atoms has a different total charge, and this total charge is the fusion of the transferred part of the charge of the other atom plus a component of its original charge.

Example 3
Consider an everyday example. Jones cuts a string with a pair of scissors. The effects are the two separate-length tropes of the cut string pieces, and a cause is the movement and sharpness of the scissors. The causal process corresponds to unstable fusion followed by fission. The string is characterized by a structural trope—its length, which consists in two string half-lengths being in a certain relation to each other, the relation of "being attached." The scissors are characterized by a movement/sharpness trope. This movement/sharpness trope comes to form part of a fused trope at the point of contact: the length of the string compresent with this movement/sharpness trope. This is an unstable compound trope. There are laws that exclude the continuation of

this trope, other things being equal. The "attached" relation is eventually eliminated. The structural trope breaks up, leaving in its wake the two string half-length tropes, half-lengths that were previously part of this compound trope formed at the point of contact. There is a general pattern here—a common two-step causal process. Two objects characterized by tropes come into contact, and an unstable complex trope is formed including these tropes. This complex trope eventually fissions, and some of its constituents emerge separately.

An objection based on this example must be considered. Can we not find a causal process of just this pattern connecting the *color* of the scissors with these effects, the separate-length tropes? Does not the color of the scissors fuse with the string length trope at the point of contact, and then does not this complex trope fission? We seem to be forced to say wrongly that the color of the scissors is a cause of the half-length tropes, which emerge from the process.

I have two responses to this objection. First, this color-length combination is not a genuine compound trope. Second, even if the color-length combination were a genuine compound trope, this does not guarantee a causal connection between the color of the scissors and the half-string lengths.

Let's look at the first response: the color-length combination is not a genuine compound trope. The general legal consequences of this combination, the compresence of these two tropes, are not different than the sum of the legal consequences of each of these tropes separately considered. Contrast this combination with that of the attached-length tropes combination. Here the legal consequences in general are quite different than those of the half-length tropes considered independently of this relation of "being attached." The law-governed consequences of two attached string lengths are quite different than the legal consequences of those same lengths when unattached. The attached lengths have different law-governed capacities than the unattached lengths.

The second response goes further and allows that even if this color-length combination were a genuine compound trope, this compound would still not necessarily be a cause of the separate-length tropes. Although the singularist component of causation is satisfied, there is more to causation than singularism. Trope persistence supplies the singularist component in the theory, but not the whole of the theory. There must also be some type-type relation between cause and direct effect, which I have assumed to be lawful connection. What is missing between the color-length combination at the point of contact and the half-lengths that emerge is a lawful connection. The same cannot be said of the movement-length trope and these half-length tropes. Causation is not just a matter of local fact. Causation also supervenes on facts about types. A one-sided theory of causation, in either direction, will generate pairing problems. An account that is overly generalist generates false pairs of the right types but the wrong singularist connections. A purely singularist account generates false pairs tied by the right singularist component but by the wrong type-level relations. Hence, the present theory: law-governed property persistence. Irrelevancies are eliminated at the level of types, and the preemption pairing problem is solved by reference to property persistence. In fact, the generalist component can be interpreted as a constraint on the singularist component. Causal laws can be read as specifying constraints on the possible combinations and decompositions of tropes.[24]

Example 4

Some causal sequences do not appear to fit these patterns. Consider the intersection of light rays of all the different visible colors. At their intersection a new color, white, is formed. This effect, however, is not a complex trope at all. Hence, this white trope cannot be a fusion of the intersecting tropes. Two simple tropes intersect and cause the appearance of a simple trope that is not a fusion of the intersecting tropes (since it is not complex).

Or so it seems. In fact, this case can be handled by challenging the claim that the intersecting tropes and the resulting trope are simple ones. Here I again borrow a point made by Armstrong about universals and transpose it onto tropes. Armstrong suggests that colors (universals) may be epistemologically simple but are in fact complex. Their actual complexity is revealed by way of physicalist reductions. Colors are light-emissions of different frequencies and wavelengths. "The differing wavelengths form a class of structural properties with a similar logical structure to lengths, if more complex."[25] If we transpose this point to tropes, we should say that each color instance consists in various wavelengths of light-emissions, or at least that different color tropes supervene on such wavelengths. The cherry-red trope of a light ray consists in or supervenes on a certain complex wavelength trope. And in our example, the color trope (the whiteness of the light) that emerges at the point of the intersection of the input light rays either consists in or supervenes on a complex property of the intersecting rays, and this complex property will be the fusion of the various wavelength tropes that characterize the intersecting rays (in which the intersecting color tropes consist or on which they supervene).[26]

This conception of causation can be further illustrated by reference to some simple chemical reactions. The relevant tropes are complex structural characteristics of molecular compounds and atoms.

Example 5

Consider the reaction that takes place when the two gases boron trifluoride (BF_3) and ammonia (NH_3) are mixed. The result is a solid white compound with the chemical formula BF_3NH_3, a compound with certain characteristics. The reactant gases are made up of molecules, each with a characteristic structure of atoms and electrons in certain arrangements, and the product is also made up of a set of molecules with characteristic configurations of atoms and electrons. The chemist can trace the chemical structure of the resulting solid back to the chemical structures of the reactant gases. The chemical structure that emerges is partially identical to the structures of the reactants. The product involves the bonding of the reactant molecules together. We can detect in the chemist's representation of this product the input structures supplied by the reactants, or at least part of those structures. The underlying chemical structure of the solid product, a complex trope, is in part a fusion of the characteristic structures of the reactants. The Lewis diagram for this reaction makes it is easier to see the partial survival of tropes through fusion. A Lewis diagram places a chemical symbol at the center of an array of dots, which represent the valence electrons of the atom. A single dot is an unpaired electron in an orbital, and a double dot represents paired electrons in the same orbital. A line represents two shared electrons.

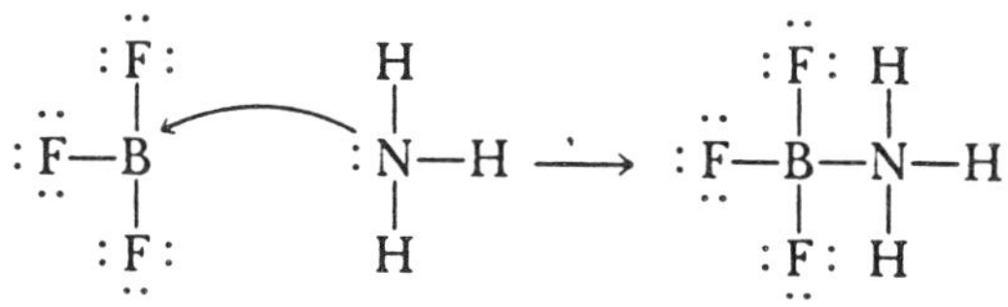

$$\begin{array}{ccc}
:\!\ddot{F}\!: & H & :\!\ddot{F}\!:\ H \\
\mid & \mid & \mid\ \ \ \ \mid \\
:\!\ddot{F}\!-\!B\quad\quad :\!\ddot{N}\!-\!H \longrightarrow\ :\!\ddot{F}\!-\!B\!-\!N\!-\!H \\
\mid & \mid & \mid\ \ \ \ \mid \\
:\!\ddot{F}\!: & H & :\!\ddot{F}\!:\ H
\end{array}$$

Figure 5.1

This diagram represents the formation of a covalent bond between the reactant molecules.

Lewis diagrams are not completely accurate. The three-dimensional shapes of the molecules are left out, and so is the fact that the shared electrons belong to a molecular shell, rather than a shared atomic shell. But these inaccuracies are not crucial. These diagrams do show first that the reactant molecules have certain complex characteristics initially, which we can think of as tropes, including the structural characteristic, in the case of boron trifluoride of a boron atom bonded to three fluoride atoms each with six unpaired electrons. The diagram also shows that this complex characteristic becomes a part of a more complex characteristic, a certain arrangement of atoms and electrons, at the terminus of the reaction. The diagram represents the relevant complex trope characteristic of the boron trifluoride molecule as persisting, at least as a part of the complex trope characteristic of the product of the reaction. We can then trace the complex trope that results from this reaction back to the complex tropes that are aspects of the reactants, through trope fusion, by way of the Lewis diagram.[27]

Example 6
Consider another fusion example. A proton accepts a pair of electrons in a bond with an ammonia molecule. The ammonia supplies the electron pair. The product is an ammonium ion with a positive charge. The Lewis diagram is as follows:

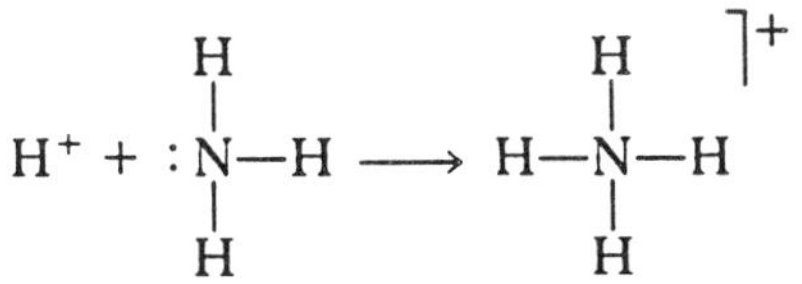

$$H^+ + :\!N\!-\!H \longrightarrow \left[H\!-\!N\!-\!H\right]^+$$

(with H above and below N on each side)

Figure 5.2

This diagram reveals that the resulting ion is characterized by a certain complex trope, a certain arrangement of hydrogen and nitrogen atoms and electrons, and that this structural trope is partially identical to the tropes that characterize the separate reactants, which come to be bonded.[28]

Example 7
Other chemical reactions illustrate causal processes involving trope fission. The breakup of ethane C_2H_6 results in the formation of methyl radicals, $*CH_3$ (the $*$ signifies an unpaired electron). The Lewis structure for this reaction is this:

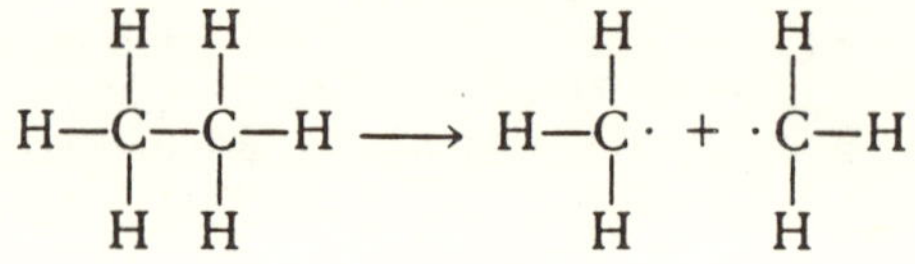

$$\text{H—C(H)(H)—C(H)(H)—H} \longrightarrow \text{H—C(H)(H)·} + \text{·C(H)(H)—H}$$

Figure 5.3

Notice that the reactant molecule is characterized by a certain complex trope—an arrangement of atoms and electrons—and that each product molecule is characterized by complex tropes that derive from the complex trope that characterized the reactant molecule.[29]

Many other examples could be used.[30] For instance, we might review the reactions and Lewis diagrams involved in the striking and lighting of a match. In the case of a "strike-anywhere" match, these reactions are multiple. One such reaction involved in the lighting of the match's head runs as follows. In the head of a strike-anywhere match is found phosphorous, which acts as an igniting agent, and underneath is potassium chlorate ($KClO_3$), which is the oxidizing agent. When the match is struck, the frictional heat causes the phosphorous to ignite in air, and at the same time the phosphorous is oxidized by the potassium chlorate. The potassium chlorate oxidizes the phosphorous to phosphorous oxide (P_4O_{10}), which generates additional heat. The Lewis diagrams for these reactions would show how various complex chemical characteristics fission and combine to form product tropes. The same could be done with many other ordinary examples of causation. The point, however, is that persistence theory clearly can handle a wide array of cases.

A Definition of Causation

We are now in a position to give a more formal account of causation. It is useful to break causal inquiry down into two stages: a preliminary stage of property analysis and a stage of causal accounting proper, property history. The explicit definition of causation I will offer applies to the second stage.

Property Analysis

Causal relata are individual properties at a time, and causation's singularist component consists in property persistence. Causal inquiry thus begins with property analysis. If P at t is the object of investigation, we must first determine whether P is simple or nonsimple. If P is simple, then the second stage of property history begins. But if P is nonsimple, then P must be further analyzed. This analysis consists in a list of P's component properties and a statement of how these properties are related. These subproperties may be organized in various ways, from conjunctive compresence to structural interrelation. Property analysis is generally an empirical matter. In order to trace the causal processes that have led to a specific trope at a time, some understanding of the nature of the property in question must be gotten by property analysis.

Property History

In the second stage of a causal account, the causal processes that have lead to P at t—which is to say a history of the component properties and their organization, if P is complex—are determined. This history specifies how these components came to be realized at t through property persistence, fission, and fusion.

In order to give a precise account of causation that will apply to property histories, I need to introduce the concept of "strong causal connection." Tropes *at distinct times*, such as P and Q, are strongly causally connected if and only if:

(1) P and Q are lawfully connected, and either
(2) P is identical to Q or some part of Q, or Q is identical to P or some part of P, or
(3) P and Q supervene on tropes P' and Q', which satisfy 1 and 2.

Clause 1 corresponds to the assumption of this study that there is some generalist component to causation. I identify that component with lawful connection here only for the sake of definiteness. The relation specified in clause 2 codifies the notion that we have been developing and constitutes causation's singularist component. Clause 2 is realized when properties persist, fuse, or fission, and it holds between direct causes and their effects, as well as across causal chains that are not very long. Clause 2 will sometimes fail for causally connected events that are linked through a long causal chain. I will take care of this limitation in a moment.

Clause 3, or something very much like it, is necessary to handle cases like the following. Suppose that experience involves simple, emergent nonreducible tropes, such as qualia of a certain type. The first two clauses, if necessary for causation, would entail that the occurrence of such qualia are not caused by the physical properties of brain states. In order to include physical-mental and mental-physical causation, we need to posit some kind of supervenient causation. Clause (3) is meant to accommodate supervenient causation, but here I do not pursue a full discussion and detailed development of this concept. I have in mind something along the lines of Kim's account of supervenient causation. Kim says that the idea of supervenient causation is roughly this: "for an instance of mental property M to cause, or be caused by, event e (let's assume e is a physical event), the following conditions must hold: there is a physical-biological property P such that (1) M supervenes on P; (2) P is instantiated on the occasion of M's instantiation; and (3) this instance of P causes e, or is caused by e (on your favorite account of physical causation)."[31] Hence, even if there are emergent mental properties that are not reducible to physical properties, these mental properties will supervene on physical properties, in virtue of which they will have mental causes and effects and physical causes and effects.

Strong causal connection does not determine causal asymmetry, since this is a symmetrical relation. The concept of "causal priority" must be brought into play in order to guarantee that causation is an asymmetrical relation. However, since the concept of causal priority is the main topic of chapter 6, I will make use of an undefined concept of causal priority here. A sufficient condition for causation is the following:

Property P at t causes property Q at t' if (A) P at t is strongly causally connected to Q at t', and P at t is causally prior to Q at t'.

This way of dividing up the analytic task (between the symmetrical relation "causal connection" and causal priority) is compatible with the fact that ordinarily we do not talk about causation as symmetric—we typically talk about "causes" rather than "causal connections." However, since "causes" comes out asymmetric on my account, this does not present a difficulty. Furthermore, there may be independent reasons for breaking the issues down in this way, since in some contexts—for example, some scientific contexts—causal connections are determined before specifying the roles of "cause" and "effect." Finally, other philosophical accounts can be read as dividing up the problems in this way. For example, the neo-Humean conditions of lawful connection and spatial/temporal contiguity can be read as an account of "either c causes e or e causes c."

Condition A is not necessary for causal connection. Events connected by a chain of indirect causation may fail to satisfy this condition. An additional sufficient condition for events that are not strongly causally connected but are linked by a causal chain must be introduced:

(B) there is a set of properties $(R_1, \ldots, R_n)$ such that P is a cause of R_1 under clause A, ..., and R_n is a cause of Q under clause A.

We may now add that P at t causes Q at t' if and only if either A or B is true.

This analysis applies to cases of property fusion and fission as well as to that of property constancy. P at t causes Q at t' only if Q at t' comes from P at t through fusion, fission, or persistence, or if P at t is connected by a causal chain to Q at t', in which the neighboring events are connected through property persistence, fusion, or fission.

Insofar as the history of the world consists in a series of momentary tropes, there is no causation. "Events" are caused only if their constituents persist from earlier moments (or at least *other* moments, if backward causation is possible). A causally structured world is not just a history of purely local facts, and momentary tropes are the most parochial of local facts. This will be so even if there are relations of constant conjunction, counterfactual dependence, or probability among these momentary tropes. For genuine causation, there must be genuine persistence between episodes. Persistent properties form the core of the causal relation, and without them there is no causation.

One consequence of this account is that a trope is caused only if there is a story of persistence to be told about its constituents. To the degree that the constituents of a complex trope have no previous history, the complex trope has no causal history. If the constitutive relation of a structural trope comes to be realized just at the point at which the structural trope comes into existence, to that extent the structural trope is uncaused. The structural trope is caused to the degree it is constituted by the fusing of preexisting tropes. New or emergent simple tropes (if there are such) that do not supervene on other properties come into existence uncaused. They can be causes but not effects. I do not assume that a world's history is limited by the simple tropes that are realized at the beginning, if there is a beginning. It is logically possible for new, uncaused, nonsupervening tropes to come into existence. Such uncaused tropes may even emerge nonaccidentally, since they may have lawful antecedents, but lawful connection is not sufficient for causal connection.

The basic intuition behind this account of causation can plumbed by way of an analogy. "Efficient causation" is similar to "material causation," with properties replacing objects. In listing the "material causes" of a house, we list the material elements that came together to form the house. The material elements, including planks and nails, come to be joined together in certain structural patterns. On the present account of causation, questions about causation run parallel to "material causation" questions, but the "materials" are tropes. A request for the causes of an event is a request for a list of the preexisting tropes which form the building blocks for the effect trope. Once we understand that causal relata are tropes, that tropes can persist, and that tropes can be complex and can be composed of preexisting constituents, the analogy becomes appropriate.

Preemption

Does this account face a preemption pairing problem? Does this account treat both preempting and preempted causes as genuine or neither as genuine? We concluded earlier that there must be some singularist component that excludes the possibility of such ties—some noncausal process by which causes bring about their direct effects. Does trope persistence supply the necessary singularist component?

Consider, again, an example. Two qualitatively indistinguishable particles collide. There is a deterministic law such that particle a will be completely annihilated and particle b will emerge with a certain property P. The effect of interest is the emergence of a particle with property P. Suppose that had a and b not collided, a would have traversed that same point at that same time with the same type of property as P. Particle b preempts a from causing a particle with a certain property P to pass that point.

A theory of causation ought to say that the particular property P of particle b, before the collision, is the cause of the final effect, but not the particular property P' of a. The present theory says in fact that it was. At the level of tropes, there is a causal process connecting P of b with the final effect, but there is no such process connecting P' of a. b survives the collision and a does not. Hence, the property that characterizes the particle after the collision is traceable to a property of b before the collision, but not to any property of a. There is a causal process that links one, but not the other of the earlier property instances to the later property instance. So even if the legal, counterfactual, or probabilistic web is insufficient to differentiate, a property history does correctly differentiate between preempting and preempted causes. A trope-persistence theory can handle preemption. Either both P and P' are each partially identical with the property that emerges after the collision, in which case there is no preemption, or one but not the other is identical or partly identical to the effect, in which case there is preemption, and the property that persists is the preempting cause.

Merely Apparent Counterexamples

Persistence theory, as we have seen, can handle a wide range of cases. Indeed, I would suggest that on deeper inspection, most ordinary cases of causation will fit this model. Still, it might be suggested that there are logically possible cases that run counter to persistence theory—cases in which a genuinely new trope is caused to be realized. A spectacular example of this would be a world in which there is persistence at every point in time except one. At this point, although there are laws that link earlier and later events on either side of this point, there are no persisting tropes. This world consists of two temporal parts, connected nomologically but not causally, according to the theory proposed here. This may initially strike us as counterintuitive. The argument that follows is meant to address these kinds of examples and others. I want to suggest that our initial impressions in such cases are in fact mistaken and that without trope persistence there is no causation.

Suppose that a particle acquires a new property after a collision but that this new trope is not transferred from the first particle and did not get generated by the fissioning or fusing of some property or properties of the second particle. Could it not be that the acquisition of that property is caused? Persistence theory entails, apparently wrongly, that the property and its acquisition must be uncaused. What are we to say about such apparently possible cases? Or imagine a world where there are no persisting tropes, only momentary ones, or a world in which earlier and later events are linked by laws but do not involve any persisting tropes. I think that the right response, as I will try to show, is that these apparent counterexamples are merely apparent. Although sequences of this type may be possible, much more would have to be said to demonstrate that these sequences are causal. I will suggest that what tempts us to judge them causal are certain misleading background assumptions. In other words, my aim here is to establish that the conditions specified so far are indeed necessary conditions for causation.

I want to suggest that the examples that might be cited against persistence theory will generally trade on an appeal to certain relations and that these examples appear to be causal only because these relations appear to be causal. I will suggest that if these relations are the only relevant features of the possible counterexamples, then on reflection we ought to reject the causal interpretation of these cases. We ought to do this because these relations can be demonstrated to lack a certain modal property (nonextrinsicness) essential to the causal relation. Here is the structure of my argument:

> (1) First, I argue that certain relations—roughly, counterfactual dependence, non-screened-off probability increase, and lawful connection—do not satisfy the nonextrinsicness principle. Hence these relations are not the causal relation.
> (2) Second, it is claimed that the apparent counterexamples are cases in which the only relations of interest (from the point of view of making causal judgments) are these three relations. Given that these three relations exhaust the relations of interest in such cases, it follows that these cases are not causal, contrary to our initial intuitions.
> (3) Finally, I try to explain why we mistakenly take these cases to be causal.

This line of argument is openly revisionist. I am suggesting that in certain cases we must choose between this deep principle about causation (its nonextrinsicness) and our intuitions. The appropriate choice is to abandon these intuitions.

Recall a certain feature of the causal relation—its nonextrinsic character. Lewis brings this feature out as follows: "Intuitively, whether the process going on in a region is causal depends only on the intrinsic character of the process itself, and on the relevant laws. The surroundings, and even other events in the region, are irrelevant."[32] This principle is not meant to entail that there is no way in which the causal relation *is* vulnerable to extrinsic changes. Insofar as causation is a matter of laws, this principle does not hold. As Lewis says, "Maybe the laws of nature are relevant without being intrinsic to the region (if some sort of regularity theory of lawhood is true) but nothing else is."[33] The causal relation is vulnerable to those extrinsic facts which are relevant to causation's generalist component.[34] However, when we set aside this generalist element, what remains is fixed by intrinsic facts. The following principle is true:

> If c causes e, and P picks out the intrinsic process that connects c to e, then c causes e in all possible worlds with the same laws of nature in which c is connected to e by P.[35]

If the laws are held fixed, the presence or absence of any events or characteristics extrinsic to the process P cannot make any difference to whether c causes e.[36] In particular, if process P is held constant with the laws, the absence or presence of would-be causes of e cannot make any difference to whether c causes e. Causation is invulnerable to mere changes in the surroundings and, in particular, to the mere presence or absence of competitors. The causal relation is not defeasible by competitors. Either there is no supervenience base for the causal relation (that is, causal realism is true) or the causal relation supervenes on the laws of nature and intrinsic facts about connecting processes. Thus, assuming that we are not persuaded by arguments for nonreductionist causal realism, any relation that does not have the same supervenience base is not the causal relation.

If we can show for any particular relation R, such that c stands in R to e, that whether or not c and e stand in R may vary across worlds in which the laws are constant and the intrinsic connecting processes remain the same, then we may conclude that R is not the causal relation. And if R is the only possible candidate in a particular case for a causal relation between c and e, we can, under these circumstances, conclude that c and e are not causally connected. This is the basis for my strategy of dismissal against possible counterexamples. The three relations I have in mind are counterfactual dependence, probability increase, and lawful connection. I will consider each in turn.

Counterfactual Dependence

Recall again the possible counterexample. Two particles collide, and one of them is (apparently) caused to acquire a new property (which cannot be traced back through trope persistence). What might make us take this underdescribed case to be genuinely causal? One possible factor might be a belief that had the first particle not collided with the second, the latter would not have acquired that property. Indeed, let us suppose there is this counterfactual dependence. Also suppose that counterfactual dependence and spatio-temporal contiguity and temporal priority exhaust the relations between these events. Now consider again whether these events are in fact causally connected. Certainly spatio-temporal relations alone will not be sufficient for a causal relation. But what about the counterfactual dependence? If this is the only other possibly relevant relation, then we should conclude that these events are not in fact causally connected.

The reason for this is that counterfactual dependence does not satisfy the nonextrinsicness principle. The possibility of preemption shows that counterfactual dependence does not have this modal property. There will exist worlds with the same laws of nature in which this collision occurs and in which the outcome is a result of preemptive causation, and in such worlds the acquisition of the new property by the second particle will not counterfactually (stepwise) depend on the collision with the first particle. The same sequence realized under different (preemptive) circumstances fails to display stepwise counterfactual dependence. Counterfactual dependence is not an "intrinsic" relation and, hence, does not have the relevant modal property. Counterfactual dependence cannot be the causal relation. If events stand in a relation of counterfactual dependence, those events are not causally connected in virtue of that dependence relation. Counterfactually dependent events may still be causally connected but, if so, not in virtue of counterfactual dependence. They would have to stand in some other "intrinsic" relation to each other. Given our assumption that the only relations of significance between the colliding particles are spatio-temporal and counterfactual dependence, we must deny that the acquisition of the property is caused. If counterfactual dependence is the only relation of significance in which these events stand, they are not causally connected, whatever our initial intuitions might be.[37]

Probability Increase
This argument works only if these events do not stand in any other significant relations. But suppose that they also stand in a probabilistic relation. Will that guarantee their causal connection?

The answer is no if we have in mind the probabilistic relation picked out by probabilistic theory. That relation also lacks the requisite modal property. Probabilistic theories tend to make non-screened-off probability increase the key relation. This relation does not satisfy the nonextrinsicness principle. Processes may satisfy this relation in one setting but not in another in which the laws are the same and the intrinsic character of the processes unchanged. Recall from chapter 1 cases in which a genuine cause is screened off from its effect by an earlier preempted cause. Now consider a process connecting c and e in which there is no preemption. Still there will be a world in which a preempted cause screens off c from e—a world with the same laws and the same connecting processes between c and e. In that world, c does not have this characteristic—of being non-screened-off-probability-increasing relative to e—even though the process connecting c and e in that world is intrinsically indistinguishable from the process that connects c and e in the actual world. The same process may have this characteristic in some surroundings but not in others. Given the nonextrinsicness principle, this means that this relation—non-screened-off probability increase—cannot be taken to be the causal relation.

Now consider again the colliding particles. Suppose the relations of significance between *c* and *e* in our example are non-screened-off probability increase and spatio-temporal contiguity and temporal priority (and perhaps counterfactual dependence). The spatio-temporal relations are not sufficient for a causal relation. If non-screened-off probability increase is the only other relevant relation that might ground a causal connection, then we must say that these events are definitely not causally connected. The reason for this is that non-screened-off probability increase is not the causal relation (since it lacks the modal property). In cases in which there is only this probabilistic relation (along with perhaps counterfactual dependence), there is no causation.[38]

Lawful Connection
The last relation that might ground a causal judgment in these apparent counterexamples is some form of lawful connection. Does this relation possess the requisite modal property? The answer depends on how this relation gets specified. In its most general form, lawful connection has this modal property. But this fact will not help, since the relation of "being lawfully connected" in its most general form is not sufficient for a causal connection. Consider that joint effects of a common cause may be lawfully connected. Like the probability theorist, a law-based theorist has a problem with epiphenomena. The probability theorist, in response to the problem of epiphenomena, modifies that basic idea of probability increase to "non-screened-off probability increase," and as we have seen, this last relation is unacceptably extrinsic. The proponent of lawful connection, however, will have to make a similar move. Even without considering how this move might be worked out, it is clear that the proponent of lawful connection will have to bring in something like "non-screened-off" lawful connection in order to take care of the problem of common causes. Otherwise he has little chance of offering a sufficient condition for causation. But this need to make reference to extrinsic conditions will guarantee that the modified relation is not the causal relation, since this modified relation will be extrinsic. The presence or absence of a common cause will determine whether this relation holds between two events. Hence, in assessing possible counterexamples we cannot rely on the fact that this relation is realized to determine that the events in question are causally connected.

These three relations seem to exhaust the relations possibly relevant to the causal question. Insofar as apparent counterexamples ultimately rely on these relations, we can dismiss them as noncausal. In particular, I would suggest that the colliding particle case as described gets a grip on our intuitions only insofar as we assume that one of these relations is realized. But that, as I have argued, misleads us into a causal judgment.

The fact that our ordinary intuitions push us in a different direction in such cases, however, requires that we explain why we tend to have these intuitions and what the price is for abandoning them. I think these intuitions result from the fact that in genuine cases of causation we do typically find probability increase, lawful connection, and counterfactual dependence. On this basis, we tend to make the mistake of thinking that wherever these relations are found, there is causation. We wrongly focus on certain features of causal sequences which, although typical, are not sufficient for causation. What is the price for abandoning these intuitions? The price is minimal if what matters most to us in typical cases of causation are just these relations. In other words, we may wrongly think that what is important in ordinary cases of causation is their causal character, when in fact what is important is that certain other relations are typically realized. If that is true, then in cases (the apparent counterexamples) in which the causal character fails but these other relations are realized, all or most of what matters to us in the central cases of causation will be realized. If that is so, then abandoning our intuition that these are cases of causation will be relatively painless.

I have not shown that these other relations are in fact what is important to us. For that I would need to explore the relation between causation and other concepts, such as action, responsibility, knowledge, and so on. This task is too large for this setting. However, I would speculate that whatever work the concept of causation appears to do in these contexts may in fact be done by certain other relations that are typically associated with causation but are not constitutive of it.

This deflationary response to counterexamples works only if all the counterexamples trade on just these relations—of counterfactual dependence, non-screened-off probability increase, and contextualized lawful connection. What if there are counterexamples that don't? In that event, persistence theory will still have a point. If there are such counterexamples, the results of this study should be viewed as having a smaller scope. The situation would be analogous to that of Salmon's theory. As he himself recognizes, Salmon's account of causal processes is not a complete theory of causation. There are events that are causally connected but are not connected by a causal process. Causal chains that include various intersections with other causal processes will not satisfy Salmon's conditions of a causal process, since the interactive links may involve breaks in the capacity to transmit marks. Salmon needs an additional theory—that of causal interactions—to tell the causal story about these breaks. For Salmon, the theory of causation divides into two separate accounts: the theory of causal processes and the theory of causal interactions. Persistence theory viewed with a smaller scope is an account of causal processes only.[39] Persistence theory on this interpretation would cover just those causal phenomena which Salmon's theory of causal processes is meant to take in.[40]

It might be thought that the causal realist is in a better position with respect to these cases, since for her, counterfactuals, probabilistic relations, and laws serve only as strong evidence that there is a causal relation present. She could argue that the reason we have strong intuitions in these cases is that we view these factors as strong evidence for the presence of a causal relation. The causal realist could contend that on her view, we need not abandon our procausation intuitions in these examples. We can simply acquiesce to the evidence. But in fact, adopting the realist line will also clash with intuitions, although not in quite the same way. The realist will have to say that in each of these cases (keeping all the counterfactuals, probabilities, and laws constant) there are at least two worlds, one in which the causal relation is present and another in which it is absent. Since for the realist these various relations are only *evidence* for the causal relation, it must be possible for these relations to be realized without the causal relation. Thus, for each such case there must be a *mix* of worlds, some causal and others not. This mixed approach is certainly no less counterintuitive than denying the causal relation in all such worlds.[41]

Standard Problem Cases

As indicated earlier, preemption is the most important problem for a theory of causation. Nevertheless, it is not the only genuine problem. An assortment of cases, problematic for various theories of causation, should also be mentioned. These phenomena include causation at a spatial or temporal distance, backward causation, probabilistic causation, transitivity, identity over time and epiphenomena.

Causation and Temporal/Spatial Gaps

A theory of causation ought to be compatible with the possibility of action over a temporal or spatial distance—that is, the possibility of non-spatio-temporally continuous causal chains. What does the persistence account entail about the possibility of "gappy" causation? On certain liberal assumptions about trope persistence, spatially gappy causation will be possible on this theory. If the same individual property can be realized at noncontiguous locations at neighboring times (i.e., if tropes can persist without being spatially continuous), then direct causation at a spatial distance is possible. And there is at least one reason for believing this possible. It is logically possible for an *object*, complete with unchanged properties, to "jump" from one location to a noncontiguous location in space, and "jumpy" objects are arguably possible only if trope persistence across a spatial gap is also possible.[42] What about temporally gappy causation? The answer depends on whether there can be temporally gappy tropes. Indeed, there is *some* reason to grant temporally discontinuous trope persistence. It is logically possible for physical objects to disappear and reappear at a later time with their properties unchanged, and if we wish to avoid saying that the object has acquired all new properties, we should grant the possibility of temporally discontinuous trope persistence.

It might be objected that in worlds in which time is discrete, there will be no persisting tropes, but that in such worlds a trope at one time can causally give rise to a trope at another time, and there can even be preemption. Hence, appeals to trope persistence cannot provide a satisfactory approach to preemption in general or constitute causation's singularist component.

This objection falters, however, on a false assumption. The discreteness of time does not by itself exclude persistence. First, consider again that it is possible for an object to go in and out of existence, intermittently. An object at t_1 may be identical to an object at t_2 even though the object does not exist at each moment between t_1 and t_2. Identity over time is compatible with intermittent existence. Second, even if this first point is rejected, the case in which time is discrete is less extreme than the case of an object that fails to exist at intervening moments. The discreteness of time does not entail that there are intervening moments when the object or trope does not exist, since it is not true that between any two moments there is another moment. An object or trope that exists through a period of discrete time may be such that that object or trope does not fail to exist during any moment in that period. Hence, even if one doubts that persistence is compatible with intermittent nonexistence at intervening times, this does not entail that identity over time is incompatible with the discreteness of time.

Backward Causation

A theory of causation also ought to be compatible with the possibility of backward causation. It should not be built into the theory that causes precede their effects. There are two ways for a theory of causation to be incompatible with the logical possibility of backward causation. The first is by the inclusion of an a priori, additional requirement of temporal priority such that there is no deeper feature of the causal relation that excludes causes preceding their effects. This is a fairly superficial way of excluding backward causation, which conflicts with the apparent ease of imagining cases in which causes precede their effects and with the possibility of a causal theory of time. The second way for a theory of causation to be incompatible with backward causation is in virtue of some deeper feature or combination of features of the theory. This more deeply grounded restriction cannot be rejected merely on the basis of the fact that it is easy to imagine stories in which effects precede their causes. An extensive examination of possible cases is necessary, along with a refutation of the various a priori objections raised to the logical possibility of backward causation. Although I do not pursue such a discussion here, I note that I don't think that there are good reasons available for ruling out the logical possibility of backward causation.[43] The theory presented so far is silent on this matter, since we have not yet said what causal priority amounts to. That is the task of the next chapter. As we shall see, there is a way of understanding causal priority that leaves this possibility open.

Probabilistic Causation

As already indicated, there has been a growing recognition among philosophers that causation is possible under indeterminism. Even if there is no deterministic law that connects c to e, it may still be the case that c causes e. Again, a theory of causation should not rule this out. Persistence theory does not make use of probabilistic notions. Nevertheless, this theory is consistent with indeterministic causation. Nothing in this theory excludes tropes whose persistence is an indeterministic matter. The current charge of a particle may be only probabilistically linked to its continuation. Neither does persistence theory preclude probabilistic forms of property fusion and fission. The laws governing property persistence, fission, and fusion may be at best probabilistic.

Transitivity

Is persistence theory compatible with causal transitivity? In our earlier discussion we found that violations of transitivity were possible given the following assumption: if some part of a complex event c is causally connected to some event e, then c and e themselves are causally connected. This assumption allows for the following pattern: c causes e by causing a part of e, and e causes f by way of a different part of e. But there are cases which fit this pattern but in which transitivity fails. These failures are rooted in the fact that c has nothing to do with f. Persistence theory seems to satisfy this assumption for compound events. Compound tropes may be connected causally by way of a causal process in which there is only *partial* trope identity at each stage. This opens up the possibility that a compound trope c is causally connected to a compound trope e in virtue of some partial identity, and e is causally connected to some trope f in virtue of partial identity, but there is no partial identity between c and f.

Under these conditions and without any further qualifications, as we saw in the section on "complex events" in chapter 3, violations of transitivity are a possibility.

In response, we cannot require partial identity across chains of indirect causation. Partial identity is at most a necessary condition for direct causation. This restriction on partial identity—as a necessary condition only for direct causation—is *not* put in place to prevent failures of transitivity. Indeed, if anything, applying this requirement more generally to indirect causation might help us with the transitivity problem. This restriction is essential, but for another reason: events connected by a chain of indirect causation may simply fail to satisfy this condition. Such cases are frequent. Not all cases of partial identity failure are associated with a failure of causation—indirect causation being the exception, at least sometimes.

There is, however, another route to resolving this issue of transitivity. The apparent inconsistency between persistence theory and transitivity arises only because we are focusing only on the theory's singularist component and ignoring its generalist component. Although the generalist component has not been developed here, the question of transitivity is properly resolved by reference to that element. For direct causation, two conditions are necessary: at least partial trope persistence and a lawful connection between the tropes at these different times. Consider an abstract example. Compound trope c causes compound trope e, and e causes trope f. There is partial identity from c to e and from e to f. Now as we have seen, if there are parts of c that are irrelevant to c's causing e, and parts of e that are irrelevant to its causing f, then transitivity may fail. But what does "irrelevancy" consist in? I would suggest that relevancy requires that there be a lawful connection between every aspect of c and e. However the generalist relation gets specified, this is one requirement. If this requirement is satisfied, then violations of transitivity cannot be generated. And this makes clear from another angle why a generalist component is important. A purely singularist account will include irrelevancies in both causes and effects. The transitivity issue trades on such irrelevancies and brings home the need for a generalist component suitably developed.

Identity over Time
A theory of causation also ought to be compatible with philosophical theories in other domains. Is persistence theory consistent with a causal theory of physical object identity? We already have seen that persistence theory is not in itself circular, since here trope persistence is not analyzed causally. Trope persistence is not a matter of any relation among temporally distinct trope stages, including the causal relation. On a causal theory of object identity, physical "object stages" are stages of the same object only if these stages are causally connected. How are we to understand this claim about causally connected object stages? A persistence theory takes causal relata to be individual properties. Given this assumption, we may read the causal theory of identity as a claim about the properties of these stages: object stages are causally connected if and only if their *properties*, or at least *some* of their properties, are causally connected. On a persistence account of causation this analysis is equivalent, roughly, to saying that two physical object stages, s_1 and s_2, are stages of the same object only if s_1 (or s_2) contains a property that is identical or partially identical to some property contained in s_2 (or s_1). Hence, there does not seem to be any circularity or inconsis-

tency in combining a persistence theory of causation with a causal theory of physical-object identity.

Epiphenomena

The problem of epiphenomena, or joint effects, is just this: a theory of causation should treat as causally unconnected mere joint effects of common cause. Although such effects have a common origin, neither is a cause of the other. What makes this a difficult demand on a theory of causation is the fact that mere joint effects may stand in relations of lawful connection, counterfactual dependence, or probability relations. Epiphenomena thus present a pairing problem. Mere joint effects ought not to be paired causally.

Consider a particular example. Suppose that a rock falls from a hill and kills Jones and Smith, hitting them simultaneously. Speaking loosely (that is, not specifying the tropes very exactly), we would say that the movement of the stone caused these two deaths but that neither death was a cause of the other. How will our three leading theories handle this case?

If there is no lawful connection between the deaths, the neo-Humean will face no difficulty. However, there is no guarantee that there will be no lawful connection. Given the circumstances and the laws of nature, Jones's death may entail the falling of the rock, and this event in the circumstances may lawfully guarantee the death of Smith. We cannot exclude this possible legal configuration. And what of the counterfactual theorist? This case will be problematic if, given the circumstances, had the death of Jones not taken place, the rock would not have fallen and Smith would have been spared. A blanket denial of this possibility would presumably depend on a denial of backtracking counterfactuals, but this is a problematic strategy in its own right, as we have seen. Probabilistic theories do no better. Suppose, for example, that there is very little chance of the rock killing both, but given that it killed one, the probability of the other death is much higher. In particular, Smith's death increases the probability of Jones's death. And under the circumstances, Smith's death is not screened off from Jones's death by the earlier falling of the rock: it is not the case that the probability of Jones's death given Smith's death and the falling of the rock is equal to the probability of Jones's death given the falling of the rock.[44] The problem of epiphenomena, however, might be resolvable if these theories can be supplemented with an independent account of causal priority. On that basis it might be possible to demonstrate that neither joint effect causes the other. How such a strategy might work for each of these theories cannot be pursued here. Nevertheless, it is important to point out that if this strategy is viable, the theory of this work will not be at a particular advantage over these other accounts, with respect to the problem of epiphenomena.

How does persistence theory fare with joint effects? However precisely we specify the tropes involved, these deaths are not strongly causally connected, since these properties are not partially identical nor do they supervene on properties that are partially identical. There is no strong causal connection present. This lack of strong causal connection does not by itself vindicate persistence theory. These events may be connected by a causal chain. Consider that each death is linked by such a process to the falling of the rock. But that fact is not enough to establish a causal chain. One further condition, that of causal priority, must be satisfied. The links in the chain must display partial identity *and* causal priority in the right direction if this is to be a causal chain connecting the deaths. In particular, it must be the case that one death is causally prior to the rock's falling and the other death is causally posterior to the rock's falling. But this condition is not satisfied, since neither death is causally prior to the rock's movement. The deaths are not connected by a causal chain. This way of resolving the problem of joint effects, however, can be made good only with a worked-out account of causal priority, the topic of the next chapter.

Summary

I have suggested the following points. Nonsimple individual properties are conjunctive/structured bundles of properties. Both simple and nonsimple properties may persist. Causation's singularist component consists in the persistence of such properties, along with the forming and unforming of such property bundles. Tropes are the alphabet of causation, and the cement of the universe consists in the constancy and survival of its properties.

6

Causal Asymmetry

I have concluded that the singularist component of causation is a matter of trope persistence. What remains to be determined is what gives causation its asymmetrical character. The account of causation in chapter 5 contains a place-holder, "causal priority," which should be replaced with a substantial analysis. The goal of this final chapter is to make that substitution.

What is it that a theory of causal asymmetry should do? An adequate analysis of causal priority will in some sense account for the following implication that we normally take for granted: if c causes e, then e does not cause c. There must be some component of a theory of causation that guarantees this implication—some asymmetrical relation R such that causes stand in R to their effects. The most familiar candidate for R, which is traditionally ascribed to Hume,[1] is temporal priority: causes precede their effects. And since temporal priority is asymmetrical, causal asymmetry follows automatically. This "Humean" account, however, although widely accepted, is not in the end acceptable for at least two reasons. First, temporal priority may not be a necessary feature of the causal relation. Various philosophers have cited what they purport to be possible and actual cases of simultaneous causation and the possibility (logical and perhaps physical) of backward causation as evidence against the temporal-priority view. Second, commitments with respect to philosophical analyses of related concepts may conflict with this reading of causal asymmetry. In particular, if the causal theory of temporal direction is correct, a temporal-priority view of causal asymmetry will be circular. In constructing an account of causal asymmetry we should at least keep open the possibility of a causal theory of temporal direction.

The purpose of this chapter is to present an alternative to the temporal-priority view, an account that does not depend on the assumption that causes precede their effects. Since the alternative I will suggest is somewhat complicated, I will begin with an intuitive sketch.

Causal asymmetry, I will suggest, is ultimately a matter of the causal independence of the causal antecedents of an effect. In order to establish which of two events in a causal pair plays the causal role and which the effect role, we need only to find an additional event (c_2) that is causally linked to one event in the pair (e, the effect) but not so linked to the other (c_1, the cause). Causal asymmetry is determined by the fact that normally, although c_1 and e are causally connected, as are c_2 and e, c_1 and c_2, the causes, are causally independent. This basic claim, which requires much refinement, is itself grounded in a deeper feature of causation—its "circumstantial" character. All causal sequences are conditioned by accompanying circumstances. Striking a match, for example, will produce a flame only if certain other conditions hold, including the presence of oxygen. One consequence of the circumstantial character of causation is that for each effect there will generally be more than one cause. In our example, not only is the oxygen a conditioning factor, it also plays a genuine causal role. Causes do their work only in relevant conditioning circumstances, which also constitute causal antecedents. Causal asymmetry is generated out of causes' independence from their conditioning circumstances, an independence that is not found between those circumstances and the effect. This, however, constitutes a very rough outline. We must now proceed to a technical development of this idea, an elaboration that is necessary if this intuition is to count as an adequate reconstruction of "causal priority."

The elaboration of this basic idea will take us through two stages. The first stage consists in deploying two preliminary concepts that will play a central role in the account of "causal priority." Causal priority can be understood in terms of the relation of *being causally connected* and the presence of a *conditioning factor or circumstance*. The elaboration of the notion of causal connection has in effect already been completed in chapter 5. However, as we shall see, the features of this relation which are important to causal priority are not those revealed by any particular substantial analysis. The logical features of this relation are the important ones here. The notion of a conditioning factor or circumstance, on the other hand, will require more work. Although the basic idea—that of a circumstance or condition on which a causal sequence depends—is straightforward, a certain amount of refinement is necessary if we are to handle complex causal situations. After completing this first stage, I will move on to working out the actual definition of "causal priority." Our discussion at that point becomes rather technical. Unfortunately, these technicalities are mandatory if we are to get from the rough idea of causal priority described above to an account that is adequate.

Two Preliminary Concepts

Strong Causal Connection

The first relation we discuss, preliminary to an account of causal priority, is that of "strong causal connection." Chapter 5 gives a substantial account of this relation. For our current task, as already indicated, this analysis is largely irrelevant. Rather, we must remind ourselves of the formal features of this relation.

What are the relevant logical features of this concept? There are two. The first is that this is a symmetrical relation. This can be brought out by recalling what we have already said about "strong causal connection." According to our definition, events (tropes at a time) are strongly causally connected just in case they are lawfully connected and their constitutive tropes are at least partially identical (or supervene on tropes that are partially identical). Asymmetry is not built in. That two events, c and e, are strongly causally connected does not entail which of the events is the cause and which is the effect, even though it will be true that either *c* causes *e* or *e* causes *c*. In other words, our truth conditions for this relation establish that the disjunction is true without determining which of these disjuncts is true. This further discrimination is the job of an account of causal asymmetry. In any case, what is important to notice at this point is that the relation "strong causal connection" is symmetrical. If an event *c* is strongly causally connected to an event *e*, then *e* is strongly causally connected to *c*.

The second important logical characteristic of "strong causal connection" is its nontransitivity. From the fact that *c* is causally connected to *e* and *e* is causally connected to *c'*, it does not follow that *c* and *c'* are causally connected. The striking of the match and the presence of oxygen may both be causally connected to the lighting of the match, but it certainly does not follow that either the striking caused the presence of oxygen or the presence of oxygen caused the striking. Joint causes of a common effect may certainly fail to be causally connected, strongly or otherwise (given that *c* and *e* are causally connected if and only if either *c* causes *e* or *e* causes *c*). The nontransitivity of "strong causal connection" contrasts with the transitivity of "is a cause of." If billiard ball *A*'s movement causes billiard ball *B*'s movement, and billiard ball *B*'s movement causes billiard ball *C*'s movement, then billiard ball *A*'s movement is a cause of billiard ball *C*'s movement. Causation is definitely transitive, but "strong causal connection" is not.

The reason for emphasizing these logical characteristics, symmetry and nontransitivity, is that it is only these features of this relation that will play a role in my account of causal priority. One advantage of this independence from the substantial analysis is that the resulting account of causal priority is compatible with other theories of causal connection. Nevertheless, the trope account of strong causal connection in combination with this account of asymmetry provides an overall theory of causation (again, in conjunction with an unsupplied theory of the generalist component of causation.)

In the following, I will shorten "strong causal connection" to "causal connection."

The Circumstantial Character of the Causal Relation

The second preliminary relation that plays a role in our definition of "causal priority" concerns the circumstantial character of the causal relation. Various philosophers, including John Anderson, C. J. Ducasse, and J. L. Mackie, have emphasized that the causal role of an event depends on accompanying circumstances.[2] The property of the match's being struck causes the match to light only if there is some set of circumstances, such as the presence of oxygen, which in some sense is causally propitious or relevant to this causal sequence. For their efficacy with respect to particular effects, individual causes depend on the specific circumstances of their realization. The circumstantial character of the causal relation is borne out by the fact that the causal role played by an event on a particular occasion does not depend solely on which generic nonrelational properties it may token. The particular effects of a given event, if any, cannot be determined without reference to the circumstances in which the event is realized. Those effects will vary with the circumstances. The property of being struck, which characterizes the match, does not cause the property of ignition, which also characterizes the match, on every occasion and in every circumstance.[3] Causation has a substantial circumstantial dependency.

Let us call such relevant circumstances *conditions of a causal connection*.[4] The presence of oxygen then is a condition of the causal connection of the property of being struck and the property of lighting, for example. This notion requires refinement before it can be of use in a definition of "causally prior." The intuitive idea at stake is that of a circumstance or condition that makes possible or is necessary for two events' being causally connected on a particular occasion. As a first approximation to an appropriate definition, let us try "an event or state f upon which the causal connection between c and e is counterfactually dependent."[5] Thus, if f had not been realized, c and e would not have been causally connected; if oxygen had not been present, the striking would not have been causally connected to the lighting. Notice that the relevant counterfactual makes reference to the nonoccurrence of an event in its antecedent and the nonrealization of a relation in the consequent clause. It is also worth noting that causal intermediaries will generally be conditions of the causal connection between the events they serve to connect.

This is the basic notion of a conditioning factor. However, this definition requires two kinds of modifications. The first modification is required to take care of the possibility that the conditioning factor may itself have a backup that would have taken over its role had it failed. In cases involving such backups, it will not be true that the causal connection of c and e is counterfactually dependent on the conditioning factor. Consider again the role of oxygen in normal circumstances with respect to the lighting of a match. Now suppose that the circumstances are not normal and that there is some gas present in addition to oxygen, gas g, which would have played the role of oxygen in the latter's absence. The oxygen, so to speak, preempts the conditioning role. On the other hand, the oxygen and the other gas may each be independently sufficient in the circumstances for the lighting (and hence for the causal connection of the striking to the lighting). In that case the conditioning role is overdetermined.

In order to handle these possibilities we need to make it clear that the causal connection is dependent on the conditioning factor in the absence of other candidates for that same role. The following incorporates that thought:

(1) f is a member of a set of events $(f, d_1, d_2, \ldots, d_n)$ each of which has been realized such that the causal connection between c and e is counterfactually dependent on each member in the absence of the other members where this set includes all and only nonredundant members.[6]

A member of the set is *redundant* if the elimination of that member does not require the elimination of some other member.[7]

Under this new definition the presence of oxygen is a condition of the causal connection of the striking and the lighting, even given the backup gas. This is so because in the absence of the backup gas, the lighting is counterfactually dependent on the presence of oxygen. In addition, the oxygen and the backup gas are not redundant for the following reason. If gas g were left out of consideration—that is, we did not suppose it to be absent—then the oxygen would not be necessary for the lighting. The elimination of gas g from the set to be eliminated requires that we also eliminate oxygen from the set of necessary circumstances. The same reasoning applies to gas g vis-à-vis the oxygen.

This definition of a condition of a causal connection requires more work, however, owing to the following difficulty. In some cases, a joint effect e' of a common cause will satisfy this definition with respect to that common cause's connection to its *other* effect e. In other words, a causal connection between c and e might counterfactually depend on a separate effect e' of the cause event in the pair, although it is not true that that effect is a condition of the causal connection of c and e. This will be possible in some cases in which the laws of nature and the circumstances conspire to make it true that c could not have failed to cause the otherwise unrelated effect e'. In that case it will be true that had e' not occurred, c and e would not have been connected simply because c would not have occurred. On the definition under consideration we would be required to say that e' was a condition of the causal connection between c and e. Our intuitive notion of "relevant circumstances," however, would exclude joint effects of c from counting as conditions of the causal connection between c and e. A joint effect never makes possible the causal connection of the cause with that cause's other effects.

The following clause, added to what has already been said, will allow us to resolve this difficulty:

(2) there is no event g on which f counterfactually depends which is not a member (either redundant or not redundant) of the set $(f, d_1, d_2, \ldots, d_n)$.[8]

A few words of clarification are necessary. This clause is meant to rule out joint effects of a cause c from counting as a condition of the causal connection between c and some other *effect* e. How does clause 2 exclude joint effects? Here is how it works:

Suppose that had e', a joint effect of c, not been realized, given the laws and circumstances, c would not have been realized, and thus c and e would not have been causally connected. So clause 1 is satisfied for e'. But e' gets excluded under clause 2. The second clause requires that if there is another event g on which e' counterfactually depends, then g must be a member of the set $(e', d_1, d_2, \ldots)$—that is, such that the causal connection between c and e depends on e' in the absence of the other members of this set including g. Now there will be an event g on which e' depends. But if g had not been realized, then in these *new* circumstances, c is not sufficient for e'. Thus, in the absence of g, c fails to be counterfactually dependent on e'. Thus g is not a member of the set $(e', d_1, d_2, \ldots, d_n)$, since the causal connection between c and e is not counterfactually dependent on e' in the absence of g (and hence in the absence of $[d_1, d_2, \ldots, d_n$ and $g]$).

Clause 2 thus excludes joint effects like e' from being conditioning factors, without excluding genuine conditions of the causal connection.[9]

Let us call an event that satisfies these two clauses a direct condition of the causal connection between c and e. I want now to extend the notion of a conditioning factor a bit further to include what I will call indirect conditioning factors. By this I have in mind primarily the following: an event that is a direct condition of a causal connection between c and f will be an indirect condition of a causal connection between c

and any event that f causes. So the presence of oxygen, in the example of the match lighting, will be an indirect condition of the causal connection between the striking of the match and any event that the lighting subsequently causes. The important feature of this case is that the indirect condition (of the causal connection between c and e) is a direct condition of the causal connection between some direct condition (of the c-e connection) and either c or e.[10] Another example of an indirect condition would be the following. Suppose that pressure from a hand on a piece of material results in the compression of the material. In turn, the compression of the material makes possible the transmission of pressure to a button. The compression of the material is a direct condition of the causal connection between the hand pressure and the depression of the button. The hand pressure compresses the material, we may suppose, only given the presence of water. The presence of water is a direct condition of the causal connection between the hand pressure and the compression of the material and, thus, an indirect condition of the causal connection between the hand pressure and the depression of the button.

One further point about conditioning factors must be made before defining "causally prior." The point is just this: conditioning factors are causes of the effects in the causal pairs they condition. Consider again the example of the property of being scratched, which causes the ignition property of the match. The property of the oxygen's being present counts as a cause of the fire.[11] The same causal relevance is evidenced in all cases of direct conditions of a causal connection between c and e: the direct condition is a cause of the effect-event in the causally connected pair. Given this conclusion about direct conditions, the *causal* relevance of indirect conditions of such a pair follows from the transitivity of the causal relation.[12] Thus in general, if d is a direct or indirect condition of a causal connection between c and e, then d is a cause of the effect of that causal pair. This general fact about conditioning factors will take on importance in our discussion of causal priority.

A Definition of Causal Priority

With the notions of causal connection and conditioning factors in hand, we can turn directly to the task of giving an account of causal priority. Recall first the rough, intuitive description of the account we now aim to make precise. The basic claim is that a cause is a member of a set of events that possess, within that set, a certain causal independence, whereas the effect-event is not causally independent of any of these events. To simplify somewhat, we may say that since every effect has more than one cause, causal priority may be read off from the causal independence among the multiple causes.[13] This basic claim, stated in this form, involves some circularity. That circularity can be avoided if we recast the claim using the notions of causal connection (a symmetrical relation) and conditioning factors. Or, to be more precise, given that every causal connection is conditioned by accompanying circumstances and that these conditions are causes of the effect-event of the causal pair, not of the cause-event, we may define causal priority by utilizing the notions of "condition of a causal connection" and "causal connection." As indicated above, since the notion of a "condition" excludes joint effects of the cause in the causal pair from counting as a condition, it follows that to establish, for example, that c_1 and e are causally connected and that c_2

is causally connected to e but not to c_1, where c_2 is a condition of the causal connection between c_1 and e, is sufficient to determine that c_1 is the cause and e is the effect.

We are now in a position to offer an account of causal priority:

> c is *causally prior* to e if (A) (1) c and e are causally connected, and (2) there is some condition of the causal connection between c and e that is not connected to c and is causally connected to e, and there is no condition causally connected to c but not to e.

In order to elucidate this account, I offer two illustrations. The first is diagrammed as follows:

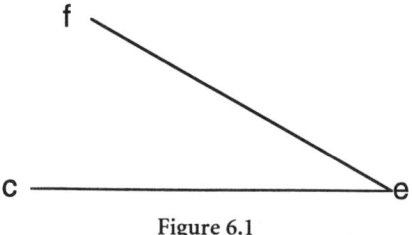

Figure 6.1

In this case there is a causal connection between c and e where f is a direct condition of that causal connection. We further suppose that there is a causal connection between f and e, but no causal connection between f and c. Given these suppositions, we may conclude that c causes e rather than that e causes c, given the definition of "causal priority."[14]

An example fitting this pattern is the following: c is the match's being scratched, e is the match's being ignited, and f is the property of the oxygen's being present. There exists a causal connection between the property of the match's being scratched and the property of the match's lighting. The property of the oxygen's being present is a condition of the causal connection between the property of the match's being scratched and the property of the match's lighting, and the property of the oxygen's being present and the property of the match's being scratched are not causally connected. From these facts it is clear that the cause in the pair is the property of the match's being scratched and the effect is the property of the match's being ignited.[15]

The second illustration, which involves an indirect condition, can be diagrammed as follows:

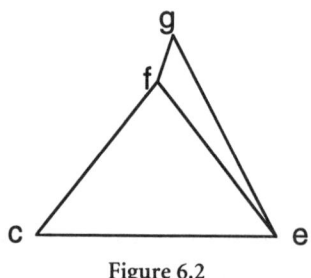

Figure 6.2

Causal Asymmetry

In this case c and e are causally connected, and f is a direct condition of the causal connection between c and e. f, in turn, is causally connected to c, and g is a direct condition of this causal connection. g, however, is not causally connected to c, but g is causally connected to e. Thus we can conclude that c causes e rather than that e causes c.

An example of this arrangement might be the following: suppose that c is a heat property not requiring oxygen, and f is the presence of oxygen. Assume further that g is the presence of some gas other than oxygen. Given the causal connections posited, the heat event c causes the property of the oxygen's being present, and this causal relation is directly conditioned by the presence of gas g. In turn, since g is a cause of f, and g and e are causally connected but g and c fail to be causally connected, we can conclude that c causes e rather than that e causes c.[16]

Although clause A is sufficient for causal priority, it is not necessary. There are cases in which the cause-event is causally connected to a conditioning factor. The conditioning factor and the cause fail to be independent. In that case we need to consider the wider causal context in which the causal pair are embedded. Here is a further sufficient condition for c's being causally prior to e:

> (B) c is causally connected to some event f, and c is a direct condition of a causal connection between f and e, and f is causally prior to e.

Clause B comes into play if clause A fails to apply. Consider the following example. Suppose that c causes e and that there is only one causal condition, f. f in turn is a cause of c (and thus of e). A rough example of this might be that c is the burning property of a match, e is the burning property of a building, and f is the property of the oxygen's being present. A diagram may help clarify:

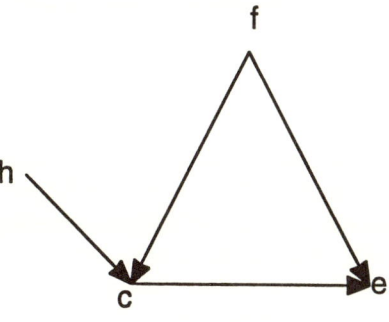

Figure 6.3

If f is the only condition of c's causal connection to e, then there would exist no condition of c's causal connection to e that was causally independent of c. Clause A does not apply. Clause B resolves this difficulty. First, we must assume that since f causes c, there exists a condition of that causal connection (call that h). h is causally independent of f. Thus f is causally prior to e. If h were to fail to meet clause A with respect to f and e, the problem would be moved back one stage. Thus f is causally prior to e. In turn, c is a direct condition of the causal connection between f and e, since c is causally between f and e. Thus, by clause B, c is causally prior to e, as we have assumed.

We can add that c is causally prior to e if and only if either A or B is true.[17]

One possible objection to this model is that it seems to rule out a priori that the total set of causally relevant conditions be called "a cause" of the effect, since there would be no further conditions. This is not a serious difficulty. We can allow such a usage as long as it is understood that the members of that set separately satisfy the definition of causal priority.

Single Causes: A Further Modification

Although this account is relatively complete, there are certain types of cases that prompt additional refinements. One obvious problem is this: suppose that e does not have multiple causes but only a single cause.[18] This account will not guarantee asymmetry for such "nonbranching" causal chains. For example, asymmetry will fail in a causal sequence consisting of a single, nonchanging trope that persists in causal isolation from other tropes. But unchanging tropes, I have said, constitute a central *causal* phenomenon. Some revision is necessary.

The appropriate revision requires reference to "negative" conditioning factors. Until now I have appealed only to counterfactuals involving positive conditioning factors, but we can extend these appeals to counterfactual truths of the form "the causal connection between c and e counterfactually depends on the nonoccurrence of some event f." "Negative events" can also play a conditioning role. For example, just as it is true that had oxygen not been present, the match would not have lighted, it is also true that had the absence of moisture itself been, so to speak, absent, the match would not have lighted. As we shall see, this extension provides a basis for determining direction in the "single-cause" cases. These negative events can, in some sense, play the role of the additional multiple causes whose mutual independence constitutes causal priority.

However, this expansion to include negative conditioning factors creates its own problem. Conditioning factors, we have said, are causes of the effect in the relevant causal pair. But negative events are not causes—or we should at least avoid that implication, if possible. Fortunately, the truth of counterfactuals of the form "the causal connection between c and e counterfactually depends on the nonoccurrence of some event f" need not commit us to negative events as causes. We can stipulate that causal relata are restricted to positive events. We can say that the absence of moisture is a condition of the causal connection between the striking property and the lighting property as long as it is understood that negative events (which happen to satisfy our definition of "condition of a causal connection") are excepted from the implication that such conditions are causes. But if negative events are to stand in for positive events in determining causal priority for isolated, unchanging persisting tropes, then some relation other than causation must come into play. These negative events must stand in some relation analogous to causal connection to the effect-event in the causal pair. Without this relation we will not be in a position to extend the present account of priority to such cases.

If we can find such a relation, then the extension will be straightforward. Let us call that relation, whatever it is, "quasi-causal connection." The absence of moisture is "quasi-causally connected to the match lighting property." The second condition of the analysis of causal priority can then be modified as follows:

(2') there is some condition of the causal connection (CCC) of c and e that is not causally connected to c and is causally connected to e, and there is no CCC connected to c but not to e, or there is some negative CCC of c and e that is not quasi-causally connected to c and is quasi-causally connected to e, and there is no negative CCC that is quasi-causally connected to c but not to e.

This modification will allow us to attribute causal priority in cases in which there is a single cause if we can find some suitable way of understanding quasi-causal connection.

How then should we define quasi-causal connection? I think the right relation here is counterfactual dependence. We can say that a negative event not-c is quasi-causally connected to e just in case had c been realized e would not have been realized. In our example, the absence of moisture is quasi-causally connected to the property of being lighted, since had the moisture property been realized, the lighted property would not have been realized. Negative events cannot in principle stand in the appropriate singularist relation to other positive events, since they are not constituted by tropes, which can persist in whole or in part, as positive events are. Negative events cannot be causally connected to positive events. Nevertheless, the quasi-causal connections of negative events will provide a basis for solving the problem of single causes.

Specifically, we can fill in 2' as follows:

(2") there is some condition of the causal connection (CCC) of c and e that is not causally connected to c and is causally connected to e, and there is no CCC that is connected to c but not to e, or there is some negative CCC of c and e on which c is not counterfactually dependent but on which e is counterfactually dependent, and there is no negative CCC on which c is counterfactually dependent but on which e is not counterfactually dependent.

How does this help in the case of a causally isolated unchanging trope? Consider this trope at two different times, t and t'. Assume that this is a case of forward causation. Now there will be some event which, had it occurred at t', would have prevented that trope from being realized at t' without blocking the realization of that trope at t. However, given the causal isolation of this trope, there will be no event that, had it occurred and blocked the realization of that trope at t, would not have also blocked the realization of that trope at t'.[19]

This is a good point at which to consider an objection from Tooley, one that is based on the possibility of very simple universes, to *any* reductionist account of the direction of causation. Here is his case: "consider a world that contains only two uncharged particles, of the same type, that rotate endlessly about one another, on circular trajectories, in accordance with the laws of Newtonian physics. Each particle will undergo acceleration of a constant magnitude, due to the force of gravity exerted on it by the other particle."[20] He claims that this world is certainly causal but that there is no feature of the situation recognized by a reductionist program on which to base an account of causal direction. A reductionist account will either collapse into a temporal-priority view or give no answer to the question of direction.

There are two responses to this case. The first is that if there really is no reductionist basis other than temporal priority for asserting a causal direction, then there is no direction. The second is to rely on negative events. Consider the negative event of the absence of a force being applied selectively to particle a that would affect the orbit of a but not the mass of the other particle, b. Call that negative event f. f is a negative *CCC* of the causal connection of the mass of b and the orbit of a, but f is not quasi-causally connected to the mass of b—because that negative event is not necessary for the mass of b—but it is quasi-causally connected to the orbit of a, since it is necessary for that orbit: if it had occurred, the orbit of a would have been different. Finally, there is no negative *CCC* causally connected to the mass of b but not to the orbit of a. Any negative event necessary for the mass of b is necessary for the orbit of a.

It is worth noting that this account of causal priority is compatible with backward causation. No special assumptions as to the specific temporal relations between cause and effect have been made. In the case of backward causation, some condition of the causal connection between, say, c and e that is causally connected to e but not to c may have been realized before, simultaneously with, or after either c or e.

Mutual Causation

We normally take for granted that causation is asymmetrical. But this assumption can be challenged. It might be claimed that "mutual causation" is possible. If so, we should take account of this possibility in our discussion of causal asymmetry.[21] In effect, to some extent we already have. Indeed, one way to think of the analysis of causal asymmetry given here is that it implicitly specifies conditions under which c and e stand in a relation of mutual causal dependence: viz., c and e are mutually causally dependent just in case c and e are causally connected and c is neither causally prior to nor causally posterior to e. In other words, if c and e are strongly causally connected but the conditions of the analysis of causal priority fail, then these events are mutually causally dependent. But if we are to recognize fully the possibility of events that are causally connected, but neither of which is causally prior to the other, one modification is required.[22] We must adjust our initial assumption that c and e are causally connected just in case either c causes e or e causes c. A further disjunct must be added:

> c and e are causally connected just in case either c causes e, e causes c, or c and e are mutually causally dependent.

We then can reinterpret the results of chapter 5 (minus the reference to causal priority) as primarily providing truth conditions for this disjunction without determining which disjunct is true.

To recapitulate, the account of causal priority elaborated here is based on the circumstantial character of the causal relation. On a particular occasion a given event c causes another event e only if there are certain accompanying conditions. These

Causal Asymmetry

additional conditions in turn are not causally relevant to (causes of) c but are causally relevant to e. If this intuition were represented pictorially we would get a view of the causal order of the world something like the following:

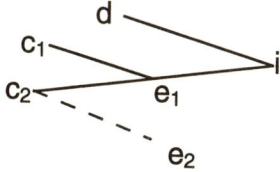

Figure 6.4

The solid line represents causal influence running from left to right. If we can discount the dashed lines to joint effects, then the direction of causation always moves in the direction of the closing forks.

Notes

Introduction

1. I will not review the many possible *responses* that these various objections have engendered within the traditional accounts. In this introduction, I go only one move deep into the causation debate.

2. D. Hume, *A Treatise of Human Nature*, ed. L. A. Selby-Bigge (Oxford: Oxford University Press, 1959); *Enquiries Concerning the Human Understanding and Concerning the Principles of Morals*, 2nd ed., ed. L. A. Selby-Bigge (Oxford: Oxford University Press, 1902); *An Abstract of a Treatise of Human Nature*, ed. J. M. Keynes and P. Sraffa (Cambridge: Cambridge University Press, 1938).

3. Hume is also known for denying that there is any empirically observable necessary connection between cause and effect.

4. For this problem see J. L. Mackie, *The Cement of the Universe* (Oxford: Oxford University Press, 1974), pp. 60–61. There are also well-known criticisms of the spatio-temporal components of the Humean account: (1) the theory is incompatible with noncontiguous events that are nonetheless indirectly causally connected; (2) *direct* causation at a spatial and temporal distance should not be ruled out a priori; and (3) neither, perhaps, should simultaneous and backward causation.

5. Other examples include joint effects of a common cause regularly found together without being directly causally connected—for example, spots on skin and an accompanying fever, both of which are caused by an underlying virus.

6. Another standard criticism of the Humean account concerns its similarity condition. If interpreted to require exact similarity, this condition is too easily satisfied (if *e* follows *c*, the generalization that events exactly similar to *c* are always followed by events exactly similar to *e* is true), and if interpreted too loosely, it will also be too easy to generate constant conjunctions. See, for example, M. Brand, "Introduction: Defining 'Causes'," in his *The Nature of Causation* (Urbana: University of Illinois Press, 1976), pp. 10–11.

7. See, for example, C. G. Hempel, *Aspects of Scientific Explanation* (New York: Free Press, 1965), p. 349.

8. More precisely, where *c* and *e* are actual events, *c* causes *e* just in case there is a law *L* along with actual background conditions *b* such that statements of *c*, *b*, and *L* entail a statement that *e* occurs, where *b*, *c*, and *L* are each essential to that entailment. Neo-Humeans also may require that causes be lawfully necessary for their effects, either in addition to or as a

replacement for lawful sufficiency. In that case, a statement of e, b, and L entails a statement that c occurs, where e, b, and L are each essential to this entailment.

9. See D. Lewis, "Causation," in his *Philosophical Papers*, vol. 2 (New York: Oxford University Press, 1986), p. 160, for these problems and that of preemption for the neo-Humean.

10. If causes must also be lawfully necessary for their effects, overdetermination becomes a problem. Overdetermining causes are not individually lawfully necessary for their effects. A death that is overdetermined by simultaneous and independently sufficient gunshots is such that no one of the gunshots is necessary. See Introduction to *Causation*, ed. E. Sosa and M. Tooley (Oxford: Oxford University Press, 1993), pp. 7–8.

11. See F. I. Dretske and A. Snyder, "Causal Irregularity," *Philosophy of Science*, 39, 1972, p. 70.

12. D. Lewis, "Causation," pp. 159–172.

13. J. Kim, "Causes and Counterfactuals," in *Causation*, ed. E. Sosa and M. Tooley (Oxford: Oxford University Press, 1993), p. 206.

14. This holds if it is true that had either joint effect not happened, the common cause would not have happened, and thus the other joint effect would not have happened.

15. Lewis himself raises both of these problems in "Causation," pp. 170–172.

16. See H. Reichenbach, *The Direction of Time* (Berkeley: University of California Press, 1956); I. J. Good, "A Causal Calculus I-II," *British Journal for the Philosophy of Science*, 11, 1961, pp. 305–318, and 12, 1962, pp. 43–51, reprinted in his *Good Thinking* (Minneapolis: University of Minnesota Press, 1983); P. Suppes, *A Probabilistic Theory of Causality* (Amsterdam: North-Holland Publishing Company, 1970).

17. One interpretation of this fundamental notion is that the probability of the effect conditional on the cause is greater than the probability of the effect simpliciter. Other conditions, however, must be stipulated. A traditional line of development requires that there is no event f earlier than c which "screens off" c from e. f screens off c from e just in case the probability of e given f is equal to the probability of e given both f and c (in other words, if and only if c adds nothing to the probability of e once f is given). Another reading of this basic notion brings in counterfactuals: if the cause had not occurred, the probability of its immediate effect would have been lower. I discuss this in greater detail in chapter 1.

18. For an explanation of these two problems see E. Eells, *Probabilistic Causality* (Cambridge: Cambridge University Press, 1991), pp. 57–59.

19. Good, *Good Thinking*, pp. 216–217.

20. Although counterfactual theory and probabilistic theory are the main contenders as replacements for nomological sufficiency accounts, there are other candidates as well. There is, for example, manipulability theory. The manipulability theorist replaces the neo-Humean emphasis on law with an emphasis on action. Our practical concerns and our concept of causation are conceptually linked on manipulability accounts. "Causes" are those events that we pick out because we can manipulate them to bring about our various goals. Roughly, a "cause" is a controllable means for bringing about some further state, and the "cause-effect" relation is explained by the "producing-by-means-of" relation rather than the other way around (D. Gasking, "Causation and Recipes," in *Philosophical Problems of Causation*, ed. T. Beauchamp [Encino: Dickenson Publishing Company, 1974], p. 131). Agency is the more fundamental notion. More precisely, one version of manipulability theory stipulates that c causes e if and only if we can bring about events similar to e by doing things similar to c. It is in virtue of the fact that we can melt ice cubes and thereby bring about a rise in the water level of the glass that the melting of the polar ice cap causes a rise in sea level. Alternately, another version stipulates that *if* we did c, then we would thereby bring about e. (For the first version see Gasking, "Causation and Recipes," and for the second, see G. H. von Wright, *Explanation*

and Understanding [Ithaca: Cornell University Press, 1971].) This version suggests that the latter is true because it is true that could we melt the polar ice cap, we could then bring about a rise in sea level.

Manipulability theories do not have many philosophical adherents. Many philosophers consider it a fundamentally misconceived theory. The lesser charges include the following: (1) the condition specified, "can bring about *e* by doing *c*," may be insufficient for causation, since I can, for example, bring about an outjumping of George by jumping six feet, but my jumping six feet does not cause my outjumping George (J. Kim, Review of von Wright's *Explanation and Understanding, The Philosophical Review*, 82, 1973, p. 382); (2) causal direction cannot be determined when at the type-level we can bring about *e*-type events by *c*-type events and *also* bring about *c*-type events by *e*-type events (Kim, Review of *Explanation and Understanding*, p. 384); and (3) this analysis implies that neural events are backwardly caused by arm raisings, since I can bring it about that these neural events have occurred by raising my arm (R. Chisholm, "Freedom and Action," in *Freedom and Determination*, ed. K. Lehrer [New York: Random House, 1966], pp. 11–44, and Mackie, *The Cement of the Universe*, p. 172). But the main reasons for manipulability theory's lack of supporters are its anthropomorphism and its obvious circularity (e.g., the expressions "doing *c*" and "bringing about *e*" seem clearly to be causal notions). See, for example, T. Beauchamp and A. Rosenberg, *Hume and the Problem of Causation* (New York: Oxford University Press, 1981), pp. 204–205.

21. She cites an example from physics: "a bomb is connected with a Geiger counter, so that it will go off if the Geiger counter registers a certain reading; whether it will or will not is not determined, for it is so placed near some radioactive material that it may or may not register that reading." She says that "if I am right, not being determined does not imply not being caused. Indeed, I should explain indeterminism as the thesis that not all physical effects are necessitated by their causes" (G. E. M. Anscombe, "Causality and Determinism," in *Causation*, ed. E. Sosa and M. Tooley [Oxford: Oxford University Press, 1993], p. 101).

22. Anscombe, "Causality and Determinism," p. 104.

23. Here I follow Tooley's reading of these comments. See M. Tooley, *Causation: A Realist Approach* (Oxford: Clarendon Press, 1987), pp. 188–189.

24. "If *A* comes from *B*, this does not imply that every *A*-like thing comes from some *B*-like thing" (Anscombe, "Causality and Determinism," p. 92).

25. Her analogy of "coming from" with "traveling from" supports this interpretation: "If we take 'coming from' in the sense of travel," it is evident that no exceptionless generalization is implied by the fact that *A* comes from *B*. If that is right, neither will *A*'s traveling from *B* on a particular occasion make it likely that *A* travels from *B* on any other occasion (ibid.).

26. Tooley, *Causation*, p. 189.

27. In particular, causal relations are theoretical relations governed by a series of postulates (described in detail by Tooley) to which the Ramsey/Lewis technique for defining theoretical terms can be applied. More specifically, causation is the theoretical relation that determines the direction of the transmission of logical probabilities (ibid., p. 252). Tooley develops this notion in such a way as to demonstrate that the formal properties of causation are preserved.

28. Tooley, "The Nature of Causation: A Singularist Account," *The Canadian Journal of Philosophy*, suppl. 16, 1990, pp. 271–322.

29. Ibid., p. 293.

30. C. J. Ducasse, *Truth, Knowledge, and Causation* (London: Routledge, Kegan Paul, 1968), pp. 3–4.

31. He also allows unchanges as causes (ibid., pp. 7–8).

32. Mackie, *The Cement of the Universe*, p. 136.

33. See B. Berofsky's "Causality and General Laws," in *Philosophical Problems of Causation*, ed. by T. Beauchamp (Encino: Dickenson Publishing Company, 1974), p. 156.

34. See Beauchamp and Rosenberg, *Hume and the Problem of Causation*, p. 109.

35. Transference theory is not meant to apply in all logically possible worlds.

36. Even if the transferences are law-governed, it does not seem to be the theory that they must be (see chapter 1).

37. c causes e if and only if (1) e is a change that cannot be accounted for without reference to other bodies; (2) the c-object makes contact with the e-object at the time of e; and (3) prior to e, the c-object possesses a quantity (e.g., energy that it transfers to the e-object) (J. Aronson, "On the Grammar of 'Cause'," *Synthese*, 22, 1971, pp. 421–422).

38. See Beauchamp and Rosenberg, *Hume and the Problem of Causation*, p. 208.

39. In addition, consider Aronson's own example: a catch is released, causing a spring to pull a weight some distance, but the release of the catch does not transfer energy to the spring. Aronson responds to this case by denying that the release of the catch is in fact a cause. The release, he says, is a "condition for making possible" the action of the real cause but is not itself a cause. Unfortunately, this distinction cannot carry the weight it is meant to bear, since many, if not all, genuine causes also make possible the action of other causes; for example, the presence of oxygen, a cause of the flame, also makes possible the efficacy of striking the match. This conditioning role is perfectly compatible with efficacy.

40. This last objection brings us to a possible dilemma faced by transference theory: either causal direction is a matter of temporal priority, and there is no room for backward causation, or the direction of transference is to be understood otherwise. However, if the transference theorist opts for the second horn, it would seem that transference itself must be cashed out in causal terms—the transferee is that which *caused* or initiated the change in possession. The account is then circular. See Introduction to *Causation*, ed. E. Sosa and M. Tooley, p. 4. This may be a false dilemma, however, because there is a third option: take transference theory as an account of "causal connection" (i.e., of the symmetrical relation "either c causes e or e causes c") and then give an independent account of causal asymmetry. The first horn, of course, has this structure, but we can replace the temporal account with one of the various nontemporal accounts of asymmetry.

41. I suggest that a generalist component is necessary to avoid the epistemological problems typically facing singularism and to circumvent the inclusion of causally irrelevant factors into the cause.

42. I argue for this account of causation's singularist component partly on the grounds that it resolves many of the outstanding problems facing generalist programs. More generally, I suggest that preemptive causation demands such a singularist component.

43. However, it is possible for the same trope to characterize two objects by virtue of distinct proper parts of that trope characterizing each object separately.

44. Properties, read as particulars, have gone under various names, including "abstract particular" (C. Landesman, "Abstract Particulars," *Philosophy and Phenomenological Research*, 33, 1976, pp. 323–333) and "particularised attribute" (J. Levinson, "The Particularisation of Attributes," *The Australasian Journal of Philosophy*, 58, 1980, pp. 102–115), but "trope" has nowadays tended to displace these other expressions. The term itself was introduced for this purpose by D. C. Williams ("On the Elements of Being," in his *The Principles of Empirical Realism* [Springfield: Charles Thomas, 1966], pp. 74–109) and is endorsed by Campbell and Armstrong in recent works (D. M. Armstrong, *Universals: An Opinionated Introduction* [Boulder: Westview Press, 1989], p. 114, and K. Campbell, *Abstract Particulars* [Oxford: Blackwell, 1990], p. 4).

45. The spatio-temporal locatedness of tropes contrasts with universals' lack thereof among those philosophers who deny location for universals. If, however, universals also can

have location, the difference remains that a trope can have only one location at a time, while universals can have multiple locations.

46. D. M. Armstrong, *Nominalism and Realism: Universals and Scientific Realism*, vol. 1 (Cambridge: Cambridge University Press, 1978), p. 121.

47. Actual co-occupation, however, is not required. Only the possibility of co-occupation is necessary, at least if there are free-floating single tropes.

48. The degree of abstractness of a trope depends on whether there are other abstract particulars that are proper parts of it that occupy its same location. From those who believe in coincident entities, we are owed a different account of the sense in which concrete objects are not, but tropes are, *abstract* particulars. If there are coincident entities—distinct concrete objects sharing the same location (such as a statue and a lump of clay)—then this characterization of concrete particulars will not work.

49. As Campbell says, a trope "is not a union of distinct elements, one particularizing and the other furnishing a nature. It is a single item, a particularized nature" (Campbell, *Abstract Particulars*, p. 2).

50. In addition, perhaps a trope is only contingently had by a given object, but it is essential to a universal exemplification that it involve the object it does.

51. Last, there is the question of the connection between language and tropes. The most sensible approach to this issue seems to be that of Campbell, who suggests a "sparse theory of tropes." On a sparse theory it is not assumed that for every meaningful predicate there corresponds a trope and that for every trope there corresponds a meaningful predicate in a language. Tropes are not just "ontic counterparts of . . . general terms used predicatively" (Campbell, *Abstract Particulars*, p. 2). A term F (such as "game") may be meaningfully applied to an object *a* even if there are no F tropes, and there may be tropes for which we lack a predicate. "There is, in short, no one-to-one correspondence between significant predicates and tropes" (ibid., p. 25). What tropes there are in the world is not primarily a linguistic matter.

52. However, not every collection of compresent tropes is sufficient for a concrete object, only the complete bundles: "[a]n ordinary object, a concrete particular, is a total group of compresent tropes. It is by being the complete group that it monopolizes its place as ordinary objects are ordinarily thought to do" (ibid., p. 21).

53. There is also a nonbundle view of concrete objects that brings tropes into play. A concrete object, on such a view, consists of a bare particular plus tropes or a substratum in which tropes inhere. This picture stays within nominalist lines, since no nonparticular elements are assumed.

54. As Williams says, "The set or sum of tropes concurrent with a trope . . . is the concrete particular or 'thing' which it may be said to 'characterize'" (Williams, "On the Elements of Being," p. 9).

55. Armstrong, *Universals*, p. 114.

56. The trope-bundle theory does not preserve the Identity of Indiscernibles as a necessary truth (which it is not), but a universal-bundle theory makes it a necessary truth. See Campbell, *Abstract Particulars*, p. 19.

57. Another advantage of a trope-bundle theory over a universals account is pointed out by Armstrong: the compresence of tropes is symmetrical and transitive and thus conducive to constructing nonoverlapping bundles, but the compresence of universals is not transitive. See Armstrong, *Universals*, p. 114.

58. See G. F. Stout, "The Nature of Universals and Propositions," *Studies in Philosophy and Psychology* (London: Macmillan, 1930), p. 391; Williams, "On the Elements of Being"; and Campbell, *Abstract Particulars*, p. 31.

59. "'Socrates is wise' . . . means that the concurrence sum (Socrates) includes a trope which is a member of the similarity set (Wisdom)" (Williams, "On the Elements of Being," p. 11).

60. Campbell, *Abstract Particulars*, p. 4.
61. Ibid., p. 23.
62. Ibid., p. 22.
63. Or as substrata with tropes.

Chapter 1

1. In addition, given a neo-Humean account of singular causal statements and this view of laws, the truth of the singular causal statement "*c* causes *e*" depends on more than relations between the token events *c* and *e*—its truth also depends on relations between types or universals.

2. D. M. Armstrong, *What Is a Law of Nature?* (Cambridge: Cambridge University Press, 1983), p. 85.

3. This criticism does not entail that lawful sufficiency is not necessary for causation, but it does undermine any claim to sufficiency.

4. D. Lewis, "Causation," in his *Philosophical Papers*, vol. 2 (New York: Oxford University Press, 1986), pp. 159–172.

5. Is this theory generalist? A generalist theory, recall, requires that causally connected token events be suitably type-type related. Lewis's theory is not strictly generalist. Indeed, Lewis explicitly denies that if *e* is counterfactually dependent on *c*, then *e* is nomically dependent on *c*; he recognizes the possibility of what he calls "inexplicable" causal dependence (ibid., p. 169, n. 11).

6. Most important to overall similarity is the avoidance of "big, widespread, diverse violations of law." Second in importance is the maximization of the spatio-temporal region of perfect match of fact. Third is the avoidance of small law violations. Of least or no importance is approximate similarity of particular facts (Lewis, "Counterfactual Dependence and Time's Arrow," in his *Philosophical Papers*, vol. 2 [New York: Oxford University Press, 1986], pp. 47–48).

7. Less clear is whether the truth of every singular causal statement requires the truth of at least some laws. Or could there be, for example, causally connected events in lawless worlds? The proper resolution of this issue would require an account of laws, an issue beyond the scope of this study.

8. Lewis, "Postscript," in his *Philosophical Papers*, vol. 2 (New York: Oxford University Press, 1986), p. 200.

9. This strategy, if successful, will work against both early nonoccurrent preemption and early occurrent preemption. What is important for this strategy is that the blocking action be initiated early; whether certain events are prevented from occurring in the alternate chain or the last event in the alternate chain is prevented from directly causing the final effect is irrelevant.

10. Lewis, "Postscript," p. 203.

11. It is worth pointing out that Lewis should recognize a third form of preemption, which we might call simultaneous preemption. Here the blocking action is initiated not by some earlier *indirect* cause in the main line or by the final effect itself, but by the event in the main line which is a direct cause of the final effect, an event that simultaneously directly causes the final effect and blocks completion of the alternate line. In the case of early preemption the roles of "blocker" and direct cause are played by different events, but in the case of simultaneous causation, those roles are played by the same event. And the blocking event in the main line occurs at the same time as would have the event in the alternate line which is in fact blocked. Now even if backtracking counterfactuals are excluded so that had the direct cause of the final effect in the main line not occurred, its earlier causes would have, the strategy for

handling early preemption will not apply. This is so because these earlier causes of the direct cause of the final effect are not the source of the blocking action; the final effect would still have occurred, without this direct cause, since without this event the alternate line would not have been (simultaneously) blocked.

12. Lewis, "Postscript," p. 205.

13. Or, more precisely, what is required is that the great majority of such other-regional processes exhibit the proper pattern of dependence (ibid., p. 206).

14. With late preemption, "what spoils the dependence is something extraneous: the presence alongside the main process of one or more preempted alternatives. Without them, all would be well. Hold fixed the laws but change the surroundings, in any of many ways, and we would have the dependence that my original analysis requires of causation" (ibid.).

15. "This means that the intrinsic character of the given process is right, and the laws are right, for the proper pattern of dependence—if only the surroundings were different" (ibid.).

16. What "spoils" the dependence in early preemption, if the dependence is spoiled, is the presence of the "extraneous" alternative line.

17. However, since the no-backtracking principle is crucial to Lewis's account of causal asymmetry, he cannot in general abandon that principle.

18. Regions can be found in which there is a process that matches the alternate line at best until a certain point and then continues on with *new* events, which lead to the final effect. There are no regions with the same laws in which the final effect is dependent on events in a process such that that process is intrinsically strictly indistinguishable from the actual alternate process. These other-regional processes include causal intermediaries that correspond to no event in the actual alternate process.

19. For the beginnings of this view see H. Reichenbach, *The Direction of Time* (Berkeley: University of California Press, 1956); I. J. Good, "A Causal Calculus I-II," *British Journal for the Philosophy of Science*, 11, 1961, pp. 305–318, and 12, 1962, pp. 43–51, reprinted in his *Good Thinking* (Minneapolis: University of Minnesota Press, 1983); P. Suppes, *A Probabilistic Theory of Causality* (Amsterdam: North-Holland Publishing Company, 1970).

20. There must be some type C, which c exemplifies, and some type E, which e exemplifies, such that the probability of an E-type event occurring, given the occurrence of a C-type event, is greater than the probability of the occurrence of an E-type event simpliciter. See Suppes, *A Probabilistic Theory of Causality*, p. 12.

21. Or, to be more precise and to bring this condition into line with the generalist reading of probability theory: c is a spurious cause of e if (1) there is some type C, which c exemplifies, and some type E, which e exemplifies such that $P(E|C) > P(E)$, and (2) there is an event f earlier than c and e and types C, E, and F that c, e, and f respectively exemplify such that $P(E|C,F) = P(E|F)$. See Reichenbach, *The Direction of Time*, p. 204, and Suppes, *A Probabilistic Theory of Causality*, p. 21.

22. The barometer reading is a spurious cause of the storm, since there is an earlier common cause that screens off the reading from the storm.

23. The difficulty is not that preempting causes are not probabilistically relevant to their effects. The basic condition of probability increase is satisfied for preempting causes.

24. E. Eells, *Probabilistic Causality* (New York: Cambridge University Press, 1991).

25. In fact, token-level causation is compatible with any possible probability relation (increase, decrease, or neutrality) between types exemplified by the token events x and y.

26. Eells, *Probabilistic Causality*, p. 279.

27. Eells also provides to-be-qualified accounts of three further causal notions: the idea of an event's happening *despite* another event, causal *independence*, and causal *autonomy*. Roughly stated: where y is short for "y's being Y" and x is short for "x's being X," and X and

Y are types, y happens despite x if x lowers the probability of y but y happens anyway. More precisely, y's being Y is despite x's being X if (1) the probability of Y changes at the time of x and (2) the probability of Y is low just after x and lower than just before x. y's being Y is independent of x's being X if the probability of Y is the same just after the time of x as it is just before the time of x. And, finally, y is autonomous of x if (1) the probability of Y changes at the time of x and (2) the probability is high just after x and higher than just before x, but (3) between the times of x and y the probability of Y drops to a low level. x is causally relevant to y if either y is Y because of or despite x's being X, and x is causally irrelevant to y if y is either is causally independent or autonomous of x.

28. This tentative verdict also applies to the temporally extended event of drug A's flowing from its source to the mechanism (from t_2 to t_1): the probability of recovery before this *extended* event is 1/2, as is the probability just after this event.

29. Notice the appeal here to type-level causation; this brings Eells's account into the quasi-generalist camp.

30. Eells, *Probabilistic Causality*, p. 132.

31. Interaction in three-factor cases is characterized as follows: a causal factor X interacts with a causal factor F, with respect to Y as the effect factor, "if X lowers the probability of Y in the presence of F and X raises the probability of Y in the absence of F (or vice versa, reversing 'raises' and 'lowers')" (ibid.).

32. Ibid.; see especially p. 362.

33. And even if we went ahead and applied qualification 2 or 3 to the release of drug B, the verdict of inefficacy for drug A would not change. If the release of drug B is held fixed (to any degree), the trajectory of the probability of survival still would not conform to Eells's characterization of the "because" pattern: the probability of survival just before the release of drug A is the same as the probability of survival just after the release of drug A—i.e., 50%—given the release of drug B.

34. For a fuller discussion of Eells's view see my "Preemption and Eells on Token Causation," *Philosophical Studies*, 74, 1994, pp. 39–50.

35. Eells, *Probabilistic Causality*, p. 346.

36. In our example, the earlier release of drug B fixes the probability of recovery at 1/2, which we assume is the physically highest possible probability for recovery. As a consequence, when the actual cause (the release of drug A) falls into place, the probability of recovery cannot be affected.

37. It is easy to devise indeterministic cases in which the theory fails. Consider this one: c deterministically causes e, but there was still some chance that e would have occurred uncaused in the absence of c. Although some of the closest non-c worlds will be non-e, not *all* of those worlds will lack e; in some, e will occur spontaneously. Hence, we are compelled to affirm falsely that c does not cause e. See Lewis, "Postscript," p. 176.

38. R. Otte, "Indeterminism, Counterfactuals, and Causation," *Philosophy of Science*, 54, 1987, p. 53 (capitalized variables have been changed to lowercase).

39. This probability is generated by conditionalizing on all that is actual in the world at t minus all that would not be actual if -c were to occur.

40. If the second probability is lower, c is a negative cause of e.

41. Indeed, in the case of Otte's formulation this strategy can be extended to the probabilistic case by reference to the transitivity clause, which Otte affirms. According to that clause, if d is a positive cause of f and f is a positive cause of e, then d is a positive cause of e. This is in effect the strategy Lewis applies to the early preemption cases. Otte might argue that although the probability of e does not depend counterfactually on d, the probability of e depends on f, the probability of which depends on d. There is thus a causal chain from d to e. d causes e in virtue of a chain of positive causation, given the transitivity of positive causation.

42. Lewis, "Causation," p. 171.

43. Lewis's defense of the no-backtracking principle is only as good as his contention that it is never true that diverging somewhat earlier, rather than just before i, involves less of a departure from actuality than diverging just before i. His basis for this contention is his claim that earlier divergence will necessarily involve more of a departure from reality than waiting to introduce a law violation. Earlier divergence involves at least two factual differences and one law violation, but the later divergence involves at least one less factual change and the same number of law violations. We depart less from actuality, then, by diverging later. This assessment of the relative closeness of these worlds to the actual world, however, would seem to rest on an assumption that is not at all obvious: all law violations are of equal significance. In fact, this assumption is false. Some laws are more important than others. In comparing worlds for overall similarity, a violation of a fundamental law of the actual world will count more heavily toward dissimilarity than a violation of a less-than-fundamental law. In the case at hand, suppose that the earlier law violation (which eliminates the blocking-initiator event) is of a less-than-fundamental law but that the later violation (which eliminates only i) is of a fundamental law of physics. In this case, it is less clear that diverging slightly sooner rather than later involves more of a departure from our world. Even though there is a slightly greater region of perfect factual match if the divergence comes slightly later, that may be outweighed by the seriousness of the law violation. Lewis owes us a reason for thinking either that all laws are equal or that maintaining a slightly greater region of perfect factual match should never be traded off to prevent the violation of a law of great importance rather than a law of little significance. He does not provide a reason for assenting to either disjunct. For criticism along this line see M. Bunzl, "Causal Preemption and Counterfactuals," *Philosophical Studies*, 37, 1980, pp. 115–124.

44. As a side note, I would also like to point out that at this stage in our discussion we cannot shift gears to another defender of counterfactual theory, Marshall Swain, and successfully invoke his notion of a "pure deletion miracle" to support the claim that had the intermediary event not occurred, the probability of the final effect would have been different (M. Swain, "A Counterfactual Analysis of Event Causation," *Philosophical Studies*, 34, 1978, pp. 1–19). Swain defines a "pure deletion miracle" as a violation of law that results in the deletion from actuality of "an event that would otherwise have occurred but which leaves the *rest* of the actual world entirely unchanged" (p. 9). Even if worlds in which there are pure deletion miracles are allowed into the comparison, there will be a (non-blocking-initiator-event, non-intermediary-event) world that is closer to the actual world than any (blocking-initiator-event, non-intermediary-event) world. In all of the latter worlds, some event on which i deterministically depends fails to occur due to a pure deletion miracle. But there will be a (non-blocking-initiator-event, non-intermediary-event) world in which both the intermediary event and the blocking-initiator event fail to occur but there is no pure deletion miracle. Since the blocking-initiator event occurs by chance, its failure in that world requires no deletion of any event on which it deterministically depends by way of a pure deletion miracle.

45. C. J. Ducasse, *Truth, Knowledge, and Causation* (London: Routledge, Kegan Paul, 1968), pp. 3–4.

46. Lewis describes this move in his "Postscript," p. 197: "It is a common suggestion to adopt extreme standards of fragility, and thereby make away with redundant causation altogether. Even if a man is shot dead by a firing squad, presumably it would have made *some* minute difference to the time and manner of his death if there had been seven bullets instead of eight . . . so if his death is taken to be very fragile indeed, then it would not have occurred without your act." Lewis goes on to reject this strategy on the grounds that it conflicts with various negative judgments we make about causation. Suppose there was a soldier on the fir-

ing squad who did not fire. In that case, if the death is very fragile, "the gentle soldier caused the death by *not* shooting, quite as much as you caused it by shooting! This is a *reductio*" (p. 198).

47. D. Lewis, "Events," in his *Philosophical Papers*, vol. 2 (Oxford: Oxford University Press, 1986), p. 250.

Chapter 2

1. It is important to distinguish between the following two claims: (1) the concept of causation is unanalyzable, and (2) causation is irreducible. Tooley, for example, denies the former but holds the latter. For Tooley, causation is a theoretical relation between events and hence analyzable by way of the Ramsey/Lewis program for theoretical terms, yet causation is not reducible to noncausal properties and relations. Here I have in mind the irreducibility thesis.

2. The theory of causation's singularist component that will be proposed is analogous only to naive transference theory. Hence, even if there are cases of preemption that naive transference cannot handle, that will not, as such, speak against the account to be offered here.

3. The realist thesis is denied by reductivist singularists, like Ducasse, who affirm that the truth values of singular causal statements are logically determined by the truth values of noncausal statements about particulars alone.

4. For discussions of simultaneous causation, see, for example, R. Taylor, *Action and Purpose* (Englewood Cliffs, N.J.: Prentice-Hall, 1966), pp. 9–39; M. Brand, "Simultaneous Causation," in *Time and Change*, ed. P. van Inwagen (Dordrecht: D. Reidel, 1980), pp. 137–153; and M. Tooley, *Causation: A Realist Approach* (Oxford: Clarendon Press, 1987), pp. 207–212. For discussions of backward causation, see, for example, A. Flew, "Can an Effect Precede Its Cause?" *Proceedings of the Aristotelian Society*, suppl. 38, pp. 45–62; M. Dummett, "Bringing About the Past," *Philosophical Review*, 73, pp. 338–359; D. H. Mellor, *Real Time* (Cambridge: Cambridge University Press, 1981), pp. 160–187; J. L. Mackie, *The Cement of the Universe* (Oxford: Oxford University Press, 1974), chapter 7; and P. Horwich, *Asymmetries in Time* (Cambridge: MIT Press, 1987), chapter 6.

5. For an interesting discussion of spatio-temporal relations and causation see J. Woodward, "Supervenience and Singular Causal Statements," in *Explanation and Its Limits*, ed. D. Knowles (Cambridge: Cambridge University Press, 1990), pp. 217–222.

6. Probabilistic theories of causation would presumably treat this as a case of (probabilistic) overdetermination, assuming that neither c_1 nor c_2 is screened off from e. But this assessment, I would contend, is too hasty.

7. H. Castañeda, "Causes, Causity, and Energy," in *Midwest Studies in Philosophy*, 9, 1984, pp. 17–27.

8. Ibid., p. 22.

9. Ibid., p. 23.

10. Castañeda supports this conception of causation (over Hume's) by way of the following case. Billiard ball A is moving toward a stationary billiard ball, B. At the moment of contact a mechanism under the table stops A and prevents B from moving. At that same time another mechanism releases B and causes B to move in just the way it would have had the collision taken place. Castañeda compares this abnormal case to a normal case of unimpeded collision and asks what is "drained" from the A-B sequence when shifting from the normal to the abnormal. His answer is that there is no transfer of energy from A to B in the abnormal sequence, although Hume's theory may be satisfied. He concludes that it is the transfer of *something* which constitutes causation. Castañeda's argument here parallels my earlier argu-

ment that preemption is more readily assessed by transference theory than by certain other accounts of causation, including the Humean account.

11. For a nice summary of Salmon's view of causal processes see P. Kitcher, "Explanatory Unification and Causal Structure," in *Scientific Explanation*, ed. P. Kitcher and W. Salmon (Minneapolis: University of Minnesota Press, 1989), p. 462.

12. W. Salmon, *Scientific Explanation and the Causal Structure of the World* (Princeton: Princeton University Press, 1984), p. 155. Salmon has recently significantly modified his account of causation. For details see his "Causality without Counterfactuals," *Philosophy of Science*, 61, 1994, pp. 297–312.

13. B. Garrett sketches but rejects this argument in "The Ship of Theseus," presented at the Pacific Meeting of the American Philosophical Association, 1993.

14. H. Noonan, "Reply to Garrett," *Analysis*, 1986, p. 209.

15. See, for example, D. M. Armstrong's claim to this effect in *What Is a Law of Nature?* (Cambridge: Cambridge University Press, 1983), p. 85. This is not to say that laws supervene on temporally global facts.

16. Woodward, "Supervenience and Singular Causal Statements," pp. 211–246; J. Carroll, *Laws of Nature* (Cambridge: Cambridge University Press, 1994); Tooley, *Causation*; Tooley, "Laws and Causal Relations," *Midwest Studies in Philosophy*, 9, 1984, pp. 93–112; Tooley, "Causation: Reductionism versus Realism," *Philosophy and Phenomenological Research*, suppl., 50, 1990, pp. 215–236; Tooley, "The Nature of Causation: A Singularist Account," *Canadian Journal of Philosophy*, suppl., 16, 1990, pp. 271–322.

17. See, for example, Woodward, "Supervenience and Singular Causal Statements," pp. 215–216.

18. This is so because they agree on their laws and their noncausal facts.

19. See, for example, Woodward, "Supervenience and Singular Causal Statements," p. 217, and M. Tooley, "Causation: Reductionism versus Realism," in *Causation: A Realist Approach*, ed. E. Sosa and M. Tooley (Oxford: Oxford University Press, 1993), p. 186.

20. There is a third response, which denies efficacy to both c_1 and c_2. Later I will argue, in effect, that the correct response is this third one.

21. A proponent of supervenience could also invoke the following principle to support the both-are-causes response, the kind of principle a counterfactual probabilistic theorist should hold: if c and e occur, and if the chance of e (at time t immediately after c) is greater than the counterfactual chance of e without c, then c caused e. (Woodward mentions this principle in "Supervenience and Singular Causal Statements," p. 222.) The same principle applied in case 2 entails that e does not occur spontaneously but is caused by c_1. One consequence of the first response to case 2 is that if there is any chance of any event causing e (including c_1), then e couldn't occur spontaneously. Some will find this consequence implausible. But is it? If one takes seriously, for example, the view of probabilistic theory, this consequence may not seem so strange. After all, for the probability theory, causation just is a certain pattern of probabilistic relations plus the actual occurrence of the cause-event and the effect-event.

22. For a similar use made by Lewis of mereological sums in place of disjunctive events, see his *Philosophical Papers*, vol. 2 (Oxford: Oxford University Press, 1986), p. 212.

23. A second indeterminacy response would extend the indeterminacy even to the "sum" event, such that there is no event for which it is determinate that it caused e.

24. A third possible way that a nonsupervenience theorist might reply to a both-are-causes response in case 2 (suggested in e-mail by John Carroll) is to add a causal law that dictates that E is not caused on any occasion by both C_1 and C_2 (and a causal law that says that E occurs only if caused by either C_1 or C_2, to rule out a neither-are-causes response). This re-

quires a certain kind of exclusiveness in the causes of e. This response is viable only if such causal laws are possible. Suppose that the laws require that C_1 and C_2 can only be immediate brute causes of E and that not both can be causes of E. Such laws would in effect dictate that the causal facts in a situation with c_1, c_2, and e do not supervene on the noncausal facts. But whether such causal laws are possible will then itself depend on the issue at stake—does causation supervene on the noncausal? The nonsupervenience theorist will insist that if there is no noncausal basis for the exclusivity clause, there cannot be such causal laws. If supervenience holds, then these kinds of causal laws are not possible, and thus, to stipulate these laws begs the question.

25. A non-c_1 world in which c_2 occurs but does not cause e is closer to w_1 than the non-c_1 world in which c_2 does cause e, other things being equal.

26. Woodward, "Supervenience and Singular Causal Statements," pp. 222–228.

27. Woodward says this is based on the more general idea "that one mark of a causal or nomological relationship is the satisfaction of an invariance condition of some kind: causal or nomological relationships are relationships which will continue to hold in a somewhat stable or systematic way, over a range of possible changes in circumstances" (ibid., p. 226).

28. Invariance is meant to be compatible with the facts that causal tendencies can be interfered with and that what effects result from a cause depends on the background conditions. Invariance demands that there not be too much such context-dependence or an unpredictable context-dependence (ibid., p. 227).

29. Ibid., p. 230.

30. It might be thought that the relevant contexts are "C_2 and E" versus "no-C_2." Invariance would then require that C_1 fail to have a perfect tendency to cause E in the former context, since it has no such tendency in the latter context. I don't think this suggestion fits with the notion of invariance. The invariance in question is relative to "background" conditions, which will include only events which could possibly make a difference to the causation of E. But then E itself cannot be part of such background conditions.

31. Woodward says that invariance does not generally require that all genuine causes produce their effects with fixed probabilities. All that is required is some stable pattern of behavior across different background conditions in the kinds of effects they produce and the way they produce them ("Supervenience and Singular Causal Statements," p. 227).

32. Ibid., p. 224.

33. Ibid.

34. The increase in probability contributed by C_1 should be invariant.

35. What does not remain constant is the frequency with which c_1 causes e on the both-are-causes response. The frequency of causation is not invariant, if we assume that whenever c_1, c_2, and e occur together, both c_1 and c_2 are efficacious. But is this any reason for rejecting the latter claim? The only way I can see to make this out is by *assuming* that a probabilistic supervenience theory is wrong and that a realist theory is correct. Without such an assumption, we get the invariance predicted by the supervenience theorist. A demand for more must be justified. The (probabilistic) supervenience theorist denies that there is an additional invariant "tendency to cause" that must be accounted for. Such a demand is legitimate only if we assume nonsupervenience or causal realism, but the point of an invariance argument was to *show* that supervenience fails and that a realist reading of case 1 is best, not to *assume* either one of those claims.

36. One further possible reason for rejecting indeterminacy should be mentioned. Causation might be thought to be too important ever to be indeterminate and a matter of arbitrary decision. Too much ordinarily rests on getting the causal facts straight to allow for indeterminacy. This objection, although intuitively appealing, rests on a mistake. The various important questions associated with causation may have determinate answers even when

causation goes indeterminate. The concept of personal identity provides an illustrative parallel. Prior to Parfit, it was thought that the importance of personal-identity-related issues required that personal identity never be indeterminate. Parfit showed that these issues can be separated from that of personal identity. Even if personal-identity facts are indeterminate in a situation S, these related questions may still have determinate answers in S. Relations that normally coincide with personal identity (such as memory) may determinately hold even when personal identity does not. And other important issues typically associated with personal identity (such as moral responsibility) can be answered by reference to these relations alone. Causation may work the same way. Even when causal facts go indeterminate, still other relations (such as lawful connection) may remain determinate and provide a basis for settling important issues typically but not necessarily associated with causation.

37. The causal realist will naturally be uncomfortable with the indeterminacy response, but an analogy will help show why the nonrealist ought not to be disturbed. Suppose that a statute entails that Jones and Smith each own exclusively anything within five miles of their houses, but there is a common object P that lies within five miles of each house. Who owns P? We might conclude that the laws don't determine ownership of P. This assessment would not be terribly disturbing, since we know all the relevant facts that can be known. An arbitrary decision assigning ownership might be appropriate. We are not realists about ownership and thus feel no great discomfort in declaring ownership of P indeterminate. We do not think ownership is some further fact over and above these legal and geographical facts. Similarly, we should be disturbed by the indeterminacy response in case 1 only if we are already committed to causal realism. The supervenience theorist who rejects realism is free to champion the indeterminacy response in good conscience.

38. And, in fact, what philosophers such as Tooley, Woodward, and Carroll seem to have in common is nonsupervenience and antireductionism.

39. Tooley, *Causation*, pp. 244–247.

40. In addition, realists assent to an epistemological thesis—that "it is possible in principle to be rationally justified in accepting some causal statement as true" (ibid., p. 247). And if one also holds that causal relations are theoretical relations, then "any knowledge that we have of causal connections must ultimately rest upon knowledge of non-causal states of affairs" (ibid.).

41. Woodward describes his own view as follows: "a singular causal claim, as ordinarily understood, does after all say more than that the events described as cause and effect occur, instantiate a law, and satisfy some additional non-causal description" (Woodward, "Supervenience and Singular Causal Statements," p. 231).

42. Imagine, for example, that there is a world with only one causal law, which says that Es occur only if caused by either C_1 or C_2 and that each of these is causally sufficient for E. On a particular occasion, e occurs and is preceded by an occurrence of c_1, and there are no C_2 events at all in this world. Given this causal law and the fact that both c_1 and e occur with no C_2s, it follows logically that c_1 causes e.

43. Thus, to establish *causal realism* about singular causal statements, we must first establish the nonepistemological side of *causal law realism*, a significantly more difficult task than proving the nonsupervenience of causal laws on the noncausal.

44. Specifically, whatever c_1 and e's causal relationship (or lack thereof), I reject the claim that it can vary across case-3 worlds.

45. Indeed, some philosophers would go so far as to say that these events must be causally connected in all such worlds. This claim could be supported by reference to a principle that has wide support within scientific methodology and philosophy. J. Carroll articulates this principle as follows: if c_1 is lawfully sufficient for e, then either c_1 causes e, e causes c_1, or c_1 and e have a common cause or joint effect (*Laws of Nature*, p. 125). This principle is weaker than

supervenience, since the consequent is a disjunction of causal configurations. Nevertheless, this widely believed principle is inconsistent with strong causal realism. Given this principle, causal facts are indeed fixed under certain noncausal circumstances. For example, a world in which c_1 and e are the only events and c_1 is lawfully sufficient for e will be a world in which c_1 and e are causally connected. Applied to our case, this principle entails that c_1 and e are causally connected in all case-4 worlds.

46. If he holds that facts of persistence are causally analyzable, a causal realist might complain that the input facts in these last two cases are causal. Later, I will indicate my doubts about causal theories of identity in light of Kripke-like arguments (involving perfectly homogeneous spheres) that make it doubtful that persistence is always analyzable causally, especially for property persistence.

Chapter 3

1. J. Kim, "Causation, Nomic Subsumption, and the Concept of Event," *The Journal of Philosophy*, 70, 1973, pp. 217–236.

2. See D. Davidson, "The Logical Form of Action Sentences," in *The Logic of Decision and Action*, ed. N. Rescher (Pittsburgh: University of Pittsburgh Press, 1967), pp. 81–96, and his "Causal Relations," in *Causation and Conditionals*, ed. E. Sosa (Oxford: Oxford University Press, 1975), pp. 82–94.

3. There is, in fact, some debate about whether Davidson actually holds this view. My main concern here, however, is not with interpreting Davidson but with representing a certain widely held view typically associated with Davidson.

4. One should not confuse the in-virtue-of assumption with the view that properties or features are the true causal relata and that the things that have those features are irrelevant appendages. On the in-virtue-of assumption, the real causes are not the features but the things that have those explanatorily relevant features. The features explain the causal efficacy of the things that have them; the features themselves are not efficacious. Indeed, on the in-virtue-of assumption, a feature (read either as exemplification of a universal or a trope) could be a direct cause in its own right only if that feature had higher-order features that explained *its* efficacy.

5. One could of course hold that events are exemplifications of properties by objects without holding that each event is the exemplification of just one property. See A. Rosenberg, "On Kim's Account of Events and Event-Identity," *The Journal of Philosophy*, 71, 1974, pp. 327–336.

6. Kim does indeed seem to hold that the constitutive property of an event is the only property causally relevant to the effects of that event. Kim says that "each event falls under exactly one generic event, and that once a particular cause-effect pair is fixed, the generic events which must satisfy the constant conjunction requirement are uniquely fixed" ("Causation, Nomic Subsumption, and the Concept of Event," p. 226). Only the constitutive property of the event, not properties exemplified by it, is relevant to its causal relations: "the property of dying is a constitutive property of the event [(Socrates, t), dying], i.e., Socrates' dying at t, but not a property exemplified by it. . . . Under our account then, if Socrates' drinking hemlock (at t) was a cause of his dying (at t'), the two generic events, drinking hemlock and dying, must fulfill the requirement of lawful constant conjunction" (p. 226). Kim contrasts his approach to the procedure in which no distinction is made between properties constitutive of events and properties exemplified by them, the view according to which an individual event is thought to fall under an indefinite number of generic events (p. 226). He says that what many have in mind who hold this view of events is "that two causally related events are such that there are at least two lawfully correlated generic events under which they respectively fall" (p. 227). He clearly means to deny that events fall under more than one generic event and that an event's causal relations depend on its merely exemplified properties. Given that Davidson does not

make a distinction between constitutive and exemplified properties of events, it is reasonable for him to assume that an event's causal connections to other events may be determined by any of the indefinite number of properties it exemplifies.

7. I borrow the example of a purple fire produced by potassium salts from J. Woodward's "A Theory of Singular Causal Explanation," *Erkenntnis*, 21, 1984, pp. 231–262.

8. F. Dretske, "Referring to Events," *Midwest Studies in Philosophy*, 2, 1977, pp. 369–378, and T. Honderich, *A Theory of Determinism: The Mind, Neuroscience, and Life-Hopes* (Oxford: Clarendon Press, 1988).

9. G. Bergmann, "Elementarism," *Philosophy and Phenomenological Research*, 18, 1957, pp. 107–114.

10. D. M. Armstrong, *A Theory of Universals: Universals and Scientific Realism*, vol. 2 (Cambridge: Cambridge University Press, 1978), p. 138.

11. It is important to note that I am not supposing that the velocity-property of the ball is a first-order feature that is made determinate only by the contingent possession of certain second-order features. I am not supposing that the ball's having a certain velocity is its having a general property of being in motion and then that general property's having the second-order property of being of a certain magnitude and direction. The second-order properties in this case are not magnitude and direction but rate of change of speed and rate of change in direction. The velocity is determinate independently of these second-order properties, which it contingently has.

12. It is worth noting a general characteristic of the argument thus far. What this argument reveals, if cogent, is an important connection between a logical characteristic of the causal relation and the limits of explanation: causal transitivity dictates that there is no explanation for why causes bring about their (direct) effects. This connection is reminiscent of a connection between another logical characteristic of the causal relation, its asymmetry, and another limit to explanation: the fact that effects cannot explain their causes. The nonexplanatory status of effects with respect to their causes is presumably founded on the asymmetric character of the causal relation.

13. c is causally connected to e just in case c causes e or e causes c.

14. If properties have higher-order features, there is still reason to think that we will reach a point at which the properties themselves do not have properties but "simply are their own unique selves" (Armstrong, *A Theory of Universals*, vol. 2, p. 138). In that case, those "featureless" properties, if efficacious, will be so not in virtue of any properties that they exemplify, since there are none.

15. J. Bennett, *Events and Their Names* (Indianapolis: Hackett Publishing Company, 1988); K. Campbell, *Abstract Particulars* (Blackwell: Oxford, 1990).

16. Honderich, *A Theory of Determinism*, p. 15.

17. Ibid.

18. Ibid.

19. "The fall that stone S underwent at time T is not the fact that S falls at T, but rather one particular instance—namely the by-S-at-T instance—of the property *falling*. If we combine this with the move from substances-at-times to zones, then the event is the instance of the property that occurred at a certain zone" (Bennett, *Events and Their Names*, p. 90).

20. Ibid., p. 16.

21. Specifically, each "S-P-T" event name refers to the instance that zone S has at T of a property P (ibid., p. 128).

22. "Namely the fact that S has P^* at T or, more generally, the fact that P^* is instantiated at a certain zone" (ibid.). The uniqueness is not strictly true unless we work with an event name used on a particular occasion by someone who has sharply made up his mind to what event he is using a given name to refer.

23. Ibid., p. 135.

24. Bennett says that events and their companion facts are not quite identical but are not deeply different metaphysical kinds. He also says that it is not deeply false to say that events are facts of a kind (ibid., p. 129).

25. One of the advantages that Campbell cites for the view of causes-as-tropes is its selectivity: "it is the weakness of this particular cable, not weakness in general . . . which is involved in the collapse of this bridge on this occasion. And it is not the cable's steeliness, rustiness, mass, magnetism, or temperature which is at all involved" (Campbell, "The Metaphysic of Abstract Particulars," *Midwest Studies in Philosophy*, 6, 1981, p. 480).

26. "When you drop it, it is the weight of this particular brick, not bricks or weights in general, which breaks the bone in your particular left big toe" (Campbell, *Abstract Particulars*, p. 113).

27. Campbell, "The Metaphysics of Abstract Particulars," p. 481.

28. Ibid., p. 480.

29. Ibid., p. 480.

30. The case for incoherence may be even stronger for the analogous spatial claim—that exemplifications of at least certain properties, such as red, are necessarily distinct if at different spatial points. If the proponent of universals denies this, then exemplifications at different places at the same time of the same universal will in some cases be identical. But then these exemplifications themselves will be universals (since the same exemplification can be wholly present at different places at the same time)—and the realist's required distinction between a universal and an exemplification of a universal seems to collapse.

31. There are at least three reasons for rejecting universals as causes. The first is simply that causes are dated particulars and universals are not. Second, a universal might exist even if a specific event instantiating that universal did not occur along with its effects. In that case, the universal is clearly not doing the causal work. Third, since the same universal can be the constitutive property of distinct events, then if we have reason to assert that a property P of one event had some effect, then we should have reason to assert that that same property instantiated by some different event is a cause of that same effect (assuming that we have in mind the universal and not a specific exemplification of it). But we would not necessarily assent to the second causal statement even if we assented to the first claim.

Chapter 4

1. The claim that there are tropes is restricted to what philosophers have called genuine properties. Cambridge properties, such as being fifty miles from a red barn, are not genuine properties and hence are certainly not tropes. The task of distinguishing genuine from nongenuine properties is a difficult one, and one that I will not pursue here.

2. N. Wolterstorff, "Qualities," *The Philosophical Review*, 69, 1960, pp. 183–200.

3. J. Levinson, "The Particularisation of Attributes," *Australasian Journal of Philosophy*, 58, 1980, pp. 104–105.

4. Ibid., p. 105.

5. C. Landesman, "Abstract Particulars," *Philosophy and Phenomenological Research*, 33, 1973, pp. 323–337.

6. G. F. Stout, "The Nature of Universals and Propositions," *Studies in Philosophy and Psychology* (London: Macmillan, 1930), p. 391.

7. Landesman, "Abstract Particulars," p. 333.

8. These cases may also be run with "quantity of matter" in place of "object," as may the discussion throughout this chapter.

9. Can relations be tropes? I suppose so. Then one question that should be raised is whether individual relations can persist. The answer seems to be yes. So long as my friend

and I are alive, then I stand in the very same friendship relation over time. If, however, my current friend dies and I become friends with a new person, then the earlier friendship trope is replaced with a new friendship trope.

10. The trope theorist's way of describing the difference between these two cases makes clear that nothing central to this example rests on our supposition that there are electrical-charge creators or electrical-charge destroyers. Outside intervention by machines can be eliminated from the first case without loss. Imagine, for example, that the particle's electrical charge disappears without being caused to do so and is instantly and spontaneously replaced by an electrical charge of the exact same magnitude.

11. I am adopting Kim's identity conditions for events, which he construes as exemplifications, for exemplifications in general, whether or not events are exemplifications.

12. If we think of this relation as "exemplification of U by x" without any reference to time, these two cases will still be treated in the same way.

13. Another reason for rejecting this analysis is that by restricting property persistence to a single object, it rules out property transfers from one object to another. For example, when billiard ball A hits billiard ball B, the energy that characterized A comes to characterize B.

14. The conclusion that trope persistence cannot be analyzed relationally is compatible with the assumption that physical-object identity and personal identity may be so analyzed. However, if objects are understood to be bundles of properties with no other constituents, then a nonrelational view of trope persistence would seem to dictate a nonrelational view of object identity. But if objects are not simply collections of their tropes, then there may be room for a relational account of object identity.

15. One might object to the claim that trope persistence is more basic than causation on the following grounds: judgments about whether one has a case of a persisting trope or of two different, successive tropes are based on the causal information one has—for example, the presence or absence of various creators, destroyers, and so on. Judgments of trope persistence are epistemologically less basic than the relevant causal judgments, and therefore it is a mistake to think that the relevant causal propositions are to be analyzed in terms of propositions about trope persistence. This objection, however, is unconvincing. It is not in all cases true that if x is more basic epistemologically than y, then x is more basic ontologically than y. Consider some examples. (1) The "macro" level may be more basic than the "micro" level epistemologically, but not ontologically. (2) Similarly, if physicalism is true, then physical states are more basic than mental states ontologically, but the latter is more basic epistemologically. (3) Or if one is a Platonist, then instances of properties get analyzed in terms of the Forms, but the former might turn out to be epistemologically more basic than the latter.

16. Even though one's judgments about these different cases are based on descriptions of various machines and their causal relations, it does not follow that there is a possible causal account that will capture the notion of qualitative persistence. Indeed, our examination of various causal accounts makes that possibility dubious.

17. There are other possible cases that are not consistent with the canceling-out hypothesis. Suppose, for example, that the destroyer machine acts by absorbing charge and the creator machine acts by transferring charge. These machines are set to operate simultaneously, with the result that at every point the particle possesses a charge of just the minimum magnitude. In the process, a charge is absorbed by the first machine, and a charge is transferred by the second machine. The proponent of a canceling-out hypothesis might suggest that the transfer of charge goes directly from the first machine to the second. At no point is there a transfer to or from the particle, and hence there is no change internal to the particle. But there may be physical reasons for excluding this interpretation: the distance between the machines may exclude any particle-independent machine-to-machine transfer, given the laws of nature. The laws and physical setup dictate a transfer from the first

machine to the particle, which at the same time transfers its original charge to the second machine. The particle undergoes nonsalient qualitative change: its original charge is replaced by a new charge of the same magnitude.

18. If objects are just bundles of properties, then immaculate object replacement is just multiple immaculate property replacement.

19. It should be noted that the argument of this chapter is independent of the debate over nominalism. Nominalists deny the existence of universals. The argument of this chapter, if successful, favors tropes but does not, as it stands, disfavor universals. No position is taken on that question. As far as this argument goes, there may exist universals alongside tropes. However, even if there are universals and exemplifications of universals, neither is capable of accounting for property persistence.

20. D. M. Armstrong, "Identity through Time," in *Time and Cause: Essays Presented to Richard Taylor*, ed. P. van Inwagen (Dordrecht: Reidel, 1980), p. 76. See also S. Kripke, "Time and Identity," unpublished lectures, for a similar example.

21. Or, more precisely, any property type that is instantiated in one quadrant will be instantiated in all other quadrants in the same relative location.

22. It is not clear that this objection will hold on the view that laws are relations between universals. However, even if laws are such relations, these laws may not always specify identity relations. See D. M. Armstrong, *What Is a Law of Nature?* (Cambridge: Cambridge University Press, 1983), p. 155, for a discussion of this possibility. If some laws are identity-neutral, even if all laws are relations among universals, consulting the laws will not always determine the identity of tropes.

23. M. Tooley, in his *Causation: A Realist Approach* (Oxford: Oxford University Press, 1987), pp. 194–197, presents the following argument, which *can* be taken as an argument against the causal theory of identity if one holds a neo-Humean theory of causation. If causal relations between states of affairs are logically supervenient on causal laws together with noncausal facts, and if rotationally symmetrical universes are logically possible, then it is impossible to give a causal account of identity over time. Tooley seems to affirm the possibility of a causal theory and the possibility of a rotationally symmetrical universe. But this argument will run in the other direction if one has a neo-Humean theory of causation.

24. This argument is adapted from ibid., p. 199.

25. See, for example, D. Lewis, "Causation," in *Philosophical Papers*, vol. 2 (Oxford: Oxford University Press, 1986), pp. 159–213.

26. A probabilistic causal theory of identity will also have difficulties handling cases involving preemption. A trope stage c_1 at t_1 preempts another trope stage c_2 at t_1, and c_1 probabilistically causes a trope stage c_3 at t_2. Suppose that the *maximum* probability of a trope stage of that type appearing in the actual world at that location at t_2, given any set of possible antecedents, is M, where M is less than 1. Suppose that the probability of that later trope stage existing at t_2 given c_1 at t_1 and the pre-t_1 c_2 is equal to the probability of that later trope occurring given c_2 before t_1—that is, M. Under these conditions, the probabilistic theory directs us to say that the existence of the c_2 trope stage before t_1 screens off c_1 at t_1 from c_3 and, hence, that c_1 does not cause c_3. This result is inconsistent with our assumption that c_1 causes c_3, and given the causal theory of identity, it is also inconsistent with our assumption that c_1 and c_3 are the same trope. This objection trades on the fact that the probabilistic theory will not always generate the correct causal story, and this deficiency will lead to incorrect assessments of the facts of identity when combined with a causal theory of identity.

27. See D. Robinson's "Re-Identifying Matter," *The Philosophical Review*, 91, 1982, p. 336, and his "Matter, Motion, and Humean Supervenience," *Australasian Journal of Philosophy*, 67, 1989, pp. 404–408.

28. Robinson, "Matter, Motion, and Humean Supervenience," p. 407.

29. Ibid.
30. Ibid.
31. M. Tooley, "In Defense of the Existence of States of Motion," *Philosophical Topics*, 16, 1988, pp. 225–254.
32. Ibid., p. 244.
33. Our reluctance to attribute velocity in such cases derives, says Tooley, "from the feeling that the velocity of an object at a time should be *causally* relevant to its positions at later times. For in the world in question, it is only the position of an object at a time which is relevant to its likely positions at later times" (ibid.).

Chapter 5

1. J. L. Mackie, *The Cement of the Universe* (Oxford: Oxford University Press, 1974), chapter 8.
2. Ibid., p. 217.
3. Ibid., p. 228.
4. Ibid., pp. 228–229.
5. Ibid., p. 221.
6. Ibid.
7. Ibid., p. 221–222.
8. Ibid., p. 222.
9. Ibid., p. 224.
10. Ibid., p. 229.
11. Mackie says that "the most we can expect is that there should be more persistence mixed with the differences." And in the case of interaction, "it seems inescapable that there should be a law of working which is not just the persistence of anything" (ibid., p. 222).
12. Ibid., p. 224.
13. K. Campbell, *Abstract Particulars* (Oxford: Basil Blackwell, 1990), p. 86.
14. D. M. Armstrong, *A Theory of Universals*, vol. 2 (Cambridge: Cambridge University Press, 1978).
15. Ibid., p. 122.
16. See D. M. Armstrong, *Universals: An Opinionated Introduction* (Boulder: Westview Press, 1989), p. 101.
17. The possibility of trope fission can also be argued for as follows. Consider again two cases: (case 5) the destroyer machine instantly eliminates a particle, and the creator machine instantly creates two particles, such that each particle has a charge and the total magnitude of their charges is equal to the charge of the original particle; and (case 6) the particle on its own divides into two particles, each with a charge, such that the total charge of the two particles equals the magnitude of the original charge. The best account of the difference (and there is a difference) between these cases is this: the particle's charge in case 6 partially persists in the charges of each of the fissioned particles, but no such persistence is found in case 5. There is partial trope overlap in case 6, but not in case 5.
18. As one might expect, the possibility of trope fusion is a prerequisite for accounting for other kinds of qualitative persistence. We must be able to account for the difference between (case 7) two particles, at the moment of collision, being eliminated by a destroyer machine and replaced by a single particle of a charge equal to the total magnitude of charges of the two particles and (case 8) two particles colliding and forming a new particle, the total charge of which equals the magnitude of the two colliding particles. The charge tropes in case 8 partially persist and come to form constituents of the complex charge of the fused particle, but in case 7, there is no persistence, or partial identity, of the charges over time.

19. W. Salmon, *Scientific Explanation and the Causal Structure of the World* (Princeton: Princeton University Press, 1984), p. 144.

20. Although in this example the process of partial destruction takes place at one moment, this type of causal process is compatible with the continuous "fading" of the trope in question.

21. Suppose, for example, that the laws entail that (1) A-type tropes are nomologically sufficient for the prior existence of either a trope of type P or a trope of type R, and (2) B-type tropes are nomologically sufficient for the earlier existence of either a trope of type Q or a trope of type R. The sum of these consequences is the prior existence *either* of one trope of type P and one of type Q, *or* one trope of type P and one of type R, *or* one trope of type Q and one of type R, *or* a trope of type R alone. But also suppose the laws entail that a nomological consequence of the existence of both A- and B-type tropes is the existence of a trope of type R. In this case, the nomological consequences of the existence of tropes of type A and of type B are different from the sum of the relevant nomological consequences.

22. This reconstruction, however, might be objected to. It might be suggested that charge characteristics are somehow logically tied to that which they characterize. Hence, charge tropes cannot be transferred from one atom to another. This objection, however, is readily disabled. We can show that charge tropes can be transferred by an appeal to a pair of cases between which there is some difference in qualitative persistence that must be accounted for. Consider a pair of cases. In the first, at the moment of impact between two atoms, one of which has a charge, a destroyer machine destroys the charge of the first atom and destroys the second atom. A creator machine replaces the second atom with another, qualitatively indistinguishable atom that has a charge independently of the first atom. In the second case, a charged atom collides with a second atom, and the second acquires a charge. There is a difference between these two cases as to the fate of the charge characteristic of the first atom. In the first case, that charge trope disappears from the scene. In the second, that is not so. The best account for this difference is to say that a charge trope is transferred in case 2 but not in case 1.

23. Some might argue that properties cannot be transferred from one object to another. This is clearly false in the case of charge. But it is also false in other cases. One object may gain a property of another object if part of that object is transferred to the first object. The only case that raises problems is perhaps the transference from one object to another of a property that is not a material quantity. Although I am not convinced that this is impossible, the issue is not particularly important for the theory of causation developed here.

24. Consider a loose analogy. In the form of painting known as pointillism, the results of painting are determined by the combinations of points of color. Different combinations constitute different paintings. Here effects are constituted by different combinations of tropes, and the causal laws are analogous to the principles of painting adopted by the painter, which dictate certain courses of development and rule out others. Statistical causal laws establish probabilistic constraints.

25. Armstrong, *A Theory of Universals*, p. 126.

26. Our picture of a causal process should thus be broadened to include "supervenient causal processes." A trope at one time is connected by a causal process to a trope at another time if these tropes supervene on tropes that are identical or partially identical.

27. P. W. Atkins and J. A. Beran, *General Chemistry*, 2nd ed. (New York: Scientific American Books, 1992), p. 302.

28. Ibid., p. 294.

29. Ibid., p. 303.

30. Another example of trope fission consists in the explosion of a liquid, nitroglycerin, which generates a number of gases. We can trace back from the chemical characteristics of

these resultant gases to the chemical characteristics of the liquid. The chemical formula for this reaction tells us that the causal process involves trope fission:

$$4C_3H(NO_3)_3 \rightarrow 6N_2 + O_2 + 12CO_2 + 10H_2O$$

Although chemical formulas don't tell us the route from reactants to products, they do tell us the beginning and end points. This is enough to determine whether causal processes involved fission, fusion, or both. In the present case, the complex trope that characterizes the reactant fissions. The result is that the part-tropes of the reactant trope now stand alone outside that structural trope. This explosion generates various gases, and the characteristics of these resultant gases are partially identical to the characteristics of the reactant liquid.

31. J. Kim, "Postscripts on Mental Causation," in his *Supervenience and Mind: Selected Philosophical Essays* (Cambridge: Cambridge University Press, 1993), p. 358. My reliance on "supervenience" here marks only one possible way of formulating this third clause, which is best thought of as a place-holder for a fuller discussion of mental and macrolevel causation.

32. D. Lewis, "Postscript," in his *Philosophical Papers*, vol. 2 (New York: Oxford University Press, 1986), p. 205.

33. Ibid.

34. There may be facts that are not local or intrinsic to the process P connecting c and e that are relevant to the laws under which c-e is subsumed. If these facts had been different, then c and e might not have been causally connected.

35. This principle is compatible with a realist view, since one can take P as referring to the causal relation itself.

36. There is no possible world in which the laws are the same and the intrinsic relation between c and e is the same but c does not cause e.

37. Lewis's extended analysis, recall, takes care of late preemption by extending causal status to those processes that fail the dependence condition if there are intrinsically indistinguishable processes that in different surroundings do display this dependence. However, he still seems to hold that in cases in which counterfactual dependence is satisfied, the process in question is causal in virtue of this dependence. But that is just wrong. In fact, what the extended analysis requires us to say is that it is not counterfactual dependence that is important to causation but whatever in the intrinsic process remains constant as we shift across worlds and lose dependence. The extended analysis is a rejection of the claim that counterfactual dependence is what causation is all about. At best, counterfactual dependence is ordinarily associated with causation and runs hand-in-hand with what is constitutive of the causal relation. But Lewis does not tell us what that is. Whatever it is has this modal property, which is the basis of the intrinsicness principle.

38. One possible reply to this argument is to modify the probabilistic analysis by generating an analogue to Lewis's extended analysis. We could construct the account such that a sufficient condition for causation is that the process that connects c and e is intrinsically indistinguishable from a process that in another setting does satisfy this probabilistic relation. But although this strategy will perhaps provide a basis for picking out the causal connections in the world, it fails to tell us anything about the nature of causation. This modified analysis confirms that the probabilistic relation lacks the requisite modal property, so we can infer that this relation does not constitute the causal relation.

39. If persistence theory has this smaller scope (that is, if it applies only to causal processes), then we must contend with certain consequences. How would this reinterpretation affect our discussion of preemption? What about cases of preemption that involve no persisting tropes? In such cases we cannot appeal to persistence theory to demonstrate that c_1 rather than c_2 is the cause of e. In fact, even if we admit the possibility of causation without

trope persistence, it by no means follows that we have to admit that this form of preemption is possible. Indeed, this description we just gave presumes that there is some difference in the causal status of c_1 and c_2 with respect to e. It is presumed that c_1 is efficacious but c_2 is not. But this may not be right. There could be a difference in causal status between c_1 and c_2 if causal nonreductionism is true, but we have already rejected nonreductionism. I think the best thing to say about these cases is that there is no causal fact of the matter. In cases in which there are no relevant facts of identity and there is more than one competitor for the role of cause, we should say that it is neither true nor false that c_1 (or c_2) causes e.

40. One consequence of taking persistence theory to have a more limited scope is that we would not have identified a singularist component that all causal sequences realize. Not all causally connected events will be connected by a causal process. This consequence would be problematic only if occurrent preemption were possible for causal sequences that don't embody persisting tropes. But since I don't think occurrent preemption is possible in such cases, there is less pressure to generate a singularist component of this type.

41. We can now return to case 1 of chapter 2, a case that was proposed to support the realist's view. Recall that in case 1 there are probabilistic laws linking C_1 with E and C_2 with E, and on a particular occasion, tokens of C_1 and C_2 and E all occur, and the probability of e is higher than it would be in an otherwise similar situation in which c_1 is absent or in which c_2 is absent. I argued in chapter 2 that the realist failed to give convincing arguments against a supervenience theorist who claims either that both c_1 and c_2 are causes of e in all case-1 worlds or that the causal facts are indeterminate in all such worlds. My own view of this case, however, which also confounds the realist, is that either there are no facts of qualitative persistence and thus no causal relation between either c_1 or c_2 and e, or there are facts of qualitative persistence that establish a single causal story. In either case, there is no more than one case-1 world.

42. Consider that if the latter is not possible, then in cases of jumpy objects we would be forced to say that after the jump we had the same object but that the object did not share any of its former properties. And that is difficult to accept if we accept the possibility of jumpy objects.

43. See, for example, Mackie's discussion in "The Direction of Causation," chapter 7 in *The Cement of the Universe*.

44. This case is modeled on a case discussed by Salmon involving billiard balls, *Scientific Explanation and the Causal Structure of the World*, pp. 168–169.

Chapter 6

1. See T. Beauchamp and A. Rosenberg, *Hume and the Problem of Causation* (New York: Oxford University Press, 1981), chapter 4, for a discussion of whether Hume ever held such a view.

2. J. L. Mackie, *The Cement of the Universe* (Oxford: Oxford University Press, 1974), chapter 2; C. J. Ducasse, *Truth, Knowledge, and Causation* (London: Routledge, Kegan Paul, 1968); and J. Anderson, "The Problem of Causality," *Australasian Journal of Psychology and Philosophy*, 16, 1938, reprinted in his *Studies in Empirical Philosophy* (Sydney: Angus & Robertson, 1962).

3. The circumstantial aspect of the causal relation does not entail that an event in the same type of circumstances always gives rise to a particular type of effect. Ducasse, for example, adopts the circumstantial account without committing himself to a Humean regularity theory construed in this sense.

4. The concept of a "condition of a causal connection" must be distinguished from related notions. First, it must be noted that some philosophers use the phrase "in the circum-

stances" to include any events or states that may be co-present on the occasion of a particular causal sequence. This notion may have its uses in certain contexts, but I have in mind a more restricted notion, requiring that the circumstances under discussion have some causal relevance to the particular causal relation. Second, the term "condition" is not employed here in order to draw a contrast between "the cause" and "causal conditions." As to the latter distinction, the definition to be offered of "condition of the causal connection" will have no direct relevance. Third, the "condition" of the expression "condition of the causal connection" will be taken to pick out a particular, occurrent event or state rather than a generic event or an "event under a description."

5. In discussing counterfactual dependence between events, this will be elliptical for counterfactual dependence between sentences asserting the existence or occurrence of the events in question. Thus, "e is counterfactually dependent on c" is short for "if c had not occurred, then e would not have occurred." In turn, statements of the form "the causal connection between c and e is counterfactually dependent on f" will be elliptical for "if f had not occurred, then c and e would not have been causally connected."

6. This definition of a condition of a causal connection is meant to emphasize that without the condition (or any occurrent "substitutes"), the particular causal connection between c and e that is at issue would fail to be realized. However, this definition does not entail that either c or e would have failed to occur if it had not occurred. Both c and e might occur but be causally unconnected, with different causal antecedents or consequences. That is not to say, however, that both c and e must occur if f fails to occur. Clearly, the relevant causal connection between c and e might fail to be realized because either c or e, or both, fail to occur.

7. This redundancy restriction blocks the inclusion of causally irrelevant occurrent events in the set.

8. The introduction of counterfactuals into an account of causation is somewhat troubling. Counterfactuals are notoriously difficult to analyze, and thus, if we could get along without them, that would be preferred. Second best would be some well-grounded theory of counterfactuals. I will not attempt to provide such a theory, and unfortunately, I can find no obvious way to dispense with counterfactuals altogether. However, I do want to make clear one constraint that this account of causal asymmetry sets on an account of these counterfactuals. Since counterfactuals play a part within the account of causal asymmetry, the truth conditions for the relevant counterfactuals cannot include facts about causal direction. Any such reference to facts about causal asymmetry would lead to circularity. There are, of course, accounts of counterfactuals available that avoid such facts, like Lewis's possible world account, but it is not clear that Lewis's account is adequate. Hence, this ends up being a serious constraint that may or may not be satisfiable. Nevertheless, I also want to make clear a burden that I do not face: a causation-free account of counterfactuals. It is not required, for the purposes of the theory of causation of this study, that an account of counterfactuals be completely causation-free. For example, a theory of counterfactuals that appeals to facts about causal connection is perfectly compatible with the theory of this study. Since I make no use of counterfactuals in my analysis of causal connection, references to causal connection by themselves in an account of counterfactuals generate no circularity in this context.

9. One might object to this clause as follows. Suppose that f is causally sufficient for a later event g, such that if g had not occurred, f would not have occurred. But g is not a condition of the causal connection between c and e, and this clause might be thought to require that g be such a condition. In fact, all that this clause requires is that g be a member of this set, even a redundant member (and hence not a genuine condition of the causal connection), which in fact it will be. The causal connection of c and e is dependent on g in the absence of the other members of this set, but g is a redundant member of the set.

10. g is an indirect condition of a causal connection between c and e if and only if g is a direct condition of a causal connection between some direct condition f, of a causal connection between c and e, and either c or e. An indirect condition may fail to be a direct condition of that which it indirectly conditions. If g, the indirect condition, had not occurred, f may still have occurred, and thus c and e would have been causally connected.

11. Whether or not the property of the oxygen's being present would properly be counted as "the" cause of the fire is not at issue, but its causal relevance cannot legitimately be denied.

12. Suppose that g is an indirect condition of the causal pair c and e. Now either g is a direct condition of the causal pair c and some direct condition f (of the causal connection between c and e), or else g is a direct condition of the causal connection between f and e. We assume that c is the cause in the causal pair c and e. If g is a direct condition of the causal pair f and c, then g will count as a cause of e, since if f is causally connected to c and f is a direct condition of the causal connection between c and e (where c causes e), then f is a cause of c, and thus g, being a direct condition of that causal connection, will count as a cause of c (and by transitivity of e). On the other hand, if g is a direct condition of the causal connection between f and e, where f is a direct condition of the causal connection between c and e, then g will count as a cause of e, since e is the effect-event of the causal pair f and e. In either case, g counts as a cause of the effect-event of the pair c and e, given the transitivity of "causes" and the fact that a direct condition counts as a cause of the effect-event of the causal pair it conditions.

13. This assumption that all effects have more than one cause will be abandoned in my discussion of cases with single causes.

14. Similar accounts can be found in D. Sanford, "The Direction of Causation and the Direction of Conditionship," *Journal of Philosophy*, 73, 1976, pp. 193–207, and his "Causal Dependence and Multiplicity," *Philosophy*, 60, 1985, pp. 215–230; and also D. Hausman, "Causal Priority," *Noûs*, 18, 1984, pp. 261–279.

15. Tooley proposes counterexamples to any reductionist account of causal direction. One runs as follows. Consider a world with time-symmetric laws. Suppose that, together, c and e' are nomologically sufficient for some later event e. Call that situation A. Since the laws are time-symmetric, we can suppose that in this world there are inverted versions of these events—call them $c_\#$, $e'_\#$, and $e_\#$—such that $c_\#$ and $e'_\#$ are nomologically sufficient for an earlier event $e_\#$. Call that situation $A_\#$. The difficulty for a reductionist account, says Tooley, is that whatever conditions are true of c, e', and e will hold of $c_\#$, $e'_\#$, and $e_\#$. If those conditions dictate that c is causally prior to e, they will wrongly dictate that $c_\#$ is causally prior to $e_\#$ ("Causation: Reductionism versus Realism," *Philosophy and Phenomenological Research*, suppl., 50, 1990, p. 181). I believe that clause 2 of the definition of a condition of a causal connnection will help with this case. With respect to situation $A_\#$, there will be an event $g_\#$ on which $e'_\#$ depends, such that if $g_\#$ had not been realized, then in these *new* circumstances, $c_\#$ is not sufficient for $e'_\#$. In those new circumstances, $e'_\#$ is not necessary for $c_\#$. In the absence of $g_\#$, $c_\#$ fails to be counterfactually dependent on $e'_\#$. Thus $g_\#$ is not a member of the set $(e'_\#, d_1, d_2, \ldots, d_n)$, since the causal connection between $e_\#$ and $c_\#$ is not counterfactually dependent on $e'_\#$ in the absence of $g_\#$ and the other members of that set. Thus, $e'_\#$ is not a conditioning factor. Situation A is different. There will be no event g on which e' depends such that g is not a member (either redundant or nonredundant) of the set $(e', d_1, d_2, \ldots, d_n)$. For any g on which e' depends, the causal connection between e and c is still counterfactually dependent on e' in the absence of g (and the other members of that set).

16. One might object at this point that consistent application of clause A will generate an infinite regress. Specifically, if c causes e and f is a condition of that causal relation, then since f is a cause of e, there must be some additional condition of f's relation to e under clause A, and so on indefinitely. But this is not a serious difficulty, since in this case there is no rea-

son to rule out c as a condition of the causal connection of f to e. In fact, this is normally the case. Generally, there will be a series of causal antecedents that mutually condition each other's causal connection to their effects.

17. The account of causal priority as represented is subject to a counterexample along the following lines. Suppose that the velocity of a billiard ball causes the velocity of a second ball. Also suppose that the velocity of the first ball has some higher-order feature—its rate of change, for example—that is quite irrelevant to this causal relation and that this rate of change is caused by some feature of the table, which is also irrelevant to any characteristic of the second ball. Suppose that had the table not had that feature, the first ball's velocity would have had a different rate of change. If the actual rate of change is an essential feature of the velocity of the first ball, then it follows that had the table lacked that particular feature, the velocity of the first ball would not have been realized. A different property, a velocity with a different rate of change, would have been realized in its place. Given the assumption that the actual rate of change is essential to the velocity, it follows then that this particular characteristic of the table is a condition of the causal connection of the velocities of the first and second balls. This is so because had that feature not been realized, the two velocities would not have been causally connected, simply because the first ball's actual velocity would not have been realized. However, we have assumed that whatever is a condition of a causal connection is a cause of the effect in the causal pair. That means we are forced to say this feature of the table is a cause of the velocity of the second ball, when in fact that velocity in no way depends on this feature of the table. We cannot, however, abandon this assumption of the efficacy of conditions of causal connections. This case is based in part on discussions in J. Lee's "Causal Connection, Causal Asymmetry, and the Counterfactual Analysis of Causation," *Synthese*, 67, 1986, pp. 213–223.

My proposal for resolving this problem is to append a further condition to the analysis:

> f is a direct condition of the causal connection of c and e only if f is not causally connected to any feature of c or e.

This additional clause will exclude the feature of the table from qualifying as a condition of the causal connection between the two velocities: since we have assumed that this feature of the table is causally connected to a higher-order feature of the velocity of the first ball, its rate of change, it is disqualified.

18. See G. Bassham, "Ehring's Theory of Causal Asymmetry," *Analysis*, 46, 1986, p. 31.

19. An assortment of problem cases to other accounts are unpersuasive against this theory. Counterexamples to "manipulability theory" involving nonmanipulable events do not constitute a stumbling block, since the theory makes no assumptions as to the manipulability of the conditions of the causal connection. In the case of regularity theory we may consider a widely discussed example. Suppose that there is a pendulum in motion and that the length of the pendulum causes the pendulum to have a certain period. Regularity theory is faced with the difficulty of excluding a causal account of length in terms of the period, given the laws covering the motion of pendulums. On my theory we need only find one condition of the causal connection between the length and the period—for example, the gravitational field—that is causally connected to the period but not to the length of the pendulum. Counterfactual theories of causal asymmetry run up against counterexamples involving preemption. Such cases do not present a problem for the theory under discussion. Suppose that c is a preempting cause of e, where d would have caused e if c had not. Since d in the actual circumstances is not causally connected to e, there are no complicating factors for this account, which emphasizes *actual* causal connections.

Various accounts of causal priority either implicitly or explicitly rely on an assumption that all causes in turn have causes, and thus they are vulnerable to examples in which the cause in the causal pair is uncaused (E. Brown, "The Direction of Causation," *Mind*, 88, 1979, pp. 334–350). Clearly, clause A may apply even where *c* is itself uncaused.

20. Tooley, "Causation: Reductionism versus Realism," p. 180.

21. Bassham, "Ehring's Theory of Causal Asymmetry," p. 31.

22. The logical possibility of mutual causation is compatible with the rejection of the logical possibility of causal processes that run in both directions. In the case of mutual causation, neither event is causally prior to the other.

Bibliography

Anderson, John, "The Problem of Causality," in his *Studies in Empirical Philosophy* (Sydney: Angus & Robertson, 1962), pp. 126–136. Originally published in *Australasian Journal of Psychology and Philosophy*, 16, 1938.

Anscombe, Gertrude E. M., "Causality and Determinism," in *Causation*, ed. Ernest Sosa and Michael Tooley (Oxford: Oxford University Press, 1993), pp. 88–104.

Armstrong, David M., "Identity through Time," in *Time and Cause: Essays Presented to Richard Taylor*, ed. Peter van Inwagen (Dordrecht: D. Reidel, 1980), pp. 67–80.

———, *Nominalism and Realism: Universals and Scientific Realism*, vol. 1 (Cambridge: Cambridge University Press, 1978).

———, *A Theory of Universals: Universals and Scientific Realism*, vol. 2 (Cambridge: Cambridge University Press, 1978).

———, *Universals: An Opinionated Introduction* (Boulder: Westview Press, 1989).

———, *What Is a Law of Nature?* (Cambridge: Cambridge University Press, 1983).

Aronson, Jerrold, "On the Grammar of 'Cause'," *Synthese*, 22, 1971, pp. 414–430.

Atkins, Peter W., and Jo A. Beran, *General Chemistry*, 2nd ed. (New York: Scientific American Books, 1992).

Bassham, Gregory, "Ehring's Theory of Causal Asymmetry," *Analysis*, 46, 1986, pp. 29–32.

Beauchamp, Tom, and Alexander Rosenberg, *Hume and the Problem of Causation* (New York: Oxford University Press, 1981).

Bennett, Jonathan, *Events and Their Names* (Indianapolis: Hackett Publishing Company, 1988).

Bergmann, Gustav, "Elementarism," *Philosophy and Phenomenological Research*, 18, 1957, pp. 107–114.

Berofsky, Bernard, "Causality and General Laws," in *Philosophical Problems of Causation*, ed. Tom Beauchamp (Encino: Dickenson Publishing Company, 1974), pp. 153–159.

Brand, Myles, *The Nature of Causation* (Urbana: University of Illinois Press, 1976).

———, "Simultaneous Causation," in *Time and Cause: Essays Presented to Richard Taylor*, ed. Peter van Inwagen (Dordrecht: D. Reidel, 1980), pp. 137–153.

Brown, Erik, "The Direction of Causation," *Mind*, 88, 1979, pp. 334–350.

Bunzl, Martin, "Causal Preemption and Counterfactuals," *Philosophical Studies*, 37, 1980, pp. 115–124.

Campbell, Keith, *Abstract Particulars* (Oxford: Blackwell, 1990).

———, "The Metaphysic of Abstract Particulars," *Midwest Studies in Philosophy*, 6, 1981, pp. 477–488.

Carroll, John, *Laws of Nature* (Cambridge: Cambridge University Press, 1994).

Castañeda, Hector-Neri, "Causes, Causity, and Energy," in *Midwest Studies in Philosophy*, 9, 1984, pp. 17–27.
Chisholm, Roderick M., "Freedom and Action," in *Freedom and Determination*, ed. Keith Lehrer (New York: Random House, 1966), pp. 11–44.
Davidson, Donald, "Causal Relations," in *Causation and Conditionals*, ed. Ernest Sosa (Oxford: Oxford University Press, 1975), pp. 82–94.
———, "The Logical Form of Action Sentences," in *The Logic of Decision and Action*, ed. Nicholas Rescher (Pittsburgh: University of Pittsburgh Press, 1967), pp. 81–96.
Dretske, Fred, "Referring to Events," *Midwest Studies in Philosophy*, 2, 1977, pp. 369–378.
Dretske, Fred, and Aaron Snyder, "Causal Irregularity," *Philosophy of Science*, 39, 1972, pp. 69–71.
Ducasse, Curt J., *Truth, Knowledge, and Causation* (London: Routledge, Kegan Paul, 1968).
Dummett, Michael, "Bringing About the Past," *Philosophical Review*, 73, pp. 338–359.
Eells, Ellery, *Probabilistic Causality* (Cambridge: Cambridge University Press, 1991).
Ehring, Douglas, "Causal Asymmetry," *The Journal of Philosophy*, 79, 1982, pp. 761–774.
———, "Causal Asymmetry and Causal Relata," *Synthese*, 76, 1988, pp. 371–375.
———, "Causal Relata," *Synthese*, 73, 1987, pp. 319–328.
———, "Closed Causal Loops, Single Causes, and Asymmetry," *Analysis*, 46, 1986, pp. 33–35.
———, "Motion, Causation, and the Causal Theory of Identity," *Australasian Journal of Philosophy*, 69, 1991, pp. 180–194.
———, "The 'only t_1 through t_2' Principle," *Analysis*, 49, 1989, pp. 176–177.
———, "Preemption, Direct Causation, and Identity," *Synthese*, 85, 1990, pp. 55–70.
———, "Preemption and Eells on Token Causation," *Philosophical Studies*, 74, 1994, pp. 39–50.
———, "Preemption and Probabilistic Counterfactual Theory," *Philosophical Studies*, 56, 1989, pp. 307–313.
———, "Probabilistic Causality and Preemption," *British Journal for the Philosophy of Science*, 35, 1984, pp. 55–57.
———, "The Transference Theory of Causation," *Synthese*, 67, 1986, pp. 249–258.
Flew, Anthony, "Can an Effect Precede Its Cause?" *Proceedings of the Aristotelian Society*, suppl., 28, 1954, pp. 45–62.
Garrett, Brian, "The Ship of Theseus," presented at the Pacific Meeting of the American Philosophical Association, 1993.
Gasking, Douglas, "Causation and Recipes," in *Philosophical Problems of Causation*, ed. Tom Beauchamp (Encino: Dickenson Publishing Company, 1974), pp. 126–136.
Good, I. J., "A Causal Calculus I-II," *British Journal for the Philosophy of Science*, 11, 1961, pp. 305–318, and 12, 1962, pp. 43–51.
———, *Good Thinking* (Minneapolis: University of Minnesota Press, 1983).
Hausman, Daniel, "Causal Priority," *Noûs*, 18, 1984, pp. 261–279.
Hempel, Carl G., *Aspects of Scientific Explanation* (New York: Free Press, 1965).
Honderich, Ted, *A Theory of Determinism: The Mind, Neuroscience, and Life-Hopes* (Oxford: Clarendon Press, 1988).
Horwich, Paul, *Asymmetries in Time* (Cambridge: MIT Press, 1987).
Hume, David, *An Abstract of a Treatise of Human Nature*, ed. John M. Keynes and Piero Sraffa (Cambridge: Cambridge University Press, 1938).
———, *Enquiries Concerning the Human Understanding and Concerning the Principles of Morals*, 2nd ed., ed. L. A. Selby-Bigge (Oxford: Oxford University Press, 1902).
———, *A Treatise of Human Nature*, ed. L. A. Selby-Bigge (Oxford: Oxford University Press, 1959).
Kim, Jaegwon, "Causation, Nomic Subsumption, and the Concept of Event," *The Journal of Philosophy*," 70, 1973, pp. 217–236.

———, "Causes and Counterfactuals," in *Causation*, ed. Ernest Sosa and Michael Tooley (Oxford: Oxford University Press, 1993), pp. 205–207.
———, Review of von Wright's *Explanation and Understanding*, *The Philosophical Review*, 82, 1973, pp. 380–388.
———, *Supervenience and Mind: Selected Philosophical Essays* (Cambridge: Cambridge University Press, 1993).
Kitcher, Philip, "Explanatory Unification and Causal Structure," in *Scientific Explanation*, ed. Philip Kitcher and Wesley Salmon (Minneapolis: University of Minnesota Press, 1989), pp. 410–505.
Kripke, Saul, "Time and Identity," unpublished lectures.
Landesman, Charles, "Abstract Particulars," *Philosophy and Phenomenological Research*, 33, 1973, pp. 323–337.
Lee, Jig-Chuen, "Causal Connection, Causal Asymmetry, and the Counterfactual Analysis of Causation," *Synthese*, 67, 1986, pp. 213–223.
Levinson, Jerrold, "The Particularisation of Attributes," *Australasian Journal of Philosophy*, 58, 1980, pp. 102–115.
Lewis, David, *Philosophical Papers*, vol. 2 (New York: Oxford University Press, 1986).
Mackie, John L., *The Cement of the Universe* (Oxford: Oxford University Press, 1974).
Mellor, D. Hugh, *Real Time* (Cambridge: Cambridge University Press, 1981).
Noonan, Harold, "Reply to Garrett," *Analysis*, 1986, pp. 205–211.
Otte, Richard, "Indeterminism, Counterfactuals, and Causation," *Philosophy of Science*, 54, 1987, pp. 45–62.
Reichenbach, Hans, *The Direction of Time* (Berkeley: University of California Press, 1956).
Robinson, Denis, "Matter, Motion, and Humean Supervenience," *Australasian Journal of Philosophy*, 67, 1989, pp. 394–408.
———, "Re-Identifying Matter," *The Philosophical Review*, 91, 1982, pp. 317–342.
Rosenberg, Alexander, "On Kim's Account of Events and Event-Identity," *The Journal of Philosophy*, 71, 1974, pp. 327–336.
Salmon, Wesley, "Causality without Counterfactuals," *Philosophy of Science*, 61, 1994, pp. 297–312.
———, *Scientific Explanation and the Causal Structure of the World* (Princeton: Princeton University Press, 1984).
Sanford, David, "Causal Dependence and Multiplicity," *Philosophy*, 60, 1985, pp. 215–230.
———, "The Direction of Causation and the Direction of Conditionship," *The Journal of Philosophy*, 73, 1976, pp. 193–207.
Sosa, Ernest, and Michael Tooley, eds., *Causation* (Oxford: Oxford University Press, 1993).
Stout, George F., "The Nature of Universals and Propositions," *Studies in Philosophy and Psychology* (London: Macmillan, 1930).
Suppes, Patrick, *A Probabilistic Theory of Causality* (Amsterdam: North-Holland Publishing Company, 1970).
Swain, Marshall, "A Counterfactual Analysis of Event Causation," *Philosophical Studies*, 34, 1978, pp. 1–19.
Taylor, Richard, *Action and Purpose* (Englewood Cliffs, N.J.: Prentice-Hall, 1966).
Tooley, Michael, *Causation: A Realist Approach* (Oxford: Clarendon Press, 1987).
———, "Causation: Reductionism versus Realism," *Philosophy and Phenomenological Research*, suppl., 50, 1990, pp. 215–236.
———, "In Defense of the Existence of States of Motion," *Philosophical Topics*, 16, 1988, pp. 225–254.
———, "Laws and Causal Relations," *Midwest Studies in Philosophy*, 9, 1984, pp. 93–112.

———, "The Nature of Causation: A Singularist Account," *The Canadian Journal of Philosophy*, suppl., 16, 1990, pp. 271–322.

von Wright, Georg H., *Explanation and Understanding* (Ithaca: Cornell University Press, 1971).

Williams, Donald C., "On the Elements of Being," in *The Principles of Empirical Realism* (Springfield: Charles Thomas, 1966), pp. 74–109.

Wolterstorff, Nicholas, "Qualities," *The Philosophical Review*, 69, 1960, pp. 183–200.

Woodward, James, "Supervenience and Singular Causal Statements," in *Explanation and Its Limits*, ed. Dudley Knowles (Cambridge: Cambridge University Press, 1990), pp. 211–246.

———, "A Theory of Singular Causal Explanation," *Erkenntnis*, 21, 1984, pp. 231–262.

Index

"Abstract Particulars" (Landesman), 92–93
Anscombe, Elizabeth, 7–8
antisupervenience, 66–68. *See also* causal realism; nonsupervenience
Armstrong, D. M., 105, 118, 126
Aronson, Jerrold, 9, 158n. 39
asymmetry, of causation, 142–53
atoms and molecular compounds, 126–28

backtracking. *See* no-backtracking principle
backward causation, 138
bare particulars, defined, 11
Bennett, Jonathan, 85, 170n. 24
blocking
   preemption and, 20–21
   stepwise dependence and, 28, 29, 160n. 9
blocking-initiator events, 38–41

Campbell, Keith
   on causal relata, 85, 170n. 25
   on tropes, 85–86, 118, 170n. 25
Castañeda, Hector-Neri, on causation, 56, 57–58, 164n. 10
causal chains
   concrete features and, 81–82
   defined, 30, 73–74
   noncomplex events and, 76
causal connections
   characteristics of, 143–46, 176n. 4, 177n. 6
   conditions of, 144–46, 176n. 4, 177n. 6
   defined, 129

causal direction, 6, 178n. 15
causal mechanism
   identity and, 51, 54–58
   Mackie on, 117
causal priority
   counterexamples to, 179n. 17
   defined, 143, 147–50
   single causes and, 150–51
causal processes
   examples of, 122–28
   fission and fusion and, 122
   persistence and, 121–22, 136, 175n. 39, 176n. 40
   pseudo-processes compared to, 120
   Salmon on, 120, 136
   tropes and, 121–22, 123–24
causal realism
   as antisupervenience, 66–68
   criticism of and support for, 61–68
   preemption and, 53
causal relata
   Campbell on, 85, 170n. 25
   Davidson on, 72
   defined, 86–87
   as events, 71–72
   as facts, 71
   Honderich on, 84–85
   Kim on, 72, 73
   mechanism and, 69–70
   as particulars, 89, 170n. 31
   as property instances, 86
   transitivity and, 73
   tropes and, 13, 15, 84, 85, 86, 121, 170n. 25

causation. *See also* property analysis; property history
- asymmetry of, 142–53
- backward causation and, 138
- Castañeda on, 56, 57–58, 164n. 10
- characteristics of, 3, 133
- counterfactual theory and, 5–6, 9, 19, 26–32, 38, 109, 162n. 37, 177n. 8
- defined, 130
- dependence and, 30, 133–34, 161n. 13
- Ducasse on, 8, 43–44, 157n. 31
- epiphenomena and, 140–41
- features and, 78–79
- generalism and, 3, 4, 10, 18, 19–20, 22, 158n. 41
- Humeanism and, 4, 5, 7, 9, 18, 155n. 3
- identity and, 51, 54–58, 139–40, 172n. 26
- indeterminism and, 38, 162n. 37
- invariance and, 65, 166nn. 28, 30
- Lewis on, 133
- Mackie on, 116–17
- mechanism proper and, 51
- methodology and, 68
- neo-Humeanism and, 4–5, 9, 22–26, 106–9
- overdetermination and, 156n. 10
- pairing problems and, 21
- persistence and, 89, 104–15, 116, 132
- preemption and, 5, 19, 20, 30, 52, 137
- probabilistic theory and, 6, 9, 111, 138, 172n. 26
- reductionism and nonreductionism and, 7, 151–52
- singularism and, 7, 19–20
- singularist component of, 1–20, 22, 116, 120, 123, 158n. 42
- sufficiency and, 5
- temporal/spatial gaps and, 137, 176n. 42
- theories of, 3–9
- Tooley on, 8, 151–52, 164n. 1
- transference theory and, 9, 44–45, 52
- transitivity and, 138–39, 147
- tropes and, 104–15, 132
- types and, 18, 22

Cement of the Universe, The (Mackie), 116–17, 173n. 11

change, qualitative, 93–94

circumstantiality, of causal relations, 144–47, 176n. 3

complex events, 74–76. *See also* noncomplex events

compound tropes, 117–18, 122–23

concrete events, 77–78

concrete features, 79–83
- causal chains and, 81–82
- transitivity and, 80–82

concrete objects, tropes and, 12, 159nn. 52, 53

conditions of a causal connection, defined, 144–46, 176n. 4, 177n. 6

conjunctive tropes, 118

constant conjunction, 18

constitutive attributes, 73, 168n. 6

counterfactual theory
- causation and, 5–6, 9, 19, 26–32, 38, 109, 162n. 37, 177n. 8
- extended version of, 32
- indeterminism and, 38, 162n. 37
- laws and, 27
- Lewis on, 5, 26, 27, 28–29, 160nn. 5, 6
- nonextrinsicness principle and, 133–34
- overdetermination and, 6
- pairing problems and, 31–32
- preemption and, 6, 19, 26–32
- trope persistence and, 109–10

dated particulars. *See* events

Davidson, Donald, 72, 73

dependence
- causation and, 30, 161n. 13
- late preemption and, 30, 161n. 14
- nonextrinsicness principle and, 133–34

deterministic early preemption, Lewis on, 38–41

Ducasse, Curt J.
- on causation, 8, 43–44, 157n. 31
- on singularism, 8–9

early preemption
- defined, 28
- indeterminism and, 39–41
- no-backtracking principle and, 30
- stepwise dependence and, 30, 161n. 16

Eells, Ellery
- on nongeneralist probability theory, 35–37
- on token causation, 35–37, 162n. 29

epiphenomena, 140–41. *See also* joint effects

events
- Bennett on, 85, 170n. 24
- causal relata as, 71–72

Davidson on, 72
  as tropes, 85, 115
Events and Their Names (Bennett), 85, 170n. 24
exemplifications
  defined, 95
  Kim on, 73, 78
  persistence and, 95–96
  transitivity and, 86
  tropes and, 13
extended probabilistic counterfactual theory, 41–43

facts, 71, 85
features
  causation and, 78–79
  defined, 84
  in-virtue-of thesis and, 79, 80, 82–83
  nature of, 79–80
  transitivity and, 82–83
first-order features, 80
fission
  causal processes and, 122
  defined, 119
  fusion and, 119–20
  persistence and, 14
  tropes and, 14, 119–20, 122, 124, 173n. 17, 174n. 30
fusion
  causal processes and, 122
  examples of, 119
  fission and, 119–20
  persistence and, 14, 173n. 18
  tropes and, 14, 119–20, 122, 124, 173n. 18

generalism
  causation and, 3, 4, 10, 18, 19–20, 22, 158n. 41
  defined, 3, 18
  Humeanism and, 4
  neo-Humeanism and, 22
  probabilism and, 33–35, 161n. 20

Honderich, Ted, 84–85
Humeanism. *See also* neo-Humeanism
  causation and, 4, 5, 7, 9, 18, 155n. 3
  criticism of, 4
  generalism and, 4
  singularism and, 7
  singularist relations, 18

identity
  causation and, 51, 54–58, 139–40, 172n. 26
  mechanism and, 51, 54–58
  persistence and, 139–40
  probabilistic theory and, 172n. 26
"In Defense of the Existence of States of Motion" (Tooley). *See* Tooley, Michael
indeterminism
  counterfactual theory and, 38, 39–41, 162n. 37
  early preemption and, 39–41
  invariance and, 65
  probabilistic theory and, 6
indirect conditions, defined, 146–47
interaction, 117, 173n. 11
invariance
  causation and, 65, 166nn. 28, 30
  criticism of, 64–66, 166n. 36
  defined, 64, 166n. 27
  indeterminism and, 65
  Woodward on, 166nn. 27, 31
in-virtue-of thesis
  Davidson on, 73
  defined, 72
  features and, 79, 80, 82–83
  Kim on, 83–84

joint effects, 5, 6. *See also* epiphenomena

Kim, Jaegwon
  on causal relata, 72, 73
  on constitutive attributes, 73, 168n. 6
  on exemplifications, 73, 78
  on in-virtue-of thesis, 83–84
  on supervenient causation, 129

Landesman, Charles, 92–93
late preemption
  defined, 28
  dependence and, 30, 161n. 14
  early preemption and, 28, 29
  Lewis on, 28, 29–30
lawful connection, 135–36
laws of nature
  causation and, 27
  neo-Humeanism and, 4–5, 155n. 8
laws of working, 117
Levinson, Jerrold, 92, 93

Lewis, David
    on blocking-initiator events, 38–41
    on causation, 133
    on counterfactual theory, 5, 26, 27, 28–29, 160nn. 5, 6
    on no-backtracking principle, 39–40, 161n. 17, 163n. 43
    on preemption, 27–32, 38–41
Lewis diagrams, 126–28

Mackie, John L., 116–17, 173n. 11
manipulability theory, 156n. 20, 179n. 19
mechanism
    causal relata and, 69–70
    defined, 50–51
    identity and, 51, 54–58
    methodology of, 68–69
    naive transference theory and, 52
    nonmechanism compared to, 68–69
mechanism proper
    causation and, 51
    defined, 50–51, 53–54
    preemption and, 52
mereological sum, 63
molecular compounds and atoms, 126–28
motion
    Tooley on, 113, 173n. 33
    of tropes, 105–10, 111–14, 172n. 21, 173n. 33
mutual causation, 152–53

naive transference theory, 44, 52
neo-Humeanism. *See also* Humeanism
    causation and, 4–5, 9, 22–26, 106–9
    generalism and, 22
    laws of nature and, 4–5, 155n. 8
    persistence and, 61, 106–9
    preemption and, 22–26
    states of affairs and, 25
    tropes and, 106–9
no-backtracking principle
    early preemption and, 30
    Lewis on, 39–40, 161n. 17, 163n. 43
nomological sufficiency, 5
noncausal theory of identity, defined, 51
noncomplex events, 76–79. *See also* complex events
nonextrinsicness principle
    counterfactual dependence and, 133–34
    lawful connection and, 135–36
    probabilistic relations and, 134–35

nongeneralist probability theory, 35–37. *See also* probabilism
nonmechanism, 68–69
nonoccurrent preemption, defined, 20–21, 31
nonreductionism, 7, 53, 62
nonsalient qualitative change
    defined, 94
    existence of, 94–95
    tropes and, 101–3, 104–5, 108
    universals and, 95
non-spatio-temporal/non-nomological theory of identity
    defined, 51, 58
    pairing problems and, 58, 59
    persistence and, 59, 61
    preemption and, 58, 59
    transference theory and, 58–59
nonsupervenience. *See also* antisupervenience
    counterfactuals and, 63–64
    criticism of, 62, 63, 64–66, 165n. 24
    support for, 62–63, 165nn. 21, 24
nontransitivity, 143–44

occurrent preemption
    criticism of, 47–49
    defined, 21, 31
Otte, Richard, 38
overdetermination, 6, 156n. 10

pairing problems
    causation and, 21
    counterfactual theory and, 31–32
    defined, 18
    non-spatio-temporal/non-nomological theory of identity and, 58, 59
    preemption and, 31–32, 58, 59, 116
    singularist component and, 18–19, 116
partial identity, of tropes, 118
partial persistence, of tropes, 117–20
"Particularisation of Attributes, The" (Levinson), 92, 93
particulars
    causal relata as, 89, 170n. 31
    defined, 10
    tropes as, 92, 101, 115, 117, 118
particulars, dated. *See* events

persistence
  causal processes and, 121–22, 136, 175n. 39, 176n. 40
  causation and, 89, 104–15, 116, 132
  characteristics of, 60–61
  exemplifications and, 95–96
  fission and, 14, 173n. 18
  fusion and, 14
  identity and, 59, 61, 139–40
  Mackie on, 116–17, 173n. 11
  neo-Humeanism and, 61, 106–9
  noncausal theory of, 59–61
  of properties, 124–25
  Salmon on, 56, 57–58
  singularist component and, 116, 123
  of tropes, 13–15, 99–114, 117, 121–22, 123, 131, 132
  universals and, 95
persistence theory
  characteristics of, 57
  criticisms of, 132–36
  epiphenomena and, 140–41
  preemption and, 131
persisting exemplifications, 100
preemption
  blocking and, 20–21
  causal realism and, 53
  causation and, 5, 19, 20, 30, 52, 137
  counterfactual theory and, 6, 19, 26–32, 41–43
  criticism of, 46–47
  defined, 20
  generalist probability theory and, 33–35
  importance of, 19, 50–70
  Lewis on, 27–32
  Mackie on, 117
  mechanism proper and, 52
  neo-Humeanism and, 22–26
  nonoccurrent, 21, 31
  non-spatio-temporal/non-nomological theory of identity and, 58, 59
  occurrent, 21, 31
  pairing problems and, 21, 31–32, 58, 59, 116
  persistence theory and, 131
  probabilistic theory and, 32–33
  singularist component and, 116
  sufficiency and, 5
  transference theory and, 45, 52
  tropes and, 131

probabilistic theory
  causal direction and, 6
  causation and, 6, 32–43, 111, 161n. 25, 172n. 26
  counterfactual theory and, 109
  defined, 32
  generalism and, 33–35, 161n. 20
  identity and, 172n. 26
  indeterminism and, 6
  joint effects and, 6
  preemption and, 32–33
  quantum mechanics and, 6
  tropes and, 111, 172n. 26
Probabilistic Causality (Eells), 35–37, 162n. 29
probabilistic causation, 138
probabilistic counterfactual theory, defined, 38, 162nn. 39
probabilistic preemption, defined, 20
probabilistic relations, 134–35
properties
  characteristics of, 120–21
property analysis, defined, 129. *See also* causation
property history, 129–31. *See also* causation
property instances, 11, 86
pseudo-processes, defined, 56, 120
pure deletion miracle, 163n. 44

qualitative change, 93–94
qualitative persistence
  exemplifications and, 96, 98
  Mackie on, 117
"Qualities" (Wolterstorff), 92, 93
quantum mechanics, 6
quasi-causal connections, defined, 150–51

reductionism, 7, 151–52
Robinson, Denis, 111–12

Salmon, Wesley
  on causal processes, 120, 136
  on persistence, 56, 57–58
second-order features, 80
self-propagation, 111–12
simple tropes, 117
simultaneous preemption, 160n. 11
single causes, 150–51

singularism
    Anscombe on, 7–8
    causation and, 7
    criticism of, 8–9
    defined, 7–9
    Ducasse on, 8–9
    Humeanism and, 7
    reductionism and nonreductionism and, 7
    Tooley on, 8
    transference theory and, 9
Singularist component
    causation and, 18–20, 22, 116, 120, 123, 158n. 42
    mechanism and, 68
    pairing problems and, 18–19, 116
    persistence and, 116, 123
spatio-temporalism, defined, 50
spurious causes, defined, 33, 161nn. 21, 22
stable fusion, defined, 119
states of affairs, 25
stepwise counterfactual dependence
    blocking and, 28, 29, 160n. 9
    defined, 30
    early preemption and, 30, 161n. 16
stepwise probabilistic dependence, defined, 38–39
    blocking-initiator events and, 38–41
Stout, George F., 92–93
strong causal connection. *See* causal connections
strong causal realism, defined, 66. *See also* antisupervenience
structural tropes, defined, 118
sufficiency, 5
supervenient causal processes, defined, 174n. 26. *See also* causal processes
supervenient causation, 129
Swain, Marshall, 163n. 44
symmetry, 143–44. *See also* asymmetry

temporal priority, 142
temporal/spatial gaps, 137, 176n. 42
token causation
    Eells on, 35–37, 162n. 29
    probabilism and, 161n. 25
Tooley, Michael
    on causal direction, 178n. 15, 151–52
    on causation, 8, 164n. 1
    on motion, 113, 173n. 33
    on reductionism, 151–52
    on singularism, 8
transference theory
    Aronson on, 9, 158n. 39
    causation and, 9, 44–45
    criticism of, 9, 158n. 40
    defined, 9, 44
    non-spatio-temporal/non-nomological theory of identity and, 58–59
    preemption and, 45
    singularism and, 9
transitivity
    and causal relata, 73
    causation and, 138–39, 147
    events and, 74–78
    exemplifications and, 86
    features and, 80–83
    persistence and, 138–39
    tropes and, 86
trope bundle theory, characteristics of, 12, 159nn. 52, 53, 56, 57
tropes
    abstractness of, 11, 159n. 48
    atomic and molecular structures as, 126–28
    bare particulars and, 11
    Bennett on, 85
    Campbell on, 85–86, 170n. 25
    causal processes and, 121–22, 123–24
    causal relata and, 13, 15, 84, 85, 86, 121, 170n. 25
    causation and, 104–15, 132
    characteristics of, 10–11, 158nn. 43, 45
    concrete objects and, 12, 159nn. 52, 53
    counterfactual theory and, 109–10
    defined, 11, 84, 86, 92, 117, 159n. 49
    events as, 85
    exemplifications and, 13, 100
    existence of, 91–93, 170n. 1
    fission and, 14, 119–20, 122, 124, 173n. 17, 174n. 30
    fusion and, 14, 119–20, 122, 124, 173n. 18
    identity and, 107–8, 118
    Landesman on, 92–93
    Levinson on, 92, 93
    motion of, 105–10, 111–14
    neo-Humeanism and, 106–9
    nonrelational view of, 100

nonsalient qualitative change and, 101–3, 104–5, 108
as particulars, 92, 101, 115, 117, 118
persistence of, 13–15, 99–114, 117–20, 121–22, 123, 131, 132
preemption and, 131
probabilism and, 111, 172n. 26
as properties, 117, 121
purposes of, 12–13
singularist component and, 123
sparse theory of, 159n. 51
Stout on, 92–93
transitivity and, 86
types and, 12–13
universals and, 11–12, 13, 87–89, 101, 117, 118
Wolterstorff on, 92, 93

types
  causation and, 18, 22
  tropes and, 12–13

unextended analysis, 32
universals
  Armstrong on, 118, 126
  defined, 10, 91–92
  exemplifications of, 11–12
  nonsalient qualitative change and, 95
  persistence and, 95
  tropes and, 11–12, 87–89, 101, 117, 118
unstable fusion, 119, 122

Wolterstorff, Nicholas, 92, 93
Woodward, James, 166nn. 27, 31, 64
working, laws of, 117